THE
STILL SMALL VOICE:

A JOURNEY IN LISTENING

The Still Small Voice: A Journey in Listening
ISBN: 978-1-60920-022-0
Printed in the United States of America
©2011 by Bob McCauley

Cover design and photo layout by Ajoyin Publishing, Inc.

Library of Congress Control Number: 2011927497

API
Ajoyin Publishing, Inc.
P.O. 342
Three Rivers, MI 49093
www.ajoyin.com

Please direct your inquiries to admin@ajoyin.com

THE
STILL SMALL VOICE:

A JOURNEY IN LISTENING

Bob McCauley

Ajoyin Publishing, Inc.
PO Box 342
Three Rivers, MI 49093
1.888.273.4JOY
www.ajoyin.com

FOREWORD

Phyllis Kilbourn

This book abounds with gripping and challenging life stories brimming with the miraculous, such as those from the author's experiences when flying in treacherous conditions in the Liberian bush or experiencing first-hand a street child's life lived in the sewers of Russia. Through recounting these stories the author teaches readers what it means to truly listen to the still, small voice of God. Additionally, the stories related demonstrate how essential such listening is to truly know, understand and appreciate God's moment-by-moment plans and guidance for our lives.

A major Scriptural principle that forms a common thread running throughout the book is the truth that having heard the "still small voice of God" we must make a choice—to obey or disobey the message conveyed. The author expands on the impact of this principle by candidly sharing from his personal life experiences the consequences resulting from his choices: regrets when he disobeyed and blessings when he did obey. Through these times of decision-making, Bob discovered another profound truth—to do God's work one must unequivocally make a total, sacrificial commitment to the will of God. There was to be no half-hearted soldiers in God's army! And that was the army this author had chosen to commit his life to regardless of the cost.

Once Bob became a "sold-out" soldier in God's army, he came face-to-face with the enemy with whom he subsequently often found himself engaged in intense spiritual warfare that usually only ceased when he was willing to make sacrificial choices; choices that launched him out of his comfort zone and required that he put God first in his life no matter the cost. Often these battles centered on his deep love for family and home.

I find Joshua's challenge put before the nation of Israel comparable to that which this author places before us in these pages. Joshua, after recounting a history of God's love and faithfulness to Israel, puts before them the challenge, "Choose you this day whom you will serve" (JOSHUA 24:15). The Israelites made a decisive response to Joshua's challenge by affirming, "The Lord our God will we serve, and his voice will we obey" (24:24). As you hear God whisper to your heart through the pages of this book may you, like the Israelites and this book's author, respond with obedience to God's voice, covenanting to keep yourself from making choices that bring regrets and to embrace those choices that bring blessing.

DEDICATION

God has placed two wonderful women in my life. Both of whom have greatly contributed to making it possible for me to follow the still, small voice of the Lord through many difficult and also blessed times.

Pat, my first wife, was completely willing to sell our home, farms, possessions, quit our jobs, lose the benefits from those jobs, and to take our children and follow the still, small voice of the Holy Spirit wherever He led us. It was her willingness to do this that made it possible for me to obey the Lord's direction for our lives. After many years of ministry together, Pat passed away.

The Lord then put another wonderful woman, named Esther, into my life. She was also willing to follow the still, small voice of the Holy Spirit, no matter what the cost, or how difficult it was. An example of this was her going down into a Russian sewer to feed and teach the Word of God to children living there. I am still amazed at her willingness to risk her health and comfort to minister in such a terrible place. Esther was very dedicated to helping start a large ministry to children living in crisis and in the prisons in Russia.

She also helped write this book, spending many hours reading and editing. I could not have written it without her dedication to make the book possible.

In thanks and love to my wife Esther, our children, family, and many friends, who encouraged me to write my experiences, and in remembrance of my deceased wife, Pat, I dedicate this book to God and His Son, Jesus Christ, that it might bring glory to Him.

Contents

INTRODUCTION

I could see nothing out of the windshield of my plane as I was flying over the African jungle at 130 miles per hour in a rainstorm! Suddenly I heard the still, small voice of the Holy Spirit speak two words to me, "Tower! Tower!" Instantly I reacted and put the plane in a steep, climbing right turn as I saw a huge radio tower flash by my left wing tip. If I had not instantly reacted to the still, small voice of the Holy Spirit, the plane would have been torn to pieces and I would have been killed.

Why was I delivered from death? First of all, it was because God spared my life by speaking two words to me in His still, small voice. Second, I had learned to hear the still, small voice of the Holy Spirit. Third, I had learned to obey His still, small voice. Was it easy for me to learn to hear and obey God's word to me personally? The answer is clearly, "No." I had to learn some very hard lessons before I learned to hear and obey His still, small voice. The lessons include deep regrets that I will live with for the rest of my life.

Am I a man of super faith? "No." There were times when I faced possible death or prison and did not have a strong faith that I would be delivered from them. Other times I had a fear of not being delivered from serious situations. At times I had doubts about God taking care of my family's needs. On occasion I lacked faith to believe God for something I needed. No, I am not a man of super faith, but rather a common person, that God used.

I was born in 1934 in a farm home located in Howard County, Indiana, which was owned by my maternal grandparents. Two years later my brother James was born. My parents were not Christians, although they both grew up in Christian homes. Though they did not attend church or claim Christianity, they did have strong values, especially in the areas of honesty and hard work. Our father started drinking when he was in his late twenties and became an alcoholic by the time he was in his mid-thirties. He was a hard worker during the day but spent most of his nights in taverns. His drinking caused a lot of arguments between him and my mother, and the arguments in turn caused a lot of stress for my brother and me.

My dad was an alcoholic who could spend late nights drinking while still being able to maintain a heavy workload the following day. He farmed 450 acres of land raising mainly corn, soybeans, and tomatoes. Most farmers at that time were farming about eighty to one hundred and twenty acres, so our farm was considered one of the larger ones in the area. We also milked twenty-four cows by hand and raised hundreds of hogs. Hard work was a way of life for us, giving Jim and me little time to play as we grew up. Our day started at daylight and usually ended well after dark. The hard work made us a wealthy family, but my father's drinking left us with no peace to enjoy that wealth.

A turning point in my life came when I was seventeen years old. It happened as a result of going to a movie called *Saint Joan of Arc*. I was deeply impressed as I watched the movie and saw the life of a woman who prayed and lived for the Lord. There was no doubt in my mind that she had something intriguing that I did not have. By the time the movie was over I knew that I wanted to have this kind of life as well; I wanted to get things right with God as soon as possible so I could start living for Him as Saint Joan did. At that time I didn't have an understanding of the plan of salvation, although I did know about Jesus. I did not realize He died for my sins, but at the same time I knew I was guilty of sin and would go to hell if I died.

The following Sunday morning I went to a nearby church and talked to the pastor after the service was over. I told him of my interest in getting right with God. He was pleased and very glad to explain the plan of salvation to me. It was then that I fully understood that I was a lost sinner on my way to an eternal hell, and that Jesus Christ died for my sins so that I could go to heaven to forever be with Him. He went on to explain that it would be necessary for me to repent of my sins and accept Jesus Christ as my Savior. This was exactly what I wanted to do, so he led me in a prayer in which I did repent and ask Jesus Christ to be my Savior. I became a born-again child of God that day, and my life was changed forever. Shortly after this, I started talking to my brother about the Lord and praying for him. Soon he also became a Christian.

About three years later I met a young lady named Patricia Lamb. We fell in love and were married in 1955 when I was twenty-one years old. One year after we were married, I was drafted into the army and sent to Korea. Pat was pregnant at the time with our son Michael, who was born while I was still in basic training. I was in Korea for the first year and a half of Michael's life, and being separated from each other during that time was very difficult for all of us. As the years passed, Pat and I had another son, Tony, and a daughter, Tanya. We loved our children very much and wanted the best for them.

Even though I was a Christian and active in church, my goal in life was to be a success on my job and to acquire as much farmland as possible. I felt this would give me and my family a better life. I knew land prices were going to increase and wanted to profit from it. To be able to purchase the land, I worked at two jobs most of the time and bought our first farm when I was twenty-six years old. I also studied and worked hard, and by the time I was in my mid thirties I was a senior engineer for General Motors.

We purchased our second farm with a lovely house on it near Kokomo, Indiana, in 1963 when I was twenty-nine years old. My wife and I had been looking for a home with farmland like this for several years. When it came up for sale, we saw it, and fell in love with it at first sight. Our large farmhouse had been completely rebuilt inside and was located about three hundred yards off the road on a small hill. Our closest neighbor was a quarter of a mile away. The view from our home in all directions was beautiful. It was our dream home. The boys loved to ride their ponies through the fields and out along the creek. I rode with them on my horse when I could. We boarded riding horses for other people and rented some of the farmland out to a neighbor to make the payment on the farm loan. The farm was paying for itself, and all of us were enjoying it.

We later sold our first farm and bought part of the farm that my grandfather McCauley and my father had owned. Our two farms were bringing in a tidy sum. The price of farmland was increasing vastly every year, adding to our net worth. I was also looking at another large farm to purchase in the area. Pat was nearly finished with her teaching degree from Wesleyan University in Marion, Indiana, and soon would be ready to start her profession as a schoolteacher. All of these things were greatly increasing our financial worth.

As time passed, my desire to serve the Lord grew deeper. The more I studied His Word, the more I wanted to. It came to the place that I was spending about two hours a day studying the Bible and in prayer. One evening I went to our guest bedroom, closed the door, knelt down, and told God He could have me and all our belongings to use for His glory. I meant this commitment with all my heart, but I did not realize the full depth of it at that time.

Although I felt completely at peace after I gave everything to the Lord, I had a strong feeling that things were going to change in our lives. God heard my prayer and would "take me up on it." I shared this with my wife and told her that I had no idea what lay ahead of us, but I wanted to do exactly what God wanted. She completely agreed with me, and said she was willing for His leading and any change in our lives as well. The changes came quickly and eventually led me from being a senior engineer for General Motors to a missionary pilot in Liberia, Africa.

During my time in Africa, I made close to four thousand flights over the African jungles. Thankfully, most of those trips turned out successfully. There were other trips though that brought me, and others who were in the plane with me, very close to death. Although I lived through each situation, there were other pilots doing the same job that did not. You will hear more of these harrowing experiences in the chapters to come. I give God the glory for all His protection during these years and am so thankful that I am still here and able to share with you God's leading in my life.

I was well educated in the dangers of flying in Liberia before I ever arrived. I knew that I would always be facing the possibility of my plane crashing due to the ever-changing jungle weather, mechanical failure, or even as a result of my own error. Every day, as I walked to the hangar to get to the plane, I walked by the grave of the pilot I was replacing. It was a stark reminder of how serious jungle flying was.

My brother's life was very similar to mine; he became a large farmer and land-owner and worked at General Motors as a tinsmith. He also made a full commitment of his life to God, and the Lord spoke to him about going to Africa as a missionary. Jim told his wife, Mary, about this, and they knew if they obeyed, it meant they would be selling almost everything they owned. They did exactly that and ended up spending the next twenty-three years in Africa.

It is hard to believe how fast the time has gone since we left our farm and home back in 1970. It is now forty years later and I am an old man today. During this time span I have enjoyed the blessings of my wonderful children and two good women in my life. (My first wife went on to be with the Lord many years ago.) However, since my prayer of dedication, our lives have been anything but normal. We have seen God do miracles, I have had a vision of hell, and we heard Him speak to us audibly. In addition to this, He also provided food and funds as well as physical things in ways far beyond what could have ever occurred naturally. We have had experiences foreign to most people. All these things came about as a direct result of hearing and following the still, small voice of the Lord.

God spoke to Elijah through the still, small voice of the Holy Spirit as we see in I KINGS 19:11-13.

And he said, Go forth, and stand upon the mount before the LORD. And, behold, the LORD passed by, and a great and strong wind rent the mountains, and brake in pieces the rocks before the LORD; but the LORD was not in the wind: and after the wind an earthquake; but the LORD was not in the earthquake: And after the earthquake a fire; but the LORD was not in the fire: and after the fire a still small voice. And it was so, when Elijah heard it, that he wrapped his face in his mantle, and went out, and stood in the entering in of the cave. And, behold, there came a voice unto him, and said, What doest thou here, Elijah?

Somewhere in Elijah's life he learned to hear the still, small voice of the Lord even in the midst of a lot of other commotion such as the wind, the earthquake, and the fire. The ability to hear the still, small voice of the Holy Spirit was not only for Elijah and other prophets in the Bible, but is for us today.

It is the work of the Holy Spirit to convict the world of sin and to bring people to repentance and acceptance of Jesus Christ as their Savior.

And when he is come, he will reprove the world of sin, and of righteousness, and of judgment: (JOHN 16:8)

How does the Holy Spirit reprove us of sin? He does it through the Word of God and as He speaks to us in His still, small voice. When the Holy Spirit reproves a person of sin, there is an inner conviction that tells them they are a sinner and need to come to Christ, repent, and be born again. It is the still, small voice of the Holy Spirit that does this.

We see in Acts 8:26 that an angel of the Lord spoke to Philip and gave him directions. I know this happens on occasion today because my brother, Jim, saw angels when God was speaking to him to sell his farms and go to Africa. In Acts 8:29 the Holy Spirit gave Philip further directions. I believe this was by the still, small voice of the Holy Spirit. In Acts 9:4-6 Saul heard an audible voice from heaven. I know this happens today because I heard an audible voice from heaven on one occasion confirming to me that my brother and I were to go into a terrorist training area and preach God's Word. The Holy Spirit not only convicts us of sin, but He also can direct and warn us of harm throughout our life by His still, small voice as He did for me when He said, "Tower, tower."

5

In 1976 the Lord gave me a Scripture found in Habakkuk 2:2-3.

> *And the LORD answered me, and said, Write the vision, and make it plain upon tables, that he may run that readeth it. For the vision is yet for an appointed time, but at the end it shall speak, and not lie: though it tarry, wait for it; because it will surely come, it will not tarry.*

This verse was an encouragement to write about the still, small voice of the Holy Spirit, but I was to wait until the right time. I waited about twenty-four years for the right time and then on the first of January, 2000, the Lord spoke to me to write this book because the time was right.

Many people and churches believe that God does not do miracles today, nor does He give personal directions to His people. They believe He only speaks through His Word. God does direct His church through His Word! This is an absolute! However God also can and does direct people personally through His still, small voice and other ways.

If it is God's will for His people to hear His still, small voice and obey, then we should be able to experience the reality of it. I know I have experienced this for the past forty years. These stories are a testimony about how God directed us with His still, small voice, and how we obeyed and made a difference for eternity in many people's lives.

I am not saying God will lead other people exactly as He did us. He works in each person according to what He wants. God directed us to sell out and go to Africa, where I became a jungle pilot. He may be calling you to stay on your job and be a witness for Him where you are. As you read this book, I hope you are encouraged to follow the Lord with all your heart and also to obey His still, small voice as He gives you personal direction in your life.

Because some people have so misused the phrase, "God told me to do it," I hesitated somewhat to even write about the experiences I have had in my life of following the still, small voice of the Holy Spirit. I need to write some guidelines a person must follow if they are to let God lead them by His Holy Spirit. The most important point of all is this: *God will never direct us to do anything that does not totally line up with His Word!* Any direction that is not in accordance with God's Word is not of the Holy Spirit; it is of a person's own mind or the voice of a demon that is directing them. I know two men that left their wives and started living with other women. They both said God told them to do it. God did not do this at all! It was their lust or a demon that led them to do it.

The second point is this: If a person is to be led by God's still, small voice, they must live a life that is totally dead to their own desires. Everything they do must be for God's glory and never glory for themselves. If in any way they feel God is directing them to do something that will bring glory to them, then it probably is not of God. The third point is that everything we do should let people see Christ in us and bring people to Him.

Ch. 1
LOVE THAT MOTIVATES ACTIONS

One day when I was working as a foreman in a large machine shop in southern Africa, my supervisor and I were walking side by side to another building on the property. As we walked by the welding shop, my supervisor noticed that one of our skilled welder employees was not working. He had a lot of welding to do that day but was not doing it. Everyone called him Sam, but that was probably not his real name because he was of the Zulu tribe and would have had a Zulu name. When we were about thirty feet from him, my supervisor said, "Sam, get to work."

Sam immediately ran at my supervisor and hit him very hard in the face with his fist. The blow knocked my supervisor backward about ten feet into a parked car. I took a quick look at him—his face was covered with blood and he was struggling to stay on his feet. I quickly turned and looked at Sam. He had run back to the welding shop and picked up a steel bar that was about one inch in diameter and about three feet long. I could hardly believe what I was seeing! Sam was quickly heading back toward my supervisor with the bar of steel raised above his head. He had a look in his eyes that told me he was going to kill my supervisor.

Within two or three seconds I evaluated the situation. My supervisor was going to be killed right in front of me if someone did not stop Sam. About a dozen African men were standing near Sam, and I thought they would stop him. However, I was amazed and shocked as I looked at them. They all had smiles on their face as if they approved of what was about to happen. Immediately I knew they were not going to stop him. That left only one man to stop the killing, and that was me! Sam was an extremely strong man, and I knew there was no way I could physically stop him, but I had to try!

As Sam was coming toward my supervisor, I threw both of my arms straight out in a defenseless manner and jumped in front of him. I started shouting, "No, Sam, no, Sam." I thought he would probably hit me with the steel bar and kill me, but he did not. Rather he tried to come around my right side, with the steel bar still raised above his head. I jumped to my right and in front of him. Then he moved to come around my left side, and I again jumped in front of him as I yelled over and over, "No, Sam, no, Sam." Then slowly he lowered the bar of steel. He seemed to have a disappointed look on his face and was looking off in the distance at something. I was a little confused at what had caused his change in behavior.

I was somewhat fearful of taking my eyes off of Sam, but I also wanted to know what was happening to my supervisor right behind me. I slowly turned my head to look behind me, trying to keep an eye on Sam as I did. I was surprised to see that my supervisor was about two hundred feet behind me, running as fast as he could toward his car. In seconds he was in it and driving away. Sam never said a word, but turned and slowly walked back to the welding shop carrying the bar of steel. I had delayed him just enough to give my supervisor time to recover from the initial blow and to run.

The whole incident took place in less than ten seconds and left me with questions. What caused Sam to react like he did to my supervisor's remarks? Why didn't Sam kill me? Why didn't the African men standing near Sam try to stop him? What made me react like I did?

I came to this conclusion: I can only account for my own actions and not for those of the other men. Every person reacts to a tragic incident according to what is deep within their heart. It is part of the person's character. Did I have something within me that caused me to react in defense of my supervisor even at the risk of losing my own life? The answer is, "Yes." Otherwise I would have stood back and not endangered my life. Did my Christianity cause me to react like I did? Again the answer is, "Yes, it did." Years before this I settled in my heart that my life was to be lived for the glory of Christ, no matter what it cost me or where it took me in the world. That included my physical life.

My testimony for Jesus Christ has to be more than just words. It has to include my actions. Someone coined the phrase, "Actions speak louder than words." A Christian's love should motivate their actions to bring glory to God in order to bring people to Jesus Christ. My faith has to be backed by my actions! I will say it this way: The Holy Spirit brings people to Jesus Christ and also brings glory to God and His Son. If I am being led by Him, I will be doing the same thing. If I say I am following the leading of the still, small voice of the Holy Spirit, and my actions, my words, and my love are not all in accordance with God's Word, then I am only following my own desires or thoughts.

Greater love hath no man than this, that a man lay down his life for his friends. (JOHN 15:13)

The big question to me is this: Am I willing to lay down my life for the cause of Christ and for my friends? Am I willing to obey the Lord even at the risk of losing my life? To me, the answer to these questions has to be, "Yes, I am willing to do that." What if I am suddenly faced with a situation in which I only have three or four seconds to decide if I am willing to risk my life for another person or for God's work? From my experience, the answer to this question has to be made before the need arises.

I could have just stood there like the rest of the African men and let Sam kill my supervisor. That would not have brought glory to Jesus Christ or to my testimony of being a Christian. Neither would it have helped me lead these people to Christ. My supervisor and the African men all knew I was a Christian, and my whole testimony was tested in front of these men. I am sure none of them had time to think about it in the seconds of time, but I am sure some of them did later. They all knew I could have been killed, and I know they had greater respect of me for what I did. As a result, they had more respect for my Christianity.

How valuable is a good testimony? I will say from experience: it is more valuable if it is tested and people see it. I did not think about it, but the African men were watching my life. As far as I knew, I was the only American Christian they had ever been around. One day a group of them wanted to talk to me after work hours, and I agreed. They asked me this question, "Umfundees (Um-fun-dees), why do you treat us different than other white men?" I was surprised by their question and also very surprised when they addressed me as Umfundees. This word is a very endearing term for father. They would only use it for someone they had very high respect for. I was their shop foreman and over them daily in their work, yet they seemed to have a great deal of respect for me.

Their question gave me a perfect opening to tell them about my Christianity and about God and Jesus Christ and what He did for them. They highly respected what I had to say. I could have talked to these African men daily about Christianity and they probably would not have heard me, but when they saw my Christianity in action, they listened.

My actions also meant a lot to my supervisor. He was one of the Hungarian freedom fighters that had fought against the Russians during their occupation of his country in 1956. After the freedom fighters lost their war, they faced long prison terms if they were captured by the Russians. My supervisor and a few other Hungarian men that escaped made their way to southern Africa and went to work for the same machine shop that I did.

These men all hated America. They said America promised them weapons if they rose up and fought the Russians. They started fighting for their freedom, thinking America was going to give weapons to them, but they never came. As a result, they had very little to fight with, and many of them were killed. Their negative feeling toward Americans made it somewhat difficult for me. At least I felt they had no respect for me, since I was an American.

After I defended and saved the life of my Hungarian supervisor, all of that changed. These men gained a respect for America that they had not had before because I represented not only Christianity to them but also America.

About five years before this incident happened, I was in Liberia, West Africa. One day three African Bible school students and one older African man named Duo and I walked about six miles from our Bahn mission station to a village named Bay-pee-a where we preached and taught the Word of God. Shortly before we left the village to walk back to the mission station, some of the Christians gave the Bible school students about seventy-five or eighty pounds of rice that was in a large bag.

Before we left the village, the African men in our group made a cushion out of dried grass and put it on the head of one of the Bible school men that was to carry the bag of rice. Then two of the men lifted the bag of rice and put it on the student's head. He carried it on his head for about a mile. Then two of the men lifted the bag from the head of the person that was carrying it and placed it on the head of the next person. This continued until all four of the African men had each carried the rice about a mile. Then they started to put it on the head of the first man that had carried it. I stopped them and said, "No, it is my turn to carry it. Put it on my head." All four men said, "No, no, white man cannot carry bag." I said, "White man can carry bag. Put on my head." They all reluctantly agreed.

I stood very straight, and the men placed the dried grass cushion on my head and then placed the bag on top of that. Each of the men could balance the bag on their heads without using their hands, but I knew I could not do that, so I used both hands to balance it. It was very heavy on my head, but I was able to carry it. We then took off walking again and I was able to carry it for my mile at the same speed that we were walking before. I will have to say, however; that I was ready for it to be taken off of my head after the mile.

About four years later, my family and I went to another mission station to take the place of a couple that was going back home for a year. As we were saying our good-bys to our friends at Bahn mission station, Mr. Duo came to me and said, "Mr. McCauley, we knew you were a good man when you put the bag on your head." I had no idea what he was talking about and thought I misunderstood him. I asked him to repeat what he said, and he said the same thing again. I then said, "Mr. Duo, when did I put the bag on my head?" Then he gave the details of our walk to Bay-pee-a four years before this.

I was shocked at how well he remembered every detail of that day. It seemed to have meant a tremendous amount to the Africans that a white man would carry a bag of rice. The fact that he used the term "we" meant all of the Africans were impressed that I carried the rice on my head. I had carried the rice about three weeks after we arrived at Bahn mission station when we first came to Africa from America. After hearing what Mr. Duo told me, I realized my actions spoke to the Africans in such a way that I had been known as a good man for the four years we had been there.

> *But wilt thou know, O vain man, that faith without works is dead?*
> (JAMES 2:20)

My faith to obey the still, small voice of the Holy Spirit and go to Africa was blessed or enhanced by my work. My work in this case actually was doing physical labor or work. I carried the bag out of love. My Christian love for these four men brought about my actions to carry the bag. Again I will say, "If I have the faith to follow His still, small voice and go to the ends of the earth and do not have love and actions or works to go along with it, I am almost useless." These all have to go hand in hand. My actions or works must also be grounded in His Word and used for His glory and not for my own benefit. My Christian love motivates my actions.

About seven years ago, my brother and I went to a Christian concert. At a break in the service, an elderly man stood up and gave a testimony with tears in his eyes. As he spoke, he pointed to Jim and me and told all of the people there that his daughter and her family would not be singing in the concert if it had not been for Jim and me saving her life fifty years before this. He thanked God for what we did to save his daughter's life. Exactly fifty years had passed since it had happened, and he remembered the event as if it was yesterday. It was a time when Jim and I put love and actions together to save a girl's life. Here is that story.

In November of 1953, Bob Dugan, Leon Horner, Jim McCauley, and I drove to Fort Myers, Florida, for a vacation. We were four farm boys looking forward to seeing the state and swimming in the Gulf of Mexico. A few days after we arrived, we drove out to the Fort Myers beach. It was a cool, windy winter day so there were very few people swimming. The waves were very large, and we excitedly ran into the water and enjoyed our time riding the waves as they flowed by.

We had not planned it, but a family from our home church was also in Florida when we were and had gone out to the beach on the same day we had. Their daughter Marj saw us riding the waves and decided to do it also. Marj's parents could not swim, so they stayed on the beach. We boys were staying in about the same location as the waves passed by us, but Marj was not a good swimmer and the waves quickly took her quite far from us and farther out from the beach. We did not notice this, however.

All of a sudden Bob heard Marj yell, "Help, help!" At that time Bob was only about 120 feet away from her. Jim and I were about 150 feet farther away when Bob yelled to us that Marj was drowning. Leon was farther up the beach from us, so he did not hear any of this. Bob took off swimming toward her as fast as he could. Jim and I could not see her because of the huge waves. We certainly wanted to help, and since we didn't know her exact location, we just swam as hard as we could, following Bob.

Our only hope was for Bob to get there quickly enough to find her. The waves were about eight feet high with large whitecaps breaking over the top. Just staying on top of them was a major challenge, and as Jim and I were struggling to get there quickly, we saw Bob disappear under the water. Bob saw Marg go under, but he could see her long hair floating above her as she went down and disappeared below the water. He dove down, grabbed her hair, and held on to it.

Bob struggled to get Marj and himself to the top, but the waves and current fought his every effort. At last he succeeded in bringing her to the surface just before Jim and I finally got to them. Bob was coughing badly, making it apparent to us that water had gotten into his windpipe. He was struggling to keep her and himself above the huge waves. My brother and I yelled to him, "Let us swim with her, and you get to shore by yourself and get help."

I was concerned about Bob's ability to make it to shore while coughing so badly and showing such signs of exhaustion; however, Jim and I took hold of Marj and held on to her arms right below her shoulders and started to swim, holding one arm each. Bob did as we suggested and headed toward the shore alone. We were about eighty yards straight out from shore and though we swam as hard as we could, we found it nearly impossible to make any progress swimming against the undercurrent.

We were farm boys from Indiana and had never experienced swimming in such adverse conditions. Both Jim and I learned to swim in a deep gravel pit about half a mile from our farm home. Almost every summer evening, covered with dirt and dust from working on the farm, we would go the pit to bathe and enjoy swimming in the cool refreshing water. This ritual began when we were in the third and fourth grades and continued every summer until we were grown and moved away from home after we were married. We both became good swimmers.

Strangely, we were somewhat driven to practice swimming underwater and, as the years passed, were able to stay underwater for long periods of time. Something was also driving us to practice swimming with one arm while we pulled the other person backward through the water, in a lifesaving manner. We would do this day after day each summer with the thought that we could save someone from drowning if the need ever came. Other boys swam with us at times, but they seemed to have no interest in doing this.

On the farm, we had learned responsibility as young people working long hours each day. Along with this, in the evenings after our work was finished, we would run and do other exercises to increase our endurance. We had a driving desire to keep ourselves in good shape and continued this through the years. When we went to Florida that special winter, Jim was seventeen and I was nineteen years old. Both of us were in very good physical condition.

Jim and I had never been in Florida before. We were not aware until later that there had been warnings that day of huge waves and undercurrents due to an approaching storm pattern. The huge waves were an exciting challenge and looked like they would be great fun to swim in. We definitely were not experienced swimming in the ocean, much less under these conditions. Marj and her parents did not know about the storm warnings either.

Marj was nearly unconscious when Bob brought her to the surface. She remained in that condition even after Jim and I took hold of her. After we had swum as fast as we could to get to her, we were already very tired. Marj was a small girl and probably weighed only about eighty pounds, but with her extra weight and with us swimming with only one arm, we had difficulty keeping her above the waves. Each wave, with its whitecap of rolling water, would break over our heads. We had to hold our breath while we were underwater, and then when the wave had passed over, we would have to get our breath and swim as hard as we could for a few seconds before the next wave came.

The waves were flowing parallel to the shore, and we were trying to swim at right angles to the direction of the waves. As a result, we made very little progress between waves. A new wave was coming at us about every ten seconds. At times, the waves would nearly roll us over with their tremendous force. Even when we were under the water, we had to exert a tremendous amount of effort to hold on to Marj and to stop ourselves from rolling end over end with the waves.

The violent force of the waves was almost more than we could handle as we struggled to get to shore. I was getting water down my windpipe during the process and knew that Jim and Marj probably were also. I started to feel extremely tired. We were swimming as hard as we could, but we were not getting much closer to the shore. We were, however, being carried farther away from the area where we had started, due to the waves carrying us parallel to the beach.

I found myself starting to get numb. My muscles seemed to be shutting down, and I knew that Jim must be feeling the same way. We were still able to keep Marj above the water except when the waves broke over us. I was very concerned about her being able to hold her breath while we were underwater. To make matters worse, there was no way we could keep her above the waves when they broke over us.

No help was in sight, and we did not know if Bob made it to shore or not. I started to realize that we might not be able to make it; however, I was determined we would keep going as long as God gave us strength. Although Jim and I couldn't discuss it, I knew we would never let go of Marj to save our own lives. That was out of the question! We would die first!

As we were moved farther down the shore, we came closer to a pier that extended into the water about one hundred yards. The pier was about twenty feet above the water and supported by poles about twelve inches in diameter. When we were about fifty yards from a pole at the end of the pier, both of us determined, at about the same time, to swim toward that pole, rather than continue trying to swim to shore. If we could get to the pole and hold onto it, it might save our lives.

Changing our direction of swimming did help conserve our strength some, but I was still feeling very numb and could hardly move my left arm. Our endurance was being tested severely even though we were in good physical condition. With all the years of swimming and holding our breath underwater, we had never experienced anything like this. The numbness in my left arm was getting stronger and stronger.

I was holding on to Marj with my right hand, so all the strength it took to swim was coming from my left arm. I am right-handed and am much stronger in my right arm than my left. Jim is left-handed and was swimming with his right arm, so he was in the same situation. We had started out opposite of what we should have. In our haste to take Marj from Bob, I had reached out to her with my right hand and Jim with his left. We did not think about the results of this seemingly small decision at the time. Now the results were showing up, but we could not change it.

As the numbness set into my muscles, it took extreme effort to keep moving my left arm. We were so busy just fighting to keep on top of the water between the waves that it was impossible to take time to trade places. Jim must have been experiencing this also because we were spending less and less time above the water between the waves. This meant that we had to hold our breath longer and longer as the waves broke over our heads. By this time Marj was more conscious than when Bob brought her to the surface. She started to say over and over, "God save me, God save me!" Jim and I were agreeing with her prayer, even though we were not praying out loud.

We kept getting closer to the pole at the end of the pier, but my strength was almost finished. It was taking extreme concentration just to keep swimming. I kept thinking, "Don't give in, keep moving, keep moving. We have to save her, we must save her." I knew that the responsibility of saving her was totally up to us, but we had to have God's strength to accomplish it. I knew that if I failed, Jim and Marj would also drown because Jim would try to save both of us if he had any strength left.

In minutes, which seemed like hours of struggling to stay on top, my muscles were completely numb. By the time the pole was just a few feet away, I had to start telling myself, "You can do just a few more strokes." I knew Jim was struggling as well because I could see him swimming deeper and deeper in the water with only his face surfacing between the waves.

Without an ounce of strength to spare, we finally reached the pole, but when we grabbed it, we found we had just traded one problem for another. The pole that we grabbed was covered with little razor-sharp shells that we later found out were barnacles. Our hands were cut instantly upon touching the pole. And to make matters worse, we were suddenly hit by a huge wave that slammed all three of us hard against the sharp, barnacle-covered pole. Instantly the water all around us was red as all three of our bodies were cut in hundreds of places.

We were too tired to let go of the pole and swim farther, and the pain was almost too much to bear staying where we were. But there were no other choices, so in spite of the pain we continued to hold onto the pole. Each wave would cause the barnacles to cut our bodies more severely. Marj was getting cut up so badly that we had to rotate our location on the pole so she was on the side opposite the direction of the waves. We did this so that the waves would pull her away from the pole rather than slamming her against it; however, the waves were pulling her away from us, and we had to hold on even tighter so she would not be torn from our grip. We were afraid she might go under immediately and we could lose her.

With all the pain and the force of the waves, holding onto the pole and onto Marj took all our strength and concentration. The waves continued to try to pull us away from the pole. Between the waves, we were left hanging high on the pole as the water dropped away below us. The waves were so high that we could hardly see anything on shore. As time wore on, we were really beginning to wonder what happened to Bob. After what seemed like a very long time, we finally saw Bob swimming through the waves toward us with a car inner tube.

We found out later that when he finally made it to shore, he saw a concession stand that rented inner tubes for swimming. He ran to the stand and took one without taking time to pay for it. He said they were screaming at him to bring it back, but he kept running. We were so glad to see him! We put Marj's arms through the center of the tube so we could hold on to her from below the tube. Now we were able to swim easily to the shore with Marj in tow. Soon our feet touched the bottom, and it felt so good to be able to stand on solid sand. Marj could not walk by herself, so we picked her up and carried her to her parents on the beach.

Since Marj's father and mother could not swim, there was no way they could help save their daughter from drowning. Saving her was totally in God's hands, and He used us to do it. Marj was covered with so much blood that her mother screamed in terror when she first saw her, and her father looked like he was ready to cry. Both, however, were so thankful to have their little girl back safe. Jim and I were covered with blood and exhausted, but we made it! Marj's parents took her to the hospital for a checkup and she was okay except for the minor cuts. Thank You, Jesus!

Was it worth it? You bet! Did we make a difference in Marj's life? Yes, we did! Today she is in her early sixties, happily married, with children and grandchildren. Marj and her husband are heavily involved in church work, and they and their family sing together at many churches. It took a total commitment on the part of three teenage boys to make a difference in Marj's life. That was over fifty years ago. I learned some lessons back then as a teenager, which I will share with you.

Our total goal was to save Marj's life. Nothing else was important to us at that time. To save Marj, we almost lost our own lives. We were willing to sacrifice our lives for her. A halfhearted effort would never have saved her. If we are going to make a difference in people's lives, it usually takes total commitment and a willingness to make sacrifices to get the job done. In God's work, I have seen many people make a big difference in other people's lives when they made an effort with a total commitment along with sacrifice. I have seen very few people make a difference by doing God's work in a halfhearted way and without some kind of sacrifice.

One of the major things I learned through this incident is this: Before we get into deep water over our heads, we must be prepared. If Jim and I had not practiced for years swimming with one arm pulling each other in the water in a lifesaving manner, we might have all died that day. Something had driven Jim and me to spend hours practicing to save someone that was drowning. It was always strange that none of the other farm boys were interested in this type of swimming. Today I believe the still, small voice of the Holy Spirit was speaking to us to do this in preparation for saving Marj.

We did not know it at the time, but I believe God had given Jim and me a special sense of taking responsibility and the desire to build up our endurance in preparation for this incident. I am convinced that God prepares us and then takes us out of our comfort zone and into strange surroundings to do His work. When we have no strength, He gives us what we need. It is at that time that we realize it is not by our strength or our own might, but by His Spirit that we can make a difference.

It was also a team effort. Without Bob getting to Marj and bringing her to the surface, and without our effort to hold on to her at all cost, and to keep swimming with all our might, she would not be here today. I have learned that in God's work, it takes a team effort to make a difference.

One of the things I have learned is how even small decisions can have major consequences in our lives. Even the thoughtless action of reaching out and grabbing Marj with my right hand and Jim with his left made a big difference to each of us. We did not think about the fact that we would have to swim with our weaker arms. Today, especially for young people, I say, "Be careful about every decision you make. They can and usually will make a difference in your life."

Another point is this: We may be the only one able to make a difference at the time. God may have called us to do a certain job and if we don't do it, possibly no one else will do it either. Some people say that if God wants something done and we don't do it, He will use someone else to do the job, but that is not always true. In Marj's case there was no one else, and if we had not accepted the responsibility and made the effort, she would have drowned. This was also the case when I saved my supervisor from probably being killed. There was no one else that was willing to do it. If it was to get done, I had to do it.

Learning to take responsibility at a young age is so important. We learned to be responsible because Dad gave us jobs on the farm, such as feeding the animals, and if we did not do it, and he did not check on us, then they would go without their food. Jim and I were accountable to Dad to do the job. We have a responsibility to obey God in His call upon our lives. We are accountable to Him for what we do to make a difference in this world. If we don't obey Him, then possibly the job He has called us to do will not get done.

I encourage you to believe that you can make a difference in this life for the cause of Jesus Christ! I also encourage you to totally commit your life to Him, and He will be your strength. Your life will be exciting! I have been able to look back as the years have passed and say, "Yes, God did give strength to Jim and me when we had none left in ourselves, and we were able to save Marj's life."

We returned the inner tube to the concession stand once we got Marj safely on shore. When the shop owners saw us standing there with blood all over us and heard our story, they wouldn't even take a cent for it.

If you were wondering if we ended up with scars on our bodies from all the barnacles, the answer would be yes. These scars were a reminder for many years of that cold winter day in Florida. But if you would ask us if it was worth the scars, the answer would also be a strong, "Yes."

As I said above, I believe the still, small voice of the Holy Spirit was speaking and driving Jim and I to practice day after day and year after year swimming underwater and with one arm pulling the other person in a lifesaving manner. We were driven so much to do this that it almost became like work. I believe God was preparing us from the time we were very young to be able to swim well enough to save Marj's life. Then on top of that, we had to put our love, according to 1 CORINTHIANS 13, into action. Love was our motivator, and our actions were the result of our love.

Just as I was motivated out of love to face possible death to defend my supervisor, Jim and I were motivated out of love to save Marj. And just as Jim and I were physically prepared to save Marj because of years of practice, I was spiritually prepared to defend my supervisor because of my decision to be willing to give my very life for my Lord and His work. This also caused me to carry the bag on my head. *A successful spiritual life has to be led by the Holy Spirit and be saturated with a love that brings about actions and works that glorify Jesus Christ.*

Ch. 2

LEARNING TO HEAR GOD'S VOICE

I was on a business trip with an older man, when a very strong thought came to my mind that I should talk to this gentleman about his soul. The farther I drove, the stronger this thought came, but I did nothing about it. I was somewhat embarrassed to ask him if he was ready to meet the Lord. I put off talking to him, thinking I would do it on our return trip as he rode back with me. When we arrived at our destination, I had a strong conviction that I had failed the Lord. I kept telling myself that I would talk to the man as we drove back, but right before we were to return, he told me that he had another ride and would not be returning with me.

I felt terrible but comforted myself by thinking, "I will talk to him the next day." However, the first thing I heard the next morning was that the older man had a heart attack that night and died. To say the least, I was devastated, and to this day I regret that I did not talk to him about his soul. As far as I know, he did not have a testimony of being a Christian, and he died instantly with no time to accept Christ as his Savior. As soon as I heard the news, I knew there was a strong probability that he would be in hell for eternity.

Then another thing happened on our farm that was very similar to the event with the older man. We had a barn made for horses, which we boarded for other people. One evening a young man came out to ride his horse, bringing another young fellow with him. When they came, I was busy doing something on the farm. Today I cannot even remember what it was, but I can well remember the same thought coming to my mind, as it had with the older man. The thought was, "Talk to the young man about his soul." I was very busy and told myself that I would talk to him the next day when he came to work with his horse. I continued with my work, and the two young men looked after the horse and left. For the second time, I had a strong feeling that I had failed to obey God. I felt badly about it at the time, but not nearly as badly as I did the next day.

Our home was right across the road and up a long driveway from the Kokomo Airport. The next morning as I was driving to work, I noticed something near the end of one of the runways that looked like a bunch of bent-up sheet metal. It was quite far back from the road, but I did notice it. Sad to say, two young men stole an airplane during the night and tried to take off in it. They crashed it before they even got to the end of the runway, and both were killed. What I saw that looked like a pile of bent-up sheet metal was the plane with the two young men still in it at the time.

One of the young men was the one that boarded his horse on our farm. I don't know for sure, but I think the other young man was the one that was with him at our farm the night before. Again, to say the least, I was devastated and have regretted for years not talking to the young men the evening before they were killed. Where are these two men today? I cannot judge for sure, but I believe this: They stole an airplane. They probably did not know they were about to crash because it was dark outside. They both died instantly, so they did not have time to think about the condition of their souls before they died. I seriously doubt that they were ready to meet the Lord when they were killed. If they had not accepted Jesus Christ as their Savior and repented of their sins, then hell will be their destiny for all of eternity.

About that same time, I made another terrible mistake that cost me a lot of money. I had rented out part of our farm to a man that planted sixty acres of tomatoes in one field. That summer a lot of weeds were growing along a ditch bank that was on one end of the field. I wanted to spray and kill them, so I waited until a day came when the wind was blowing away from the field. I did not want the spray to drift over the tomatoes and damage them.

As I got the sprayer out of the barn and hooked it to my tractor, I started to hear this voice in my head saying, "Don't spray them, don't spray them." I checked the wind direction again and thought, "It won't hurt the tomatoes because the spray will drift in the direction opposite of them." I ignored the warning and drove the tractor and sprayer to where the weeds were. I turned the pump on and picked up the handheld sprayer tube. Just before I squeezed the trigger to spray the weeds, I again heard this voice in my mind saying, "Don't do it." As I had done before, I ignored the voice and sprayed the weeds.

About two weeks later, the man that rented the land came to me, very upset. He told me that I had severely damaged his tomatoes when I sprayed the weeds. I told him that the wind was blowing away from the tomatoes when I sprayed them. He told me that the spray was still on the weeds, and when the wind later blew toward the tomatoes, it picked up enough spray that was still on the weeds to damage his tomatoes. He then said that it happened at the worst possible time because they were in bloom when I sprayed the weeds.

I immediately remembered the strong thought that came into my mind to not spray the weeds. I also knew I was responsible for the damage and that I needed to pay for it. I told him that I would pay him in full what I owed him. He hired an independent group that assesses the damage to a field of crops from spray, etc. They set a price, and even though it was a lot of money, I paid it with no questions at all. For one thing, I did not want to hurt my Christian testimony, and I did cause the damage.

I started to think about the strong thoughts or feelings that I had concerning talking to the men about their soul and the same thought warning me not to spray the weeds. The more I thought and evaluated what had happened, the more I knew beyond any doubt that it was the Holy Spirit that was speaking to me. Before this, I thought it might just be my own mind that was bringing these thoughts to me. When I finally came to the conclusion that it was the Holy Spirit that spoke to me, I regretted my failures more than ever. I regretted losing all of the money when I sprayed the weeds, but I could overcome that. The worst part was in knowing that I was the last person that could have talked to the three people about their soul, and I failed to do it. This was an eternal failure on my part that I could never redo and will regret for the rest of my life.

I finally came to this conclusion: I never will get back the chance to witness to these people again, but I will do everything possible in the future to make sure it does not happen again. The only way I could do this was to make a firm decision to follow the voice of the Holy Spirit regardless of what it cost or where it took us. I then did this the best I could at the time. I did not, however, realize how much the full cost would be until God required it of me. I did ask God to forgive me for my failure to witness to these people, and I am so thankful that I know He has.

Ch. 3
Victory Over Satan's Attacks

When I worked in engineering, we tested every new part to see if it would fail. We took the part through every adverse condition that it would ever be in to see if it would still function. We did this for sixteen thousand to thirty thousand times. If the part still functioned after that, we accepted it as suitable for manufacturing. If God is going to use us in His work, He is going to let us be tested and proven just as He did with His own Son and Joseph of the old Testament.

Then Jesus was led by the Spirit into the desert to be tempted by the devil. (Matthew 4:1, NIV)

Jesus Himself was tested and proven before His ministry was started.

And he sent a man before them—Joseph, sold as a slave. They bruised his feet with shackles, his neck was put in irons, till what he foretold came to pass, till the word of the LORD proved him true. (Psalms 105:17-19, NIV)

God gave Joseph a word that his brothers would bow down before him, but before this came to pass, he was tested and proved.

In this you greatly rejoice, though now for a little while you may have had to suffer grief in all kinds of trials. These have come so that your faith—of greater worth than gold, which perishes even though refined by fire—may be proved genuine and may result in praise, glory and honor when Jesus Christ is revealed. (1 Peter 1:6-7, NIV)

Dear friends, do not be surprised at the painful trial you are suffering, as though something strange were happening to you. (1 Peter 4:12, NIV)

According to 1 Peter 1:6-7 and 1 Peter 4:12 our faith will be proved or tested. We are not to be surprised when this happens as though some strange thing is happening to us. I believe every person that is going to be used of God will be tested in some way, and I certainly was not exempt from this.

When I first made the decision to obey the still, small voice of the Holy Spirit, I thought it would be easy no matter where it took us in the world. This was not the case at all, however. My decision had to be tested and proven to see if I would really go through with it regardless of the cost. At the time, it did not even enter my mind that my commitment to follow the still, small voice of the Lord would be tested, nor did I have any idea of the severity of it.

Not long after I made the decision to obey the still, small voice of the Lord, He spoke something to me that was frightening! He told me to quit my job and go to Bible school for one year in preparation to go to Africa. Now my decision to obey the Lord took a whole different commitment on my part. It was going to require the job that I loved so much and all of the benefits that it brought to my family. I quickly found that it was easy to make the commitment in words, but putting those words into action was much different. It was now going to require a great sacrifice on my part.

My first thoughts were, "I hope it goes away." It did not, however, and as the days and weeks passed, it continued. Constantly I kept hearing this in a very peaceful still, small voice. It was much stronger every time I went to prayer and nearly every time I was by myself. These words scared me! I wanted God's will in my life, but going to Africa was another matter. I was not afraid of being in Africa, but I feared quitting my job and losing the security it gave to me and my family. One day I happened to pick up a book, and as I turned the pages, I came to a picture of Mount Kilimanjaro in Africa. It was almost like it jumped off the page at me. I could hardly get my eyes off that picture. Then again there was the still, small voice saying, "I want you in Africa."

By this time in our lives, I had nearly eighteen years seniority with General Motors. I worked hard and was promoted to the level of senior tool engineer. My salary was very high, and I had many benefits, such as being able to drive a new car every year. I loved my job and the security it brought to our family.

As I thought about what the still, small voice of the Holy Spirit was telling me to do; I became desperately concerned about what my obedience would do to my children and their future. Was it fair to them? Was it fair to Pat?

On top of that, I had worked so hard to get my job, and I would lose all the results of my labor. I would also lose my retirement from General Motors. In addition to this, I wondered how I would ever be able to put my children through college without the income I was making. Things were looking much different now to me because God was taking me up on my commitment to Him.

It was a major decision for me, and one that I did not want to say yes to! It was the most difficult decision I had faced in my life. I did not say yes immediately, and as the days and weeks passed, the still, small voice of the Holy Spirit kept saying the same thing to me.

A few months passed and I still had not told the Lord that I would obey Him. One day in 1970, a close friend of mine told me about a revival they were having at Asbury College in Wilmore, Kentucky. He had attended Asbury when they had the 1950 revival, and he wanted us to take our family and attend the revival during the weekend. It sounded like a good plan, so after I got off work on a Friday evening, we made the four-hour drive and arrived there around 11:00 p.m.

When we walked into the sanctuary, the presence of the Holy Spirit was overwhelming. I had never experienced anything like it. It seemed as if no one was leading the service, but it was going on with young people singing, testifying, and praying. The service had been going powerfully around the clock for several days and was still going that way when we arrived. At about one o'clock in the morning, our friends and my family went to their rooms for the rest of the night, but I could not leave the presence of the Holy Spirit.

About four o'clock in the morning, I went to the altar and knelt down to pray, joining about twenty other people. I opened my mouth to pray, but no words came out. I tried over and over to pray, but my vocal cords just would not work, or at least I could not speak words. I tried and tried but it was hopeless; I was unable to speak and could not even make a sound. Suddenly I realized that I was mute. I stopped trying to speak and started listening to the still, small voice of the Lord. Soon I realized that it was the Lord doing this, and I said with my mind but not with words, "What is it, Lord?" Then in that still, small voice I heard Him say, "You know what I want and you won't do it. I will only hear you pray for Me to use you full-time."

I knelt there for a long time after that, thinking how serious this was and knowing that if I prayed that prayer it meant business with God! Finally, with tears in my eyes I said, "Lord, use me full-time," and I knew He was going to do it. I also knew that this was a major event and that our whole life was going to change.

I dreaded to tell Pat what had happened because I did not know how she would take it. Her lifestyle would change greatly if I quit my job and we went to Africa. When I told her, she said, "You are my husband and the authority of our house. I believe God will give you the directions for us, and I will follow what you say. If you say we need to go to Africa, then it is my responsibility to go where you go, and I will do it." I was somewhat shocked at her complete willingness to obey God's word to me. It seemed to me that it was much easier for her than it was for me.

I knew I had to tell my supervisor that I would be quitting my job, and I really dreaded it. I was concerned how he would take my resignation. I wondered if he would ridicule or laugh at my decision and feel that I was very foolish. He might even be very upset with me. I just did not know how he would react. I also knew that telling him would be the start of leaving my job, and I still had a dread of doing this in my heart.

I finally told my supervisor that I wanted to have a meeting with him, and the two of us went into one of the conference rooms. I then told him about the call of God on my life to go to Africa. Instead of being upset or ridiculing me, he said, "I have heard of other people being called to do a ministry like that, but it has never happened to me. I do, however, believe it does happen." Then he said, "I was planning on giving you a promotion to be the top engineer over one of our plants."

I knew right then that this would have been a major promotion for me that would have greatly increased my salary, along with other benefits. The temptation to take the job was there and probably was one of my first tests to come, but I knew I could not take it regardless of the money. I thanked him for his willingness to promote me to the position, but I told him that I still had to leave my job. He understood and I left my job four months later after training my replacement. When I walked out of the plant on my last day, I had a bit of a sickening feeling in my stomach, knowing that I had just burnt a bridge behind me.

I knew God had required my job of me, but I hoped He would let us keep our farmland and home even though we were in Africa. I had worked very hard for years at two jobs getting enough money to buy the farms, and I could hardly stand the thought of selling them. Before I got into engineering, I worked as a tool designer during the day and as a tool and die maker building sheet metal dies in the evenings. After I got my engineering job, I could no longer work at a tool and die shop because of the company's policies. Then, to bring in more money, I started a backhoe business putting in septic systems, etc. I kept very busy at that in the evenings, plus I farmed and raised hogs. To say the least, I was very busy.

Then one night after I quit my job, the Holy Spirit again spoke to me in His still, small voice and said, "Sell your land." I was on my knees at that time praying, and I started to weep after I heard this. My heart was nearly broken. God was requiring something of me that was so dear to my heart. It was also very dear to Pat and my children's hearts. I knew beyond any doubt that it was the voice of the Holy Spirit saying this to me. With tears streaming down my face, I said, "Lord, I will sell it as you say." After that I started to think and say to myself, "The Lord is requiring me to burn every bridge behind me as I serve Him! I will sell our land, but there is no way we can ever go back as a family to what we had before this. Yes, the bridges are being burnt behind us, and we can only go forward after this."

The Lord then spoke to me in His still, small, voice, telling me that I was to get all the Bible training I could in one year. I enrolled at Wesleyan University in Marion, Indiana, and planned to start my Bible classes in September of 1970. Later I would find out how important it was for me to follow this direction.

After hearing God speak to me to sell out, I did some painting and made a few repairs on the buildings to make the farm look nice to sell. This did not take long. Then I went to prayer and prayed, "God, everything is ready to put the farm up for sale. How do you want us to do it?" I was asking if we should sell it ourselves or should we put it in the hands of a realtor. To my surprise, God said, "Don't sell it yet." This word to wait did not concern me that much at the time. Later it would concern me a lot. This was in the summer of 1970, and I felt that within a few days God would tell us to sell it.

I should have known that Satan was going to test us on our call to go to Africa, but I didn't. At that time I had a lot to learn about his attacks to either stop or discourage a person from fully following God as we were trying to do. As I look back on this time, years later, I realize that I had no training on the type of attack Satan was going to test me with. In church we were told many times how Satan tempts us to sin. This was almost always related to the temptation to lie or steal or do some other sinful act. This type of temptation would have had no effect on me, and I could have easily resisted it. What I was about to face was far different than this, and I was so unprepared for it.

Shortly after the Lord told me not to sell the farms yet, I started to feel like my mind was a battleground. It was like I was surrounded by voices shouting at me such things as, "You are a fool! You quit your job! You will not be able to support your children or your wife! You have wronged them! You lost your retirement and insurance and you are not going to make it without those! You won't be able to put your children through college! You did this and there is not even a God! You blew eighteen and one-half years of seniority with the largest company in the world! That was stupid!"

On and on this went and I could not stop it. It was with me almost twenty-four hours a day. If I woke up at night, this battle in my mind was raging within me. Throughout every hour of the day it was there. It was almost like I was losing my mind, and I could not stop it. The battle raging in my mind was as real to me as the call from the Lord was to go to Africa. My desires to keep my job and land, which included the security they brought to my family, were being used against me. It was a weakness I had, and Satan was using it against me but multiplying it one thousand times over in my mind.

I tried to reason within myself that I had made the right decision to follow the Lord no matter where He directed me to go. However, as hard as I tried, I could not get the raging within my mind to stop. Constantly I was hearing, "You are stupid; there is no God; you quit your job; you cheated your family."

Then on top of that, many of my friends and family started to criticize me severely for quitting my job. One of my close friends said, "Bob, you should be castrated." He felt that I was so unfair to my family that I should never be allowed to have any more children. His statements were very hurtful. Another friend (who went to the same church as we did) went around our community telling people that I had gone completely insane. His words got back to me and again they were very hurtful.

I knew I could not be a missionary unless I overcame this battle in my mind. I also knew I could not do it on my own, because I had tried and it had not worked. I was desperate! I wanted God to do something special in me to remove these attacks, but I could not see how this was possible.

PSALMS 37:4 says, *"Delight thyself also in the Lord; and he shall give thee the desires of thine heart."*

I was delighting myself in the Lord. In my heart I knew I had done the right thing by quitting my job and getting our farm ready to sell, but with my mind I was facing these doubts that kept coming in. I became desperate one night and prayed, "God, if you will give me a faith that does not doubt you, I will give you ten years off of my life." I meant this prayer with all my heart. I was thirty-six years old and did not know how long my life span would be, but regardless of how long I had to live, it would be worth it if God would give me peace and confidence of His very existence and the call He had on my life to go to Africa.

About a week later, my brother came over one evening and told me about a meeting he went to where some Christian laymen gave their testimonies. During that time, a young man told Jim about the baptism of the Holy Spirit. Jim said he wanted that, and some men laid hands on him, and he started to pray in a different language. He was more excited than I had ever seen him. Shortly after relating this to me he had to leave, so I didn't get a chance to question him further.

I went to the extra bedroom in our home where I did most of my praying, knelt down and said, "God, I would like to have the same thing Jim received." I continued praying, but to my surprise the words came out in a different language! I started to praise God in a way I had never experienced before! I was speaking in a different language, praising God, and I knew what I was saying even though I did not know the words!

I was describing all of the wonders of God's creation and praising Him for them. This went on for a few hours. Then I started to praise Him for whom He was, and this went on for about an hour. After that I praised and thanked Jesus for the wonderful things He had done. My love for Christ intensified many times over, and I knew He had answered my prayer. I would never doubt His call on my life or His existence again, and I never have. I can truly say that I have never had to fight those doubts again. I know my God lives, and I know He called me to Africa. Praise His holy Name!

God made a change in my life that night and I have never been the same since. He gave me the baptism of the Holy Spirit! It was something I knew little about, since our church did not teach it. I received a power far beyond anything I could comprehend. He and He alone made a difference in my life. Satan's plans were thrown back into his face. God, in an instant of time, gave me victory over Satan. God's Holy Spirit then started to work in my life in a wonderful way with His spiritual gifts and power.

As a result, He has used me many times since, in many different groups and countries, to make a difference in other people's lives. He became so close to me that communication with Him has, at times, been like talking to my best friend, but He is much more than that. He is the God that created the world and everything in it, and He saw fit to bless me in a way that I never thought possible. Yes, it was God and God alone that did this. Praise His holy Name!

I learned a lesson from this. If I am going to make a difference in this world for Christ, the Holy Spirit has to make a difference in my life first! Also, if I am really delighting myself in the Lord, the desire of my heart will be to obey Him with all my heart, and He will give me what I need to do it.

Satan had his demons shouting in my mind all the words of doubt as he tried to discourage and keep me from going ahead in my service to the Lord, but God outsmarted him and did something wonderful for me. Outside of my salvation, the baptism of the Holy Spirit has been extremely wonderful to me in my Christian life. After that I was able to move in the Lord's work with a power beyond anything I ever thought possible and have had no problems with those doubts that Satan was throwing at me since that time.

I started going to Bible college, and Pat started her student teaching in September of that year. After Pat finished her eight weeks of student teaching, she would have her teaching degree finished. We had some money in the bank to live on, but nearly all our funds were tied up in the land. That fall we had a very large farm payment to make. When the time came, we made the payment, but after that we had little money to live on. We also had a $330 payment to make that fall and did not have enough money left to pay it. If we would have been able to sell our farm, we would have had enough money, but God was continuing to say to me in His still, small voice, "Don't sell it yet."

As the day of the $330 payment came closer, I became quite concerned. Never before had we had a loan that we could not pay, and I sure did not want this to happen now. On the other hand, I was determined I was not going to disobey the still, small voice of the Holy Spirit and sell the land. Land was selling well at that time, and we could probably have sold our farm within a couple of days.

We had a lot of equity in our farm, so we would have had plenty of money if we sold it.

God was leading my brother to sell his farmland and go to Africa as a missionary at the same time He was speaking to me in His still, small voice to do the same. It was a major sacrifice in his life plans to sell the land he had worked so hard for and loved so much. Jim and Mary had three farms at the time, totaling 295 acres of land. Each of the farms had a nice house on the land. God directed Jim to keep the fifty-five-acre farm that he and Mary and the children lived on and to sell the other two farms.

Jim was a very successful farmer and was the largest hog producer in Tipton County where he lived. At that time he had thirty-three sows that he was getting ready to sell. He told me that a man had offered him one hundred dollars each for the sows, but Jim was not comfortable with that price, and he asked me to pray with him concerning this.

We prayed and God spoke in His still, small voice to tell the man that Jim would sell them for $110 each. Jim told the man this price and the man said that he would not give that much for them, so he removed his offer and said that he was going to buy sows from someone else. The one hundred dollars offer for each sow was a good price, but God had said it was to be $110. Jim stuck to the price that God had given us even though it seemed he lost the deal because of it. About two weeks went by and Jim had no more offers for the sows. Logically, he should have taken the one hundred dollar offer because now he might have to sell them for much less.

The days were quickly passing, and Pat and I still had no money to pay the $330 bank loan. I prayed every day asking God if we could sell the farm now, but God continued to give me the word to wait, so we continued to have no money to pay the loan. Then something happened that changed all of that. The man that had made the offer of one hundred dollars each for the sows called Jim and said, "If you still have those sows, I will give you the $110 for each of them." Within hours the man came and paid Jim for the sows.

Since Jim was originally going to sell them for one hundred dollars, he decided to give me the ten dollars extra from each of the sows, which came out to $330—the exact amount I needed for my payment. I had the money the day before the bank note was due, so we went to the bank and paid off our loan. God used His still, small voice to make it possible for us to have the exact amount of money that we needed exactly when we needed it. On top of that, He was teaching me a lesson about waiting on Him and hearing and obeying His still, small voice.

The day before Pat finished her student teaching at our local school, the board decided to hire another teacher. Since Pat was already there as a student teacher, they hired her. She went to work as a teacher the day after her student teaching was finished. This was a miracle of God for us! Since we had not been able to sell our farm, our funds were depleted. All the money I had made for years was tied up in farmland, and we could not get to those funds until we sold the land. Pat's job gave us just enough money to live on while I was going to Bible college.

I continued to go to Bible college, but we had another very large farm payment due on March 15, 1971. There was no way we could save that much money from Pat's wages, so I knew we desperately needed to sell the land in order to make the payment. Daily I kept praying about selling our farm, and God kept saying in His still, small voice, "Not yet." The days, weeks, and months passed. I kept praying and God kept saying, "Not yet." I knew God had told me that I was to sell the farm, and now He was continuing to say, "Not yet."

By the time February came around, I was getting very concerned, because if God did not release me to sell the farm, we would lose it. By the first of March I had to make a vital decision—either sell the farm and disobey the still, small voice of the Lord, or obey what the Lord was saying to me even if we lost the farm. Knowing we had a large payment on March 15, I prayed this prayer, "God, I am not going to disobey You, even if we lose the farm, and I am going to stop praying about it and trust You!"

On about the first of March I stopped praying about selling the farm, knowing we would lose all the funds we had in it if we did not sell it. I turned it completely over to God and was able to be at peace with trusting God to do something. On March 14 as I was praying, the Lord spoke to me in His still, small voice and said, "Rent your farm." I said, "Lord, You know most people rent their land in November and here it is the middle of March, which is almost too late to rent. If You want me to rent it, then have someone call me within two hours and ask to rent the land." One hour after this prayer, I received a phone call. A voice on the other end said, "Bob, I want to rent your farm." I was surprised and yet not surprised because God had answered my prayer.

The man said, "I will pay you this certain amount for the year and I will give you half of it now. I can send the check right away or you can come and get it." I told him that I would rent it to him for that amount and that I would be right there to get the advance payment. I drove to his house right away, and by the time I got there he had the check made out. The check was one dollar more than our payment. On March 15 I went to the bank and made our payment right on time. I know God was testing me regarding my obedience to the still, small voice of the Holy Spirit. Later the Lord told me it was time to sell the farm and it quickly sold.

It is now about forty years later, and I can look back at this time with an insight that was impossible then. I know God let me be tested to see if I would obey His still, small voice, and I am very glad I did. When I quit my job, I felt I had lost all of my retirement and security and would not be able to care for my family. God took care of all of that in miraculous ways. He even put me back into General Motors years later at a very high salary, and I ended up with a higher-paid retirement than if I had stayed. God even blessed us with a beautiful home located on a large body of water. Today I regret that I doubted Him as I did.

I have seen firsthand what God will do when we obey His word to us personally. I have done my best to obey His direction, and it has been a very special forty years. This does not mean everything was easy, but I always had the knowledge and peace that we were where God directed us and doing what He called us to do. Then on top of this, I ended up with the wonderful baptism of the Holy Spirit, for which I will always be grateful.

Ch. 4

"Lord, Give Me a Vision of Hell"

After making a total commitment of my life to Jesus Christ, I found myself wanting to witness to people about Him wherever I went. Even though I witnessed about the saving power of my Lord Jesus Christ to many people, I started to wonder if I really had a burden for these people like I should.

One evening as I was praying in our extra bedroom, I started to think about my burden for people that were going to hell. I felt that I did not have enough of a burden for these lost souls and I wanted to have a deeper desire to be a witness for my Lord. I prayed, "Lord, give me a vision of hell like I have never had before so I will have more of a burden for the lost." I did not know what I was praying for, and totally did not expect what came about immediately after I prayed.

Suddenly I felt like I had died and was not a Christian. A terrible fear came over me instantly! I cannot even express in words how terrified I was. It was a hopeless terror and I started to scream, "I cannot get it back, I cannot get it back!" It was like I knew that I was lost and was going to burn forever, and I could never get an opportunity again to be saved. This horror went on for a short time and then suddenly changed. It was like I had been thrown into something that caused every nerve and fiber in my body to be in extreme pain. My jaw started to slam from the extreme left to the right and back again during this process. My teeth sounded like they were being torn out of my mouth as they ground against each other. My arms and legs were jerking and flailing around, and every nerve in my body seemed to be reacting and jerking. I do not have words to rightly describe how terrible this was! Nothing on this earth could be as bad as what I was experiencing!

I could not make it stop, and it kept going on and on. Finally, during all this torment and fear, I heard the Lord speak to me in His still, small, voice and say, "You asked for this, and it won't go away until you ask for it to stop." Immediately I shouted, "God, take it away." Instantly it went away, and I was left sweating and exhausted on the floor. I was extremely shaken up from my experience. I did not experience pain but my body reacted as if I was burning in flames and it was terrible. On top of that was the terror of knowing it was going to be for eternity. It was a hopeless terror beyond what I can describe!

I am thankful that God, in His mercy, kept me from feeling the pain of the fire. I don't think I could have ever been normal again if I had felt the actual pain. My body, however, reacted in such a way that I knew I had experienced some of the horrors of hell. Again I will say, "There are no words to express how bad it was!"

As I lay there on the floor, I thought, "I can never be happy again in all my life. My life has totally changed. How could I ever laugh or be happy again after experiencing this terrible thing of hell?" I felt a tremendous combination of discouragement and depression upon my shoulders, knowing that millions and millions of people were going to experience what I had just gone through. They would also feel the pain of the burning in addition to what I had experienced. They would never be able to pray and have it go away as I had just done. They would scream for eternity for it to leave and also plead for one more chance to repent and accept Christ as their Savior. Nothing they would do could change their destiny forever and ever. They would be in that terrible place burning forever, a time without ending!

My burden for the lost was now almost more than I could carry. God had given me exactly what I had prayed for, but it was at a tremendous cost to me. I continued praying, but this time it was in a very weak voice saying, "God, I will never laugh again as long as I live after seeing how terrible hell is going to be for the lost." My prayer was very simple and short. I could not pray beyond what I had just prayed because I was so burdened. I felt like I was in a hopeless state. I crawled back to a chair where I had first started my prayer time. I just knelt there for a time, feeling extremely depressed thinking about the horrors of what I had experienced.

Suddenly, as I knelt there, the Lord gave me an inner vision. I saw a large water fountain. As I looked at the fountain, the words came to my mind, "Living water." Then I saw a large wooden cross behind the fountain. I looked at the cross, and suddenly my eyes fell upon a very narrow door directly behind the cross. As I looked at the door, I said out loud, "No person could go through that door, because it is so narrow, without going through that cross."

Then it was like I knew Jesus was standing with outstretched arms on the other side of the cross, waiting for anyone that would come through the cross and the door to Him. Then another scene popped into the picture. Above and behind Jesus was a golden city with golden beams of light shining out from it. It was beautiful. I started to laugh and say, "There is a hell, but no one has to go there, because they can go to heaven if they will come to the Living Water and go through the cross and the door to Jesus Christ."

God in His mercy gave me this last vision. It gave me hope for the future. There is hope for the world to escape hell, but it is only through Jesus Christ. I had known this fact for years, but God was bringing me back to a balance. Right after the vision of hell, I could only think about how bad it is going to be for billions of people that are going to that terrible place. The second vision brought my mind back to the place of knowing that not one of them has to go there if they will accept Jesus Christ as their Lord and Savior and then live for Him the rest of their lives.

My life has never been the same after this vision of hell. I probably have thought about this vision and how terrible it was every day for forty years. I would not pray that prayer again for any amount of money. I would not go through one minute of what I experienced for all the money in the world! The sad thing is that all of the millions and millions of people that have died or will die without Jesus Christ will go through this hell for eternity. It is extremely serious, and every pastor should clearly warn his flock about this place of eternal torment.

Ch. 5

"I Have Sinned against the Holy Ghost"

Pat and I went to a missionary meeting at Jim and Mary's church in the fall of 1970. It was about the same time God furnished us the three hundred and thirty dollars to make a payment. God had taught us a lesson on trusting, and now He was in the process of doing something else in our lives. After the service, I asked the missionary if his mission had work in Africa. He said they did not have an official work there, but a few of their missionaries had gone to Africa with WEC mission. I had no idea who WEC was or what it stood for but the Lord spoke to me in His still small, voice and said, "Get their name and address."

The missionary was glad to give me an address as well as a contact person. He also told me that the mission was called Worldwide Evangelization for Christ (WEC) and that they were a large nondenominational mission. From our conversation, I learned that the WEC headquarters was located in Fort Washington, Pennsylvania. When I got home, I wrote to WEC, and in a short time they replied with information about their mission. The Lord spoke to me again in His still, small voice and said that He wanted us to go to Africa with WEC.

I finished my year of Bible school in the spring of 1971, which was about two weeks before Pat finished her teaching. A friend of mine wanted me to run his backhoe on a job, so I did that for two weeks and made some money. Then the Lord again spoke to me in His still, small voice and said that we were to sell all of our household furniture, etc., and go to the WEC headquarters that summer. By this time we had sold one of our farms and the land was rented out for the year on the other one, so we were free to go.

After we sold our household items, we loaded our car and drove seven hundred miles to the WEC headquarters in Fort Washington, Pennsylvania. The headquarters compound consisted of about forty acres located on a beautiful heavily wooded hill on the northern edge of the city limits of Philadelphia. It was called Camp Hill because George Washington and his troops camped on that particular hill for a time during the Revolutionary War. At one time, the estate was owned by a very wealthy family who built a mansion there as their summer home. When the mission purchased the property, the large home was in terrible disrepair, and the WEC personnel rebuilt it themselves to save money. They made the old estate into a beautiful setting for a mission headquarters.

Through the summer, I became very involved in doing maintenance at the mission headquarters. The old buildings took a tremendous amount of work to keep them going. Since I had electrical wiring, plumbing, and general building skills, I was kept very busy. Pat was very busy helping to run the household jobs such as cooking. In September of that year, we were to start our missionary candidate training at the WEC headquarters, which would last four months.

God also led my brother Jim and his wife Mary to the WEC headquarters, and to the same candidate program that Pat and I were in. It was there that we met Esther and her husband, who were on the WEC staff at the time. Pat, Mary and Esther became good friends during the months we were there. Our children, Michael, Tony, and Tanya and their cousins, Belinda, Mark, and Debbie all got to know Esther and her husband's children, Kevin and Miriam. Kevin was just three weeks younger than our four-year-old Tanya, and Miriam was eighteen months at the time. They all had a good time together during those months.

By the first of September, about thirty young missionary candidates were at the WEC headquarters eager to start their candidate training, Jim and Mary and Pat and I being among them. Part of our candidate training was to spend every Friday afternoon witnessing to people in the city about Jesus Christ.

A young missionary named Allen (not his real name) came on a Friday in late October to visit our WEC headquarters. When he found we were going to witness in the city, he wanted to come with us, and it was decided that he and I would go as a team. We decided to drive to the center of Philadelphia, park our car, and walk around, letting the Holy Spirit lead us to the right person.

As Allen and I walked down the streets, trusting God to direct us to the right person, we entered into light conversation, getting to know each other. We were dressed in casual clothes with light jackets due to a slight breeze and chill. Allen was about twenty-five years old from New Zealand, and I was thirty-seven from Indiana. We had grown up in different parts of the world but we had the same goal of bringing people to the Lord and were both going to be missionaries in a foreign land.

40

As we walked into a small park right in the center of the city, we saw an elderly man who appeared to be in his late seventies or early eighties sitting alone on a park bench reading a newspaper. He was neatly dressed in a gray suit with a white shirt unbuttoned at the collar and no tie. He had the appearance of being a businessman that might be retired. He seemed to be out enjoying the outdoors while it was still warm enough to do so.

The man was probably about five foot nine inches in height and weighed about 150 pounds. His white hair and general appearance gave me the first impression that he might be rather distinguished, and a man that was in control of whatever he was involved in. As most of us know though, first impressions are often wrong, and this was no exception. I looked around and noticed that the three of us were the only people in the area. There were a few trees and a small fountain in the center of the park that was surrounded by very tall, majestic-looking buildings.

Allen went up to the older man first and spoke to him with his New Zealand accent, saying, "Sir, may we talk to you about your eternal destiny?" When the older gentleman said, "Yes," Allen began to talk to him about God's plan of salvation. Allen took about twenty minutes, explaining in detail God's plan for us and how we had all sinned and came short of His glory due to sin in our lives. It wasn't until Allen started to tell the elderly man how he could be saved, that the man interrupted for the first time. What he said startled us both. He said, "Wait, boys, you don't know me. You are wasting your time on me. It would be better if you talked to someone else who can be saved. You see, I have sinned against the Holy Ghost and can never be saved. I am eighty-four years old and will soon die. Then I will have to go to hell because I have committed the unforgivable sin."

At that time I entered into the conversation and said, "Sir, what have you done to sin against the Holy Ghost?" He said, "Years ago I committed adultery, and that is the sin against the Holy Ghost for which I can never be forgiven." Then the old man brought a small pocket Bible out of his suit pocket and quoted a scripture that he said proved he had committed this unforgivable sin.

My heart went out to this man as I could see the deep pain he felt as he spoke. The elderly man totally misunderstood the verse he was quoting. I realized the pain that he had in his heart for all of these years, and said, "That is not the sin against the Holy Ghost, sir. God will forgive adultery!" The old man's voice

41

cracked as he answered and said, "You mean I can be saved?" I said, "Oh, yes, God will forgive you for that." I asked for the Bible that he had carried for years, and the old man handed it to me. I opened it to the passage he had quoted and explained the right meaning of the verse. Then, still using his Bible, I went through the story of David and other scriptures, and after I had finished, I said, "You see how God forgave these people. He is no respecter of people, and He will do the same for you."

Suddenly the old man started to cry with his head bowed between his hands. He cried and prayed, "Oh, God, forgive me." We watched and prayed with him as tears fell from his eyes and made a puddle on the concrete below him. After about ten minutes, he suddenly started to laugh and cry at the same time. He stood up and hugged both Allen and me, shook our hands, and thanked us over and over. I had never seen a person so excited after accepting Christ as his Savior. Then he said something so touching. He said, "Now I can go home; I have not seen my daughter in eighteen years due to my guilt. Now I can go home and see her." We prayed with the gentleman and then said good-by to him. Neither Allen nor I ever saw that elderly man after that day, but for years I have had a special joy in my heart that we obeyed God and went to the streets of that city on that day.

Did we make a difference in that old man's life back then and also for eternity? Yes we did! This happened over forty years ago. I am sure the old man is in heaven today, and Allen and me will see him someday. God led both Allen and me in different directions after that day. It was the only time we ministered together in our lives. I went to Africa shortly after this as a missionary bush pilot, and he went to some other part of the world to serve God as a missionary. We have lost track of each other over the years. However, I will never forget how God brought the two of us together from different countries and faraway places to make a difference in one old man's life.

Why did God use us to bring this elderly man to Jesus Christ? I don't know, but why not us! We were both willing to go and to let God use us to make a difference. It was as if God was saying to me personally in His still, small voice, "I want to use you to make a difference in people's lives. I will do it if you will let Me lead you." Since then, I have never forgotten that special day. The results of it have made a lasting impression on my life. By being obedient to God's still, small voice, I know I can make a difference. God wants my obedience! As I obey Him, it is exciting to see Him do the rest, and great things happen!

God will use you to make a difference in people's lives as you decide to follow Him all the way. If you are fully following Him, you are making a difference!

Ch. 6

"Preach My Word First and Fly the Plane Second"

For some unknown reason, the WEC plane in Liberia, Africa, crashed in the jungle, and all on board were killed. The pilot, Don Collins, a German nurse, and an African young man lost their lives in the crash. It was a terrible tragedy for Don's wife, Shirley, and his son, Steve, and daughter, Suzanne, as well as every missionary with WEC and the African Christians. Pat and I first heard about this tragedy when we went to WEC for our candidate training. The WEC staff was praying for a pilot to replace Don. Although I was a pilot and had hundreds of hours of experience working on aircraft engines and airframes, God had not spoken to me to be the mission pilot, so I prayed along with everyone else for God to send a pilot!

I started to fly when I was eighteen years old, and my cousin and I purchased our first airplane when I was twenty-two. I loved flying, which made this opportunity look like a perfect fit for me, and I really wanted to be the mission pilot, so it would have been easy for me to agree to be their pilot, but I had no intentions of getting ahead of the Lord. If this were the job for me, I would wait until I heard the Lord's still, small voice in this matter.

As I stated above, our official candidate training was from September to December of 1971. WEC had a policy that all of their candidates would live together in a type of communal living for the three months of their classes. They would work and have meals together during this time. The WEC staff would evaluate how each candidate behaved in the close living and working conditions. Most candidates had no problems living and working together with other people, but some just felt the conditions were too stressful, and they could not handle it and dropped out.

Each day of the week we would go to classes in the morning, where we would study such things as the cultures of the different countries and other missionary-related subjects. In the afternoons we would do physical jobs such as cleaning and building. Jim and I both had experience in building and plumbing, and they used us in a large remodeling project. On Friday we would go into different areas of Philadelphia and witness to people about Jesus Christ.

On Saturdays, we all worked at the mission compound for four hours in the morning and then were free for the remainder of the day. Jim and I often used this free time to continue working on the remodeling project. On Sundays we were free to attend the church of our choice. Many times Pat and I would take our family on the weekends to visit some of the historical sites around Philadelphia such as Washington's Crossing, Valley Forge, and many others.

Before the end of our candidate training in December, the WEC staff wanted each missionary candidate to announce what country they felt God calling them to. Three days before we finished our program, Pat and I still did not know where God was calling us. This concerned the WEC staff and also concerned Pat and me, but it was not enough to cause me to announce something that God had not yet spoken to me.

That night at 1:00 a.m., I suddenly woke up from a sound sleep. The presence of the Lord was upon me, and I knew God was going to speak to me. I quietly slipped out of bed so as not to wake Pat, and I went into our little living room and knelt down on my knees. I said, "God, what is it?" I knew He was going to say something to me. Then, in that still, small voice that I knew so well, He said, "Go to Liberia, Africa, and preach my Word first and fly the airplane second."

I immediately knew God wanted us to go to Liberia. I also knew that my first emphasis was to be on preaching the Word, and my second was to be on flying the airplane. The next morning I told Pat what had happened during the night and she was very happy. Then, that morning I told the WEC staff what God had spoken to me, and they were very pleased. They had been praying for a pilot, and I was to be that person.

At the end of the program in December, the staff made a decision as to which candidates they felt could live in stressful conditions working with other missionaries in foreign countries. All of the candidates in our class were accepted except one couple. They did not have trouble getting along with other people. They were rejected because they could not get along with each other!

WEC had the policy that every missionary had to have a minimum of one year of Bible school. Before Pat and I went to our WEC candidate training, the Lord had directed me through His still, small voice to get a year of Bible training at the Wesleyan College, which I did. Pat graduated from Wesleyan College and had enough Bible training to be accepted. As a result, we were both accepted to go to the mission field right away.

Jim, from the beginning of his call of the Lord, knew that God wanted him and Mary in Swaziland, and even though WEC did not have a mission outreach in Swaziland, Jim felt God wanted him and Mary to come to the WEC candidate program. This was a little confusing to them, but they obeyed God anyway and came. During their candidate training, God spoke to Jim in a very special way that He wanted them to put their call to Swaziland on hold and to go to Liberia.

God simply had a detour for Jim and Mary! Some missionary women who lived in the Bassa tribal area had prayed for years for a man to come to their mission station and build a Bible school for their people. God needed someone to build a Bible school in Liberia, and Jim was the man for the job!

Jim and Mary did not have Bible school before they came to WEC, so they were required to get one year of Bible school, and in addition to that they were to get teaching in linguistics. After they finished Bible school and linguistics, they went to Liberia as missionaries.

A young man named Bob Gilbert had gone to Liberia to fly the mission plane until WEC could get a full-time pilot who had gone through their missionary candidate program. After the Lord spoke to me that I was to be the mission pilot in Liberia, I remembered the seven thousand dollars I still had in my GI Bill that I had not used. It would be enough to get my commercial flying license with a multi-engine rating before I went to Africa. Since Bob was already flying the plane, I felt that he would be willing to stay a bit longer until I received my training. I talked this over with the WEC staff, and they wrote to WEC in Liberia with this proposal. The WEC staff at the headquarters and those in Liberia all agreed to have me delay going to Liberia until I received my commercial license with the multi-engine rating.

Wings Field Airport, a twenty-minute drive from the WEC headquarters, had a very good training program for receiving a commercial license with a multi-engine rating. I signed up for it, and soon after starting my training, I got a job working there under their top mechanic when I was not flying. I wanted to get all the experience I could on maintaining planes before I went to Africa. I enjoyed both the flying and my hands-on work on the planes. The mechanic I worked under was very good and did all he could to train me. The lessons I learned from him would be a great help in maintaining the mission plane in Liberia.

My flight training went very well, and I passed my written test and my flying check rides the first time for both my commercial and multi-engine rating. By the time I had the ratings, I had used up all of my GI Bill except fifty dollars, which the government got to keep. Previous to coming to WEC, I had used some of my GI Bill funds to go to Bible college.

Pat and I were now ready to go to Africa. But before we left, we needed to make a trip back to Indiana for a last visit and to take care of a very emotional situation in regards to our sons.

Liberia did not have a school for missionary children, and our sons would have to go to the neighboring country of Ivory Coast to the WEC Missionary Children's School as soon as we arrived in Liberia. They would be separated from us and would be in a school and environment completely foreign to them. This would be very difficult for them as well as for us, so after a lot of prayer and discussion, we decided that it would be best for them to finish their school year in Greentown, Indiana, where they had been attending before we went to WEC. They would be going to school with friends they knew and would be living with David and Mary Anne Long, close friends of the family, until the time came for them to join us in Liberia. This was a very difficult decision for us, but in the end we felt that it was the best for the boys.

Pat and I made the seven hundred-mile drive back to Indiana and took care of the details to leave Mike and Tony with the Longs. When the day finally came for us to leave for Africa, Pat and I took Mike and Tony to school that morning with very heavy hearts. It was extremely difficult for us as we dropped them off at school and watched them walk down the sidewalk and through the school doors. We watched them as long as we could, but when the doors closed behind them, we could no longer see our beloved sons. We also knew that we would not see them for a long time.

Both Pat and I started to cry uncontrollably. I was crying so badly that I could hardly drive. We cried for probably the next one hundred miles of driving. I knew in my heart that God had promised to bless our children if we obeyed Him, but it was still very hard to leave our two sons and head on our long trip to Africa.

When we arrived back at the WEC headquarters in Fort Washington, we purchased our tickets to fly to England and then on to Liberia. Then we packed a few barrels of supplies that we sent to Africa by ship. We would be there before they arrived. We flew to England and spent ten days at the WEC

International Headquarters near London, where we had a few days to visit some of the sites in London, and flew on to Liberia.

I still remember stepping out of the plane at the airport near Monrovia, Liberia, and taking my first breath of air. It felt like I was breathing in an oven because it was so hot; however, soon I would get used to this heat. WEC Mission in Liberia was called Liberia Inland Mission, and their business agent was at the airport to get us. He took us to the mission headquarters in Monrovia where we spent three days checking into the government offices. I also had to get my Liberian flying license, which required a physical examination.

From Monrovia we went with the field leader, Wesley Bell, on a two hundred-mile drive on a jungle road to Bahn mission where we would be living. The road was dirt and gravel, so it was very dusty and extremely rough. The drive gave us our first look at the thick jungle where the trees and vines were so close together that it looked impossible in some places to walk through. As we drove, we were able to see many villages with their mud houses covered with grass roofs. Each village had poorly dressed, barefoot children playing in the dirt or kicking a coconut around as a football. Then there were the women and girls cooking, in big black pots, which were sitting on three rocks over a fire. Each village had a few chickens running around, plus some jungle goats. The women were colorfully dressed and all wore a scarf on their head. Even though many of the children looked poor, all the children and adults were very clean.

It was a hot, hard drive, but after about five hours we arrived at Wesley's mission station, called Flumpa, which was located on the same road that led to Bahn mission. We arrived at Flumpa around noon and ate a meal prepared by the missionary ladies, and after lunch Wesley took me out to see the Flumpa airstrip. When I first saw it, I wondered if a person could land a plane on it because it was so hilly and rough. Later I would find out that it was the best airstrip that the mission had.

When we arrived at Bahn mission late that evening, the missionaries had lined the path to our house with arches covered with jungle flowers. It was beautiful, and I am sure that they had spent many hours making the arches with the flowers. Many African Christians were there to greet us; all standing on the sides of the path to the house, and each greeted us as we walked down the path and through the arches. They treated Pat, Tanya, and I like royalty.

Next the missionaries had a very delicious African meal for us. It consisted of some foods that we never had in America such as cassava, plantain, and paw paw.

Cassava is a root of a tree that can be boiled or fried, while plantain is like a large banana that is fried. Paw paw is a fruit that looks like a muskmelon but has an entirely different taste. Their main staple was rice with greens and gravy on it.

That evening we were taken to our house. It was a very small two-bedroom house with a kitchen and living room, built out of sun-dried mud blocks with a concrete floor. The house had a lot of termites in it that had eaten large portions of the ceiling. The bedroom was filled with mosquitoes that came into the room by going through the roof vents and down through the holes in the ceiling. With so many mosquitoes in the room, sleeping under mosquito nets was a necessity.

Like all of the missionary houses, our rooms had little lizards that walked around on the ceilings eating mosquitoes. No one paid much attention to them, and neither did we. Our first night included all of this plus the jungle sounds, as well as the Devil Society drums beating until the very early hours of the morning.

The missionaries at the station were Bill and Jean Kimbery from England and their two little girls. Bill was the station leader, and he and Jean were both teachers in the mission school. June Harper from Ireland was the mission nurse. Shirley Collins was a teacher in the mission school; she and her two children were from Canada. Shirley was the widow of the pilot that was killed in the plane crash. Pat was also going to be teaching in the mission school, and I was to be the pilot.

We were now at our home in Africa, living with the people that we would be working with. God had used many ways to get us there, which had included speaking to me with the still, small voice of the Holy Spirit and also through prophecy, tongues and interpretation, and what I call inner visions. It also included being struck mute at one time. To get there I had left my engineering job with General Motors and as far as I knew at the time, I had lost my retirement income. On top of that, our family was now separated with our sons still back in America. With all of this in mind, we knew we were where God had called us, and He was going to use us in a wonderful way right where we were at the time.

The next five and one-half years would include a series of events that are too numerous to write down. I have written several of them in this book and will not expand on the stories at this time. Mike and Tony did join us after their school year had finished in Indiana. We found out about a very good correspondence school out of Chicago called The American Correspondence

School, and we signed the boys up. Mike could finish his high school and Tony could take all of his high school by correspondence. Now the boys would be able to live with us year-round and take their schooling right in our own home, and we loved being together again as a family.

Ch. 7

"The Plane will Crash and All Will be Killed"

The first time I saw the mission plane was exciting for me. I knew I would soon be flying it across the jungle nearly every day. The body of the plane was painted yellow and white and the wings were an unpainted aluminum. A missionary woman had painted the words "Wings of Service for Jesus" across each side of the cowling. I liked this inscription on the plane because that was what I wanted to use it for.

Bob Gilbert, the pilot that went to Liberia to fly the plane until WEC got a full time pilot, took me up for my first flight over the jungle. On our first takeoff, I was amazed at the power the Maule plane had with its large IO-360A engine. I had never flown a small plane with the acceleration that it had or one that could get a large load off the ground as quickly as it could. It was a very good plane for flying in and out of the very short jungle airstrips. I continued to fly with Bob for about three months to all of our village airstrips and mission stations. Bob did all he could to ensure that I knew their location and how to land at each station and village airstrip.

About three months later, the plane was turned over to me, and I started flying as the mission pilot. I never forgot about God's word to me in His still, small voice that I was to preach His Word first and fly the plane second. I was the mission pilot, but I was first and foremost a minister of God's Word.

Most of my flying with Bob was during the three months of dry season in Liberia when it hardly ever rains. I took over just about the time the daily jungle rains came, and these gave me some real challenges. About six months after I started to fly the plane, I had a very unusual experience. I had no idea what was going on at the time, but I now know that Satan and his demons were planning to kill me and destroy the plane. How do I know this? It came from a word of prophecy from someone who was demon possessed.

The power of Satan can be great in an area where people worship and make sacrifices to him. God, however, is much greater, and His power outperforms Satan's every time. I am sure the devil wanted to attack me all the time, but he could only go as far as the Holy Spirit let him. When we are fully living for Jesus Christ, we are under God's protection. I know this to be true, but I also believe if we get out from under God's protection by allowing sin into our lives, then we are open to the attacks of the devil without God's protection. Satan attacked Job and we see in the scriptures that his problems were not of his own making. There was so much more involved that Job did not know.

One Sunday morning Pat, Jean, and June were walking to our church in the village of Bahn. The mission station was located on top of a hill near the edge of the village. At the bottom of the hill was a small stream with a few rocks laid in the water as stepping-stones for walking across the water. As the ladies neared the stream, they saw a woman lying on the ground, moving around like a snake in the mud at the edge of the stream. She had no clothes on, was filthy, and verbally abused the missionary women. It was obvious to the missionaries that she was demon possessed. Demon possession is common for people that have been involved in witchcraft, and the missionary ladies had seen this type of thing before.

The missionary ladies ministered deliverance to the woman and cast out the demons. The woman was set free, and her mind became normal. She told the missionaries that she became demon possessed when she went to a witchdoctor and paid him to cast a spell on her husband because she was angry with him. At one time this woman was a Christian, but she stopped serving the Lord. Now she was set free to serve the Lord once again. The three missionary women took this woman back to the mission station to get her cleaned up. Next they gave her a clean African dress, and they all went on to church. The Christians at church knew this woman, and they also knew that she was demon possessed, but they had not been able to minister deliverance to her. They were all very excited to see her come into the church clothed and in her right mind.

This woman continued on with the Lord for a while, but again became very angry with her husband and went back to the witchdoctor, paying him once again to put a curse on her husband. Satan is a hard taskmaster and he and his demons will take every chance they have to possess someone who involves themselves in witchcraft. Again this woman became demon possessed, and was probably worse off than before, according to MATTHEW 12:43-45.

When the unclean spirit is gone out of a man, he walketh through dry places, seeking rest, and findeth none. Then he saith, I will return into my house from whence I came out; and when he is come, he findeth it empty, swept, and garnished. Then goeth he, and taketh with himself seven other spirits more wicked than himself, and they enter in and dwell there: and the last state of that man is worse than the first. Even so shall it be also unto this wicked generation.

To my knowledge I had never seen or spoken to this woman, but little did I know what an input she would have on my life!

We had been attending the yearly conference of the Gio and Mano Christians at a mission station called Garply. The road to Garply was in bad shape, and it took a full day or two for many of the Christians to walk back to their villages. About one thousand Christians attended the week of meetings, and after the last service, I planned to fly as many as I could back to Bahn in an effort to help them get back to their villages as easily as possible.

The last meeting was on a Sunday afternoon, so as early as possible on Monday morning I took Pat, Tanya, and another person back to Bahn on my first flight out. They were going to prepare food for those that came to the mission station later that day. The flight from Garply to Bahn only took twelve minutes, but it was a twenty-five-mile walk or about a day of driving by car, because the road went in the opposite direction from Bahn mission station to another village and back around to Bahn; the roads were so bad the trip took almost the whole day. I planned to fly back and forth all day carrying people from Garply to Bahn, so I had a heavy day of flying ahead of me.

That morning after we got into the plane, I turned the starter key, and it roared to life instantly. We then taxied to the end of the airstrip. I checked the engine, and it ran and sounded perfect; I checked the controls and they checked okay also. We had our normal prayer for God's protection, I gave the engine the power, and within seconds we were above the trees, on a heading for Bahn. After about six minutes of our flight, I thought I heard a strange noise in the engine. It only lasted about one second, but it concerned me. I had spent hundreds of hours sitting behind that engine, and I knew it's every sound. I looked my engine gages over and everything looked okay, but I was still concerned about that strange sound.

53

Then, all of a sudden, I heard another sound like that of a twelve-gage shotgun. Instantly, I heard a high-pitched screeching noise that sounded like the engine was being torn apart. Once again I checked all the engine gages over, and they still looked okay, but I knew something was being torn apart in the engine. I still had full power, but the sound was almost unbearable.

Pat heard the sound also, and she started to pray. Although I was praying too, I was also looking for trees in the jungle where I could have a controlled crash if it quit running. I knew it could not last long, so I had to be prepared to come down in the jungle. There were a lot of palm trees in the jungle that had very few leaves and very solid trunks. I had already planned that if I ever had to come down, I would try my best to avoid an area with a lot of palm trees, because their solid trunks would tear a plane to pieces.

The tall trees with a lot of small branches would be the best to bring a plane down in, because the branches would help slow the plane before it hit the ground. Many of us pilots had talked for a long time about how we planned to slow our plane down right above the tall trees in case we ever did have to crash-land. We hoped that our wings would settle into the small limbs and take away most of our speed, which would ease our crash some. Our plan was like trying to make the best out of a very bad situation.

If the engine completely quit running, it would be harder to pick out a softer place to bring it down. The Maule was a good, short field plane with a lot of power, but when it was loaded, as we were, it had a terrible glide ratio. It would come down fast if it had no power. I quickly thought it over and decided to continue to fly as long as I could. We only had about five more minutes to go, and how I prayed and hoped it would keep running that long. The five minutes seemed like a very long time as I kept watching and picking out places with larger trees.

I did not know it at the time, but the front ball bearing in my generator had broken. The loud screeching noise was the gear on the front of the generator being torn up by the big ring gear which also drives the camshaft and the magnetos. If one tooth on the ring gear broke, the engine would stop immediately, and we would come down. I also did not know it, but the front of the generator had a hole torn in it that was getting larger by the second. The hot engine oil was being dumped out of the hole in the front of the generator. It was spilling out into the engine compartment and along the sides of the plane.

The villagers in one of the small villages that I passed over were telling each other that Mr. McCauley was pouring oil on them.

Back at Garply mission station, a line of Gio and Mano people were waiting for me to return and bring them to Bahn. I did not know it, but right then as I was flying, the demon-possessed woman was standing in front of the line, making fun of the people for standing there waiting for me to return. She kept saying to them, "The plane is going to crash, and all in it will be killed." She was laughing at the people as she said this. It was evident that the demons in her knew that I was going to have engine trouble, and they planned that we would be killed as a result.

I don't know all the details of what was going on in the spirit world at the time, just as Job did not know all the details of what was happening to him, but I do believe the demons had something to do with the bearing breaking, or else they would not have known about it. I am sure they wanted to kill us and stop what God was doing through us. God, however, would only allow them to go to certain lengths when they attacked us. God probably agreed that they could cause the ball bearing to break. Of course that is only a guess, as I don't know the full story. I do know that the bearing broke and that the demon-possessed woman was making fun of the people for waiting for me, and that she was telling them that we would be killed. She knew something was going to happen to the plane, and I believe she knew it as a result of her demon possession.

When I saw our runway at Bahn mission I felt better, but I knew I had to fly past the runway and then make a turn and get lined up on my final approach. I also would have to slow the engine down and slow down my airspeed. The worst part of this was in knowing that if the engine quit during my approach when we were slowed down to land on the short runway, the plane would drop out from under us quickly and we would be killed. I planned to make my landing pattern as short as possible, but I also knew that I might have only one chance to make it. I could not afford to miss my landing spot and have to make another go-around.

Landing on Bahn mission airstrip had its own peculiarities. A pilot could only land on Bahn runway from one direction because of a hill. Most of the jungle airstrips were this way. There was a lower level of ground and then a hill and a higher level of ground. A pilot had to get the plane on the ground on the lower level and then let it roll up to the top level as he was applying the brakes to stop. There was also a very tall, dead cottonwood tree about one hundred yards straight out from the end of the runway. These are the tallest trees in the jungle in Liberia, and they stand about one hundred feet above all the other trees. This tree was about twenty feet across at the base of the trunk. I found that the best way I could get around it was to come in on my approach at forty-five miles per hour and then make a slight cross control slip to my left, and then one back to my right, and then slow the plane down to about forty miles per hour in order to get stopped after getting the plane on the ground.

This time I needed to get by the tree while not coming in too fast. I flew past the end of the runway, but only about one fourth as much as I normally did. I made my turn, slowing it down as I did. I made my turn so close to the end of the runway that I did not have to go around the tree. When I straightened it out, the engine was still running. I pulled the flaps right at the last second as I crossed the end of the runway, and then pulled the power all the way off, pulled back on the yoke, and we were on the ground. I immediately turned the engine off and we had just enough speed to roll up the hill to the second level. It worked out perfectly, and I thanked God for this.

I got out of the plane and could hardly believe what I saw; the sides of the plane were dripping with engine oil. I opened the engine compartment, and the entire engine and everything in there was covered with hot oil—even the hot exhaust pipes were covered with oil. As I looked at the amount of oil on everything, I was amazed that it did not catch on fire. The outside of the plane and the engine compartment looked a mess, but I was thankful that my passengers and I were safe. We came very close to death that day, but I praise God—we walked away from it with no harm to us.

The demon-possessed woman was not in error when she said something was going to happen to the plane, but she was in error when she said we would crash and be killed. God had not allowed Satan to kill us that day, and we survived to win more people to Jesus Christ. As far as I know, the demon-possessed woman never got delivered again after that.

The Gio and Mano Christians had a good week of hearing the Word of God taught and preached, but getting home was quite a task for them. Most were unable to catch a ride by car or truck, so they walked the twenty-five miles back to their villages.

It's possible, perhaps, that the devil wanted to hurt them as much as he wanted to kill us. I don't know. Whatever it was, God was the winner as He always is for those that will serve Him with all of their heart.

Very quickly I found the problem with the engine. I removed the generator and was amazed at how large of a hole had been torn in the front of it, where the oil was leaking out. I closely examined the teeth on the ring gear and they were okay.

About two years earlier, a "Flying Club" made up of Europeans working at an iron ore mine crashed a Maule plane about one hundred miles north of us. The mission field leader and I went there with a large truck and bought the plane for one thousand dollars. It had many good parts on it, which we could use. The generator was one of them; I put the used generator on the engine. It worked great, and we were back flying within a few days.

Ch. 8

"Tower, Tower"

One day during the rainy season, I flew our mission airplane to a village called River Cess in order to pick up a German nurse and take her to a village called Botawea. From the air I could see thunderstorms in nearly every direction. My flight was very important because many people's lives could be compromised if I did not get the nurse to the village. The whole area was expecting us to treat their sick people that day, and from past experience I knew many of them would be very ill. People from far-off villages would carry their ill people for a day's walk or more to get medical treatment when they knew we were coming to set up a clinic. Some people would be deathly ill and could not be properly treated by the nurse in the village, so I would fly them to the mission hospital, which was about one hundred miles away.

My biggest concern in getting the people medical help was the weather. If a jungle storm was over Botawea, it would be impossible for me to see well enough to land the plane. Botawea's very short, rough airstrip was tricky to land on because I needed to maneuver around some small trees and a hill before touching down. Any rain during my landing would make it nearly impossible to see and avoid these obstacles.

My flight to River Cess would take me right by Botawea, so as I was flying and watching the different storms, I anxiously waited to see what the weather was like at Botawea. About forty-five minutes after I took off, I could see Botawea about two miles off to my left as I passed by. I was very happy to see that the weather at that time was clear. I did, however, notice a storm front approaching the village from the south, so I knew I only had a short time to get the nurse back before the rain came. If I had no delays, I had just enough time to pick her up and fly her back there.

As I got closer to River Cess, I saw rainfall over the village and surrounding areas. However, I could see that the airstrip outside the village was still clear. Now I faced a decision. I could avoid the rain, land at the airstrip, and wait out the storm, or I could fly through the rain and pass over the village to let the nurse know I had arrived. Then she would drive her motor scooter to the airstrip after seeing my plane over the village. I could then fly her on to Botawea, and we should get there before the storm. I knew hundreds of sick people waiting on the nurse would be extremely disappointed if she did not arrive, and some might even die. Therefore, in spite of the rain, I decided to fly over the village.

I saw no hills to worry about and began to feel comfortable with my decision. After all, I had flown in rain many times before at other locations. I soon discovered, however, that this would have been a terrible choice without the Lord's intervention. I was unfamiliar with the River Cess area, but thankfully God knew what to expect.

I dropped down to about fifty feet above the trees and headed straight toward the village. I was flying about 130 miles per hour at low altitude when I entered heavy rain. Immediately, I could see nothing out of my windshield, so I held my altitude by looking out the side windows. After about thirty seconds, I could see village huts, confirming my course was perfect, and I could proceed to fly over the village.

The raindrops were making extremely loud cracking sounds as they hit the front window. With the noise from the rain and the roar of my engine, the noise level inside the cockpit was very loud. Despite this noise I suddenly heard a very still, small voice faintly whisper two words: "Tower, tower." Instantly, I realized this voice was the Holy Spirit.

I shouted to myself, "There is a tower in this town!" and immediately yanked the control yoke back. For some reason, I made a sharp climbing right turn. The left wing and nose of the plane came up in a split second, putting the plane in a steep right-hand climbing turn. Then, through my left window, I saw a huge tower flash by my eyes. My left wing tip missed the center of the tower by just a few feet, and my wheels missed a large support cable by about two feet. My wings were nearly parallel to the cable as I passed over it, otherwise my left wing probably would have hit the cable.

The shock of seeing the huge tower flash by my wing tip at 130 miles per hour and realizing how close my wheels came to the cable stunned me for a few seconds. I knew that I had just come extremely close to losing my life. If I had not reacted instantly, I would have hit that tower right in the center and died. Also, if I had not given the plane a very strong right bank and right climb, I would have crashed into the support cables. If I had delayed one quarter of a second, I would not be here to testify of God's deliverance. In addition to knowing how close I came to death, I also knew I was only alive because the Holy Spirit had spoken to me in His still, small voice.

I could not dwell on these thoughts, however, because I was still flying a plane in a storm with almost no visibility out of my front windshield. By this time I was well out over the ocean since the tower was located right at the edge of the water. I stopped my steep climb while I continued to make a right turn and flew over the water following the beach until I saw the little airstrip. By this time I was out of the heavy rain.

I slowed the plane and landed on the little airstrip outside the village, and the nurse arrived a few minutes later, just as planned. We quickly put her medicine and other supplies in the plane and set out for Botawea. We arrived shortly before the storm got there, so the nurse was there to treat the sick people just as planned. I never told her how close I came to losing my life that day because I did not want her to feel badly. I have, however, told this story to others many times for the glory of God. I thank Him for my life and for the extra time He has given me to proclaim His Word to people who are lost and on their way to an eternity in hell unless they are born again through the blood of our loving Lord Jesus Christ.

Over thirty years have passed since I heard Him whisper, "Tower, Tower." I reacted instantly. I have asked myself a thousand times since then, "What if I had delayed one second?" The answer is clearly this. I would have died if I even delayed for a second. A second is so short but it would have been long enough to have cost me my life.

Today I want to hear and instantly obey His voice just as I did that day. Perhaps you too need to hear God's voice to help you avoid a "tower" in your own life. However, you will never hear Him if you are not praying and living according to His Word. Obey Him at all cost and never compromise. Totally commit every area of your life to Him and ask Him to lead you in every way. Delight yourself in Him. Choose to please Him no matter where that choice takes you in this world or what it costs you. Study and believe His Word. As you do these things, you will hear His still, small voice and know His will for your life. And, as a result, you can have an eternal impact on the lives of others by helping them also seek the Lord's voice and His will.

Ch. 9

God Made a Tunnel in the Fog

My wife and I and our eight-year-old daughter, Tanya, were on a week's vacation near an iron ore mine and village named Yekepa that was located on the northeast side of Liberia. A local missionary family went on a trip and wanted someone to stay in their house while they were gone, so we volunteered. We were enjoying ourselves, but a lot of our time was spent thinking and talking about our two sons, Michael and Tony, who were still back in Indiana finishing their year of school before they came to be with us. During this time I made a few flights for our mission flying out of the local landing strip that week, but most of my time was spent with my wife and daughter. The iron ore company had a swimming pool and we were able to spend a lot of time swimming and relaxing around it. They also had a pool area that was especially made for young children, and Tanya was having a good time playing in that pool.

The week quickly came to an end, and some missionaries drove us about ten miles to the local airstrip. The mission plane was sitting where I had tied it down after my last flight. As usual, I was relieved to see that the plane was still there and okay. This was especially true when the airstrip was far from home and in a location where there were no lights or security.

The plane looked good as it sat there with its yellow and green fuselage and aluminum wings with their short field takeoff and landing tips painted green. The plane's identification letters were ELAGO and they were painted on the fuselage. The plane had flown through many jungle storms, which had eroded the paint from the leading edges of the wings and nose cowling many times, but I always tried to keep the paint looking good, so I had repainted these surfaces several times.

I checked out the plane from the outside and everything was in good condition, so we were ready to get in. I looked up in all directions at the weather and it looked okay from the ground; however, I had no way of checking the conditions between where we were and our mission station. There were no weather reports in Liberia, and the weather could change very quickly in the jungle.

I knew that the rapidly changing weather conditions had caused major problems for many jungle pilots, including myself, and several had been killed as a result; the weather was a constantly changing force that bush pilots had to deal with and respect.

I knew the dangers of the ever-changing weather, but everything looked good, so we said good-by to our friends and climbed on board, strapped ourselves into our seat belts, and I started the engine. We sat there for a short time letting the engine warm up. I checked out the engine and controls and taxied out on the airstrip. Just before we took off I had my usual prayer for God's protection on the flight. After the prayer, I pulled the flap lever up to fifteen degrees for takeoff, and then pushed the top of both rudder pedals down to lock the brakes. I checked to make sure the prop control was in the takeoff position and did a second quick look around to make sure no other planes were landing, etc., then I pushed the throttle full forward.

Within a few seconds, the engine was running at full rpm and at full power. I released the brakes, and down the runway we went. Within about four hundred feet we were up to flying speed; I pulled up on the flap lever a little with my right hand and back on the yoke slightly with my left hand, and we were flying. I kept my eyes on the trees in front of us that we had to clear, and within seconds we were over them. When we were above the trees and small hills in the area, I saw that there was a heavy overcast, but outside of that the weather looked good for our flight home. The humidity, however, was very high, so I knew that the weather conditions could change very quickly.

About fifty miles later, the weather changed for the worse. We started to get into rain and fog on our heading, and I was starting to get concerned. As a result, I decided to make a return trip to the airstrip from where we had started. As I was making the 180-degree turn, I saw that the weather back toward Yekepa was completely closed in. It looked like a large jungle storm had developed in that area. There was no way that I could see well enough to go back and land at that airstrip, and there were no other airstrips in the area that I could get to. We had to go through the rain and fog and continue on heading to our mission station. This was not the first time I had seen the weather change this drastically, and it was never a welcome sight.

I knew that we were getting into trouble; I had to fly low enough to stay below the overcast, and yet high enough to miss the small hills. The worst thing we could do now was to go on top of the overcast, because if we did we would not be able to find our mission station or know where we were at. To make matters worse, there were no radio signals from the area that we could use to locate ourselves. The visibility kept getting worse, and I kept lowering the plane's altitude to stay below the overcast until I was flying just a few feet above the trees and making sharp turns to miss the hills. We were in big trouble!

Soon we came to an area where the fog was solid to the ground. I could see nothing ahead of us. I also knew that we were flying below the tops of many of the large hills in the area. The only thing I could do was pray as I gave the engine full power to climb out as steep as it could in hopes of getting above any hills ahead of us. The Maule Rocket plane had a lot of power, so it had a very steep rate of climb, and soon we were above the hills. I could see nothing outside the plane except the gray fog, so I was flying completely on instruments.

What made this flight even worse was that the mission plane had only the very basic instruments in it. It did not have a vacuum system, so there were no instruments such as an artificial horizon or any of the other instruments to assist in instrument flying or flying in bad weather. I was taught how to fly using only your basic instruments during my commercial flight training as preparation for this type of situation. The instructors told us if you lose your vacuum system and get into blind flying conditions you can use this procedure, but it is very difficult. I remember thinking at the time that a person would probably never get in this kind of situation, but now that I was in it I was certainly glad for the training I had.

The decision to purchase a plane without bad weather instruments was made by a few people on a mission board committee. The people that made this decision were not pilots, and their reasoning was completely flawed. They felt if they purchased a plane with no bad weather instruments, it would force their pilots to stay out of bad weather, thus keeping their pilots safer. It had just the opposite effect, putting them and those that flew with them at a much greater risk of being killed. The risk of flying without the proper weather equipment was greatly heightened for a pilot flying in tropical rain forest conditions, where the weather changed very quickly.

I was watching the basic instruments closely and praying desperately as we were making the steep climb in an attempt to avoid the tall hills. When we reached an altitude that I knew was safely above the hills, I was relieved to be past that danger, but I was extremely concerned about even more severe conditions we were now in.

We were in solid fog, and I knew that when we broke out on top of it, our chances of finding a hole that we could come down through would be almost zero. Even if we did find a hole down through the fog, I would not know our exact location. I would have to know our exact location in order to get to an airstrip. The trees all look alike from the air, and it is extremely easy to get lost in bad weather. I was aware that if I missed the airstrip by even one quarter of a mile, I would most likely fly right by it and not see it at all.

We continued to climb, and soon we broke out on top of the overcast. The sun was shining and it was beautiful; however, we could not enjoy it because of the seriousness of our situation. The fog below us looked like a level white sea; it was all we could see in every direction. There was no indication at all of an opening down through the fog. I decided to keep the plane on the same heading that I was on when we were going toward our mission station—just in case we did crash, someone would know what heading we had been going.

As I was trying to evaluate our possibilities, it occurred to me that not only did we just have about forty-five minutes of fuel left, but it would also be dark very soon. Both of these factors presented a huge problem, as the only airfield with lights was in Monrovia, the capital city, and that was still one and one half hours away. In addition to that dilemma was the knowledge that a heavy overcast fog can sometimes stay in an area for days, making the chances of finding a hole in the short time span we had a near impossibility.

If we ran out of gas or daylight, we would have to come down in the jungle and probably would be killed, and if we did survive, it would be nearly impossible to live long enough to find our way out of the jungle. I knew that we probably could not survive even one night in the jungle with all the deadly snakes and animals that prowl in the night.

At this point, I was checking my watch closely as each desperate minute passed by with ever increasing speed. I asked my wife, sitting beside me, to pray, which I am sure she was already doing. She knew we were in trouble, but seemed relaxed as she prayed for the Lord's deliverance from our impossible situation. The time was quickly passing and soon I was aware there were only fifteen minutes before total darkness would set in. At this point I said to myself, "Bob, you just killed your family." My heart was heavy and my prayers became more desperate. If God did not make a way, there would be no way we could survive, and He only had fifteen minutes left to do it.

Suddenly I saw what looked like the possibility of a hole through the fog straight ahead of us about a mile away. Could it be true? My heart was in my mouth as I waited. It was a hole! It was very small and almost round. It was like looking down through a pipe, but it was a hole down through the fog! I made a circle around the hole and could hardly believe my eyes, because I could see all the way down through the overcast to the one mountain in all of Liberia that I knew from the top.

This mountain had a very large flat rock on top that I recognized. Some of the pilots called this mountain Old Baldy because the huge flat rock on top of it prevented any trees from growing on it. Although I knew exactly where we were, I still had many questions spinning through my mind. Was the fog down to the ground around the base of Old Baldy? If we got down through the small hole, would we be able to fly to an airstrip from there? Despite the unanswered questions, we had no choice but to go down through the hole and see what awaited us there.

To get through the hole, I had to put the plane in a very tight spiral. This required dropping one wing nearly straight down and making sharp descending turns. I told Pat and Tanya to hold on, and I dropped my left wing nearly straight down and made rapid dropping rotations. Right above the mountain I leveled off and started to fly around the base, but to my disappointment, as I made the turn flying very close to the edge of the mountain, I saw that the fog was all the way to the ground. I could not fly through that fog even though I knew exactly where we were. We still were in trouble. I continued making the circle until I came to an area that was on the three hundred-degree side of the mountain. Once again, I could hardly believe my eyes because there was a tunnel about the height of a telephone pole above the trees and about one hundred feet wide on an exact heading of three hundred degrees.

Flumpa mission station was on a three hundred-degree heading away from Old Baldy. They also had an airstrip, and it was only a ten-minute flight away. I still could hardly believe it. The tunnel through the fog was on a three hundred-degree heading away from Old Baldy! I made a sharp turn and brought the plane around to a three hundred-degree heading and flew down the tunnel. Although I could not see much, I could see enough directly in front of us to keep flying—it was as though the fog kept clearing only in the direction we were going as we went. As we kept looking around the plane, we could see that there was solid fog right above us, and the fog was to the ground only a few feet beyond the wing tips. I hardly looked at my instruments, but rather just followed the tunnel.

This was absolutely amazing! We were flying through a tunnel in the fog. This type of setting was impossible! The fog just does not react like this! It could not have happened in the natural! Only God could be doing this! We were in the middle of something that only God could have made for us. He was making a way where there seemed to be no way!

This amazing adventure lasted about ten minutes and ended at the Flumpa airstrip. This airstrip was very short, and still we could not see the full length of it but only the end. The direction of the tunnel came exactly to the end of the strip. About fifty feet beyond the end of the runway, the tunnel ended and the fog was again completely down to the ground. We made a turn at the end of the runway and landed. By the time we stopped our landing roll and got out of the plane, it was totally dark. We would not have had another thirty seconds of light to land.

This was truly a miraculous landing provided by God, and I will thank Him for it as long as I have breath. There is no doubt that He delivered us from certain death on that day. I am sure the question has come to your mind, as it came to mine: "Why did God save our lives and yet let other Christian pilots in similar situations die?" Only God knows the answer to the times and ways He takes His dear children home. The joy is in knowing that He uses our lives or our deaths to accomplish His work. His work will go on, and His Name will continue to be praised. Although I don't know every answer, I do know that God can make a way where there is no way, and we are alive today because of the way He made for us on this particular day. I thank Him for this and have fully dedicated the remainder of my life to His service. And after that, I will have all eternity to serve Him more in His heavenly kingdom.

Ch. 10

I SAW THE LORD

Bahn was a large African village of about ten thousand people. It was about two hundred miles inland from the capital city of Monrovia, which was located at the edge of the ocean. About 70 percent of the people were from the Gio tribe and the rest were from the Mandingo tribe. It was a very busy place with about half a dozen small stores operated by Lebanese traders. They sold items that the Africans needed such as cloth and clothing, canned fish, bread, paint, building hardware, etc.

Every morning the center of the town was filled with African women sitting either on a cloth on the ground or on a small stool selling different items such as rice, vegetables, dried fish, a piece of cloth, and mats and other items that they had woven. One woman even made and sold peanut butter. It was common for the prices to be bartered, so there were always long discussions between the buyers and the sellers to determine a price. When they finally agreed upon a price, they were all happy and laughed and seemed to appreciate each other in spite of the bartering. We bought almost all of our food from these women.

Our mission station was on a small hill at the edge of town. We had a grade school with about one hundred children attending and a Bible school with twenty-four students. My wife, Pat, was a teacher in the mission school. I flew the plane almost every day, but I could not start flying until nine thirty or later because of heavy fog nearly every morning. This gave me an opportunity to teach the early morning Bible school class and then get the plane ready to fly before the fog lifted. When I was not at the mission station due to my flying, my class was omitted from the schedule.

Tanya was going to our mission school, and her friends at the school were children from the Gio and Mano tribes. She was quickly learning both the Gio and Mano languages. Both languages were tonal, and this made it very difficult for western people to learn. Tanya was learning the two languages very quickly, however. She even helped me with the languages many times, as I had a very hard time understanding or speaking them. Mike and Tony were in Liberia at this time and were taking their high school by correspondence, so their classroom was in our home.

I was flying the plane almost every hour I could be in the air. Each morning just as soon as the fog lifted about two hundred feet above the trees, I would take off for my day of flying. Some of my flying consisted of taking missionaries to various places, and flying needed supplies and mail to the different mission stations. The mission stations that I serviced were located in the Gio, Mano, and Bassa tribal areas. However, my main flying was reserved for medical evangelism. My job was to get doctors and nurses to the villages so that the people there could receive medical treatment. Many of the villages were so far back in the jungle that it took days for them to walk to a place where they could be treated for any illness. As you can imagine, many people died because they could not walk that far.

When we flew to the village, I was the pilot, but when we landed I became the assistant to the medical personnel and also the preacher and teacher. If someone was too ill to be treated properly in the village, I would fly them to the hospital. About 350 people's lives were saved physically through the years as a result of our medical evangelism flying. Also during this time, hundreds accepted Jesus Christ as their Savior.

I usually had very busy days of flying, but when I had room for an extra passenger, I would take either Mike or Tony with me. I let them fly the airplane, under my careful instruction. Both boys were very quick to learn how to control the plane and to keep it straight and level while keeping it on a heading to get us where we needed to go. I would even let them make some landing approaches, but I always took over the controls to actually land the plane, since landing in the short strips was very critical. Both Mike and Tony enjoyed doing this, and it also gave us some very good quality time together, which I enjoyed. Both of the boys ended up with a lot of hours flying over the jungle.

Our mission station had a boarding school for the Africans students who lived in villages that were far away. We also had a medical clinic on the station where our nurses treated many people daily for different sicknesses and injuries. Our nurses would also deliver one or two babies every day in the clinic.

As I stated earlier, before I arrived in Liberia, the mission's airplane crashed in the jungle and burnt. The pilot (named Don Collins), a missionary nurse, and an African young man were all killed in the crash. No one knows what caused the plane to go down. It was a terrible tragedy and a time of great sorrow for Don's wife and their two children, as well as for all the missionaries and the African Christians. Don was buried on the mission station near the school.

Shirley Collins, Don's widow, had a beautiful bronze plaque made for a marker on Don's grave. Shirley and her son and daughter were living on the mission station when we arrived. Wesley Bell, the mission field leader, lived on a mission station called Flumpa, which was about a two-hour drive down a jungle road from Bahn. Wesley had driven to Bahn early one morning, and he and I spent the day mounting the plaque in concrete at the head of Don's grave. It was a very sad day in many ways for us as we worked making the forms, digging the foundation, mixing the concrete, and mounting the plaque in the fresh concrete. We could not help but think about Don and his family, the nurse, and the young man that had died in this tragedy, and all of the sorrow that it entailed. We felt a strong obligation to mount the plaque, but it certainly was not a joyful thing to do.

Little did I know that by the end of the same day, I would have a death experience! Things can change extremely fast, as they did on this particular day. Wesley had a pickup truck with a metal topper over the bed that he had made himself. It was about the size and height of a normal truck bed topper that you can purchase. He did a good job making it, but the rough African roads had caused the metal frame to break in several places, and after we finished our work on Don's grave, Wesley asked me if I would weld the broken steel tubing in his truck topper before he made the two-hour drive back to his mission station. I brought a new portable Arco Welder / AC Generator with us when we came to Liberia, and I told Wesley it would not take me long to weld the tubing, and I would be glad to do it. Wesley went to one of the mission houses to visit with the missionaries while I welded the topper, so I was alone.

It was late in the evening, and I was in a hurry to get the welding done while I still had some daylight. I pulled the welder up behind the truck, plugged in the cables, got my mask in place, flipped the switch from AC Generator to Welder, and started the gasoline motor. A warning sign on the side of the machine said that the ground rod must be driven into the ground before being used as a welder. In my haste, I did not drive the ground rod into the ground, and this proved to be a terrible error. The purpose of the ground rod was to prevent the possibility of the operator being electrocuted.

I welded most of the broken steel tubes very quickly while standing on the ground outside the truck, and after I finished welding all of these places, I carefully looked the topper over to see if there were any other places that I needed to weld. As I looked, I saw one broken place on the frame that was located at the inside center top of the topper. I would have to get inside the truck bed to weld it.

I jumped up inside the bed with both cables. I hooked the ground cable on one side of the broken brace and got myself in place to weld it from the bottom side. I found that the topper was too high to weld while sitting down and too low to stand up. I would have to weld it in a crouched position. It was going to be an awkward position for welding, but I felt I could do it. I moved the tip of my welding rod close to the steel brace that I was going to weld, and then lowered my welding mask over my head.

At that instant, I lost my balance in this awkward position and stumbled backward. My reflexes then took over to keep from falling, and I grabbed the steel brace that I was getting ready to weld. In the process, I lost my hold on the welding rod holder, and as it fell I grabbed the end where it held the welding rod. This all took place in probably less than a second, but it was a major error. My left hand was holding the steel brace that was connected to the negative side of the welder, and my right hand was holding the positive side of the rod holder. This allowed the electricity from the welder to flow right across my chest.

The error of not driving the ground rod into the ground added to my problem. I was the conductor between the positive and the negative sides of the strong electric power. The force of the electrical power was so strong that I felt like I had been hit with a ball bat swung at full force, nearly knocking me unconscious. The electrical current stuck my left hand to the steel brace that I was going to weld, and my right hand stuck solid to the rod holder. Immediately I started jerking badly as the electricity flowed through my body. I could hardly think, but I knew that I had to get away. I tried to pull away but could not do it. My left hand was stuck to the brace like a strong magnet. I had to get away! I leaned forward as much as I could, and very quickly threw my full weight backward. This broke the hold my left hand had on the steel tubing, causing me to fall out of the back of the truck and into a pile of sand.

Suddenly I could not get a breath of air. My lungs were not working properly, and I struggled with all my might just to get a slight amount of air. The next breath, however, was harder than the first, and I realized that I was dying but kept struggling with every effort to breathe. I knew I could not continue this very long before death would overtake me.

One or two minutes after I fell out of the truck, my two sons and Steve Collins, the son of the pilot that was killed, came out of the jungle on a path that went right by where I was lying. They saw me and asked, "What is wrong, Dad?" I replied as best I could, "I am hurt badly; go get Uncle Wesley." I knew they would also get their mother, and within seconds, my wife, my children, Wesley, and the mission nurse arrived along with all of the African Bible school students.

They saw how badly I was hurt and all started to pray. My wife and children were crying and praying. In a weak voice, I told my children that I was dying, and I asked them to live for the Lord. At that time the African Bible students put their hands under me, lifted me above their heads, carried me to our house, and laid me down in our living room on the couch.

By this time I no longer had strength to keep fighting for breath, and I was becoming paralyzed. I knew that death was very close. I lost all feeling except a slight quiver around my heart area. Within a minute after I was placed on the couch, I was totally paralyzed. I could not even move a finger. I could still whisper very weakly, and my wife was kneeling over me with her ear right against my mouth to hear me say, "I love you and I am going." Pat was crying as she spoke back to me, "I love you too."

I wanted to die with my hands lifted and praising the Lord, and I managed to speak the words to her, "Lift my hands." She repeated my words to the others, and Michael lifted one hand and Wesley lifted the other. Right after they lifted my hands, the presence of the Lord came on me like I had never experienced before. It was like my whole body was filled to the brim with His presence. There was absolutely no fear whatsoever of death. I knew my body was going to die, but I would live a new life in His kingdom. The real Bob McCauley was not going to die at all. I had ceased to think about dying because I knew I was going to live. What happened to my body at that time seemed insignificant. I was going on to heaven to be with my Lord Jesus, and this is what I wanted to do!

Not only did the Spirit of the Lord come upon me as I went through the process of dying, but also the most wonderful peace and joy that I have ever experienced came over me. It was so wonderful that I do not have words to express it. I lay there and thought, "All my life I have wondered how it would be to die and here it is and it is the most wonderful thing I have ever experienced." I totally lost all desire to stay in this world and wanted to go on to be with Jesus.

Then I could feel my spirit leaving my body, and at that instant I saw the Lord above me, waiting for me. He was dressed in a pure white robe. Today I cannot remember any of His facial features or even His hands or feet. I only remember the robe. As I looked at Jesus, I wanted desperately to go on and be with Him, but at the same time I felt He had called me to Africa, and the work He called me to do was unfinished. Somehow I knew that I did not have to speak to Him with my mouth but with my mind. I said to Him, "Jesus, I am ready to meet You, but people are going to hell, and I pray that You will give me a little longer to preach." Jesus spoke back to me and said, "I will give you a little longer."

Immediately, I no longer saw the Lord and I could breathe again, and I started to shout with a very loud voice, "O death, where is thy sting, O grave, where is thy victory. I have come to the edge of death and looked in and I saw nothing but glory in Jesus Christ." I then shouted, "I am going to live; stand me on my feet!"

Mike took my left arm and Wesley my right, and they lifted me to my feet. Mike let go of my left arm, but Wesley held on to my right arm. I almost fell over to my left side, and I would have except Wesley held me up. I was totally paralyzed on my left side. I could move nothing on that side no matter how hard I tried. As you can imagine, everyone in the room was staring at me.

By this time, the house was surrounded with Africans, and the room was full of people. I said to them, "I cannot move anything on my left side." I stood standing on my right foot and looking down at my left leg. This went on for a short time. No one said a word, but they all just looked at me in a startled way. All of a sudden I realized I could move one toe. I started moving it and then I could move my foot, and leg, and up to my left arm and hand. Soon I could move my left side, and within minutes I could move my whole body.

By this time, I felt totally exhausted. All of the fight to breathe, etc., seemed to have caught up with me. I was completely worn out. I sat down on the couch and told everyone that if I could get a good night's rest, I felt that I would be fine by morning. I asked Mike and Wesley to help me into bed, which they did. They put me in bed quickly, not even taking time to take off my shoes. Everyone left our home except Pat. My children went with the other missionaries to have dinner with them, and Pat made something to eat, but I was too exhausted to feed myself, so she helped me.

After I had a taken a few bites, I told Pat that I needed to sleep, so she left the room and I lay on the bed for about ten minutes. All of a sudden, a surge of energy went through my body, and I felt more rested than I had in years. I was full of energy and jumped out of bed, shouting to my wife, "A surge of energy came upon me, and I feel more refreshed than I have in years. I don't think I have felt this refreshed since I was a child. God has touched me."

Pat and I went to the other missionary house where they were having the evening meal. They were surprised to see me walking in and told me that the African Christians were having a special prayer meeting for me at the church. I walked to the church quickly, and when I entered, they were down on their knees praying for me. When they saw that I was there and looking well, they started to praise the Lord. After a time of praising Him in the church, they went outside, got palm branches, and started dancing and praising God.

The sight of all these African Christians waving the palm branches in step with their dancing was something to behold. As I looked on just standing there, I started to think, "They are dancing and praising God as a result of me being healed." I got two palm branches and started dancing with them and praising God. We danced and praised God all around the village and then danced up the hill to the mission, praising God all the way. When we got to the mission, we danced and praised the Lord all around it as well. This went on for about three hours. This kind of celebration consisted of a lot of exercise, and yet I still felt very refreshed.

What a day this turned out to be. It started off with building a memorial for the pilot that was killed; to having a death experience, and becoming totally incapacitated, experiencing God's healing and refreshing; to dancing before God for three hours in praise for what He had done. This was certainly a day I would never forget.

The experience had a life-changing effect on my life, and I learned some things as a result of what I went through. The process of dying can be extremely difficult; we can suffer in pain and agony as we move toward the time that this body will die. Many people fear the actual death more than they fear the pain and agony that can lead up to it. The actual dying is the wonderful part of the death process, however. The suffering that leads up to dying can be terrible, but if a person dies in Jesus Christ, the actual time of moving into death can be the most wonderful time in a person's life. The peace and joy at the time of a believer's death will be far more glorious than anything they have ever experienced while living on this earth.

Each morning at 8:00 a.m., our six mission stations had a fifteen-minute talk on their two-way radios. During our radio time the next day, Wesley told the other mission stations about my experience. They were all happy that I was well, but they did have one request. They believed God had touched me, but because I was their pilot, they felt I should have a physical exam before flying again. I was in total agreement with them. Wesley offered to drive me to Monrovia that very day.

While we were making the two hundred-mile drive, Wesley asked me why I was crying as I was going through this experience. He thought I was crying because I was facing death. I saw that appearances can be deceiving, as they were in this case, and I was glad I had an opportunity to let him and others know what had caused my tears. I told Wesley I was not actually crying at all, and I think this surprised him.

I told him that when I fell out of the truck, I fell on the sand pile that was right behind the truck. My head hit the sand so hard that my eyes were filled with sand, and I was struggling so hard to breathe that I did not have time to think about my eyes and the tears. Other people could see the tears, so they thought I was crying, but it was only the natural reaction of my eyes having sand in them. If I had died, I would have hated to have my family and others think I was crying because I was fearful and sad, when I was actually enjoying the peace and beauty of it.

The next morning after our drive to Monrovia, Wesley and I went to the Sudan Interior Mission Hospital, where I saw a very good doctor from the States and told him what had happened. He gave me an electrocardiogram and it showed my heart to be in excellent condition. The doctor told me that my heart had been knocked into fibrillation as a result of the electric shock, and that there was no way that my heart should have started to beat correctly again on its own. He said the only way a heart could be restarted is by using a shock from a special device that puts an electrical charge through the heart in an attempt to restart it, but that there were none of these machines in all of Liberia. Three different times the doctor said to me, "Boy, you should be dead; only God saved you." I knew then that he was right, and I still know it nearly forty years later.

I know that I am alive today only by the grace of the Lord. I asked for more time to preach because people are going to hell. I want to do everything I can to warn people about that terrible place so that they might repent and accept Jesus Christ as their Savior and live for Him. They then can have the joys of dying in Jesus and have His blessings in heaven for eternity.

I well remember my vision of hell and how terrible it was, and I well remember how wonderful it was to experience dying in Jesus Christ. I died that day as a born-again Christian. God's Word confirms the joys that I experienced. His Word also confirms the terrors of dying without being born again. The difference is as far as the east is from the west. One is complete terror and suffering. The other is complete joy, peace, and beauty in Jesus Christ. I hope everyone that reads this will choose the latter and live for the Lord Jesus Christ.

Ch. 11

GOD MADE A WAY TO SEE

Many jungle pilots have died from the inability to see in bad weather or darkness. Almost all of them have the ability to fly at altitude on instruments when the visibility outside is down to zero, but they have to be able to see outside to land on the short airstrips in the jungle. If they cannot see due to darkness or bad weather and are forced to land, they are probably going to crash and possibly get killed or injured badly. The wonderful thing is, we serve a God who can make a way when there seems to be no way!

I took off from the airport in Monrovia, Liberia, one morning with about six hundred pounds of supplies for our mission stations that were about two hundred miles back in the jungle. I did not have the plane overloaded, but it was heavy enough that I had to have a fairly long runway to land on and get the heavy load stopped. I knew Flumpa mission station had the longest runway, so my plan was to land there first and unload their supplies. Then I would have a lighter load for the other stations.

When I got about forty miles from Flumpa, I saw a dark storm front coming toward their runway from the opposite direction. I did not like what I was seeing because I could not land on any other runway in the area with the load I had on board. I needed at least nine hundred feet to get down and stop the plane with this load. If the rain beat me there, I would not be able to see well enough to land, and I would be in big trouble. I sped the plane up to about 140 miles per hour in an effort to beat the approaching storm. When I was about ten miles from the runway, I saw that I was going to lose the race unless the storm front slowed down.

However, it did not, and when I was about two miles from the runway, I watched the heavy rain come across the Flumpa station and runway. I was flying well over two miles per minute, which made the timing very close. If I had two minutes more, I could have landed the plane and been safe on the ground when the rain came. I clearly had lost the race, but there was nothing I could do about it at this time except to trust the Lord to safely get me down on the ground someplace.

I quickly made a right turn to avoid the rain for a short time, so I could still see well as I looked around the area from my plane. I knew the directions to all of our other mission stations in the area, and I could see they were all having heavy rain as well. This eliminated the possibility of going on to a different runway to land. The only area that had clear weather was toward Monrovia where I just came from, and I did not have enough gas on board to go back there. I made a slow circle while I was still outside the rain to give me time to evaluate my situation. There was no other place I could land. I did not like my conclusion at all, but I had no other choice. I had to try and make a landing at Flumpa in the heavy rain!

Having no alternative, I began flying toward the Flumpa runway at a reduced speed of 120 miles per hour and within seconds was in the rain, which caused my visibility out of the front windshield to decrease greatly. You could compare it to driving a car at 120 miles per hour with no windshield wipers. I could see the runway out of my side window until I made the turn for my final approach; then the runway was so blurred that I could not distinguish the runway from the trees. It just looked like a blurred brown area surrounded by green, and I could not tell where the sides were, nor the ends of the runway.

I slowed the plane down and was trying to line it up with the runway for a landing, but I just could not see out of the front, even at the slower speed. From the side windows I could see that I was about twenty-five feet above the trees, but I could not tell where I was in relationship with the runway. I knew I would crash the plane if I tried to land, so I gave the engine power to make a go-around.

I climbed up to about one hundred feet above the trees and made a left turn in an attempt to land again. I could see the runway out of the left side window as I went by it on my downwind leg, so I thought I would try it again. I turned and lined the plane up for a final approach the second time. Once again the runway looked like such a blur that I could not tell where the edges and ends of the runway left off and the trees began. The runway was narrow so I only had about forty feet on either side of my wings before they hit the big trees. This gave me very little room for error.

If I did hit one of the trees, it would most likely spin the plane around and tear off both wings high above the runway, which would cause it to drop to the ground, and possibly burn. I knew I was in trouble, and would probably crash, but I had no other option. I had to land here, so I planned to bring it on down and trust God for the rest.

From the side windows I could see that I was still high and needed to lose some altitude. I quickly did a cross controlled slip to get a little lower. I brought my left wing around in front of me in the slip. This meant I was flying somewhat sideways. When I did this, I was looking out of my left side window as I made the sideways slip. To my surprise, I could see the runway perfectly because the rain was hitting the top of my wing, and I was looking at the runway out of my left window, which was below the wing. The wing was a roof over my window.

I continued to bring the plane down, but held it in the left sideways slip. With my left wing leading the plane and protecting my side window from the rain, I could see perfectly. I was still heading exactly toward the direction of the runway, but I was flying sideways. I held that heading and lowered the plane until I was about ten feet above the ground directly over the runway. Then I quickly brought my nose around so it was lined up with the runway, cut the power, and landed it, looking out the side windows as I did. It worked perfectly! It felt so good to hear and feel the wheels rolling on the ground. By looking out of the side windows, I was able to keep the plane in the center of the runway as I came to a stop.

I very sincerely thanked God that I was safe on the ground. He and He alone gave me this way to see. I know God somehow took control of my flying in such a way as to cause me to be a little high and to put the plane in the left sideways slip so I could see out of my left window. I never would have thought about this. I certainly was never taught this procedure in any private or commercial training I had. God had just taught me a new way to land a plane in very heavy rain. I was able to add this type of landing to my ways to save lives in an emergency.

Not once did I become fearful even when I knew I could be killed, nor did I panic. I did not want to die and I certainly did not want to tear up the mission plane, but despite these concerns, I had an amazing sense of peace that only the Lord could have given me during this whole ordeal. He did give me calmness and peace, but the wonderful part is this: "God made a way for me to see!" This happened over thirty years ago and I still say, "Thank You, Lord!"

Ch. 12

A Hole in the Wing

I purchased a small box of sheet metal screws to have on hand in case I needed them to make any repairs around the mission station. We had a small tool shop in our mission airplane hangar where I planned on putting the screws. As I was walking to our airplane hangar carrying the small box of screws to put in the tool shop, the still, small voice of the Holy Spirit spoke to me and said, "Put them in the airplane." Even though this seemed like a strange request, I recognized the voice of the Lord, opened the door of the plane, and put them in the small toolbox that I carried under my seat. I had no idea why the Lord had directed me to put them in the plane, but I obeyed what He said.

A village named Nee-aa-ka Town was in the process of making a new village airstrip. Whenever a village was making a new airstrip, I liked to go and check their work to make sure they were doing it the right way. I did not want to cause them extra work, and this meant that it was important that they do it right the first time. The easiest way for me to get to Nee-aa-ka Town was to fly to Boya Town and then make the three-hour walk from there to Nee-aa-ka Town.

I figured that the airstrip was about done, so I decided to go there and check things out. I flew to Boya Town and made the three-hour walk to Nee-aa-ka Town. When I looked the strip over I saw that it was nearly ready to fly into, but it was about fifty feet short of what I needed to land and get stopped before I hit the tall trees on the end of the strip. The pastor and people of the village told me that they had many ill people in the village, and they wanted me to fly back there right away with medical personnel to treat the sick people. I could see that they were very sincere in their request, so I told them I would return in one week, but they had to extend the airstrip by fifty feet. I showed them how far to clear the bush and told them to level the ground the best they could.

There was one tree right in the center of the extension that I needed to have removed, but the people of the village asked me if they could leave that tree in place. I told them and the local pastor that the tree had to be removed because I had to have that extra length to get stopped. The first part of the strip was on a slight incline, but the extra length was downhill at a fairly steep decline. I would not be able to see this part of the strip when I landed because it was on the other side of the hill, but it would give me a few more feet to get stopped. The pastor promised me that he would see to it that the tree was removed.

One week later a nurse named Elizabeth Bowman from Switzerland and I got into the plane, with medical supplies in the back. It was a very clear day outside so we expected no difficulties with weather, but we had our usual prayer for God's protection and blessings. Then I yelled, "Clear prop," and started the engine. After doing my preflight check, I gave the engine full power and we were off the ground and flying within seconds, headed toward Nee-aa-ka Town. This town would have been a very hard ten-hour walk from the mission station, but we were there in ten minutes.

I made a quick flight over the village and then flew back to the airstrip and started my approach for landing. I lined the plane up with the five hundred-foot strip, slowed it down to about fifty miles per hour, and pulled full flaps for my landing. I then slowed down to about forty-five miles per hour, and then very slowly started to lower my flight speed to forty miles per hour. I controlled my descent with my engine power and was lined up well to make my touchdown right at the end of the airstrip. Because the strip was so short, I would land with my brakes partly locked but not enough to nose the plane over. I cut the power at the beginning of the strip, and we were on the ground. I pushed very hard on both brakes and we were quickly slowing down, but I would need the extra fifty feet to get fully stopped.

Within seconds we came over the crest of the hill. I was shocked at what I saw. The villagers had cut the bush back for the extra fifty feet, but they left the small tree right in the center of that area. I was going to hit it straight on with the nose and propeller of the plane! In a split second I thought, "Save the propeller," which would also save the engine. I jammed the left rudder down and the plane reacted instantly, turning slightly to the left. The entire rotating propeller cleared the tree, but the right wing hit it very solid. The impact of the right wing hitting the tree made a loud crunching noise, and we stopped instantly.

I looked over at Elizabeth and said, "Are you okay?" I knew the sudden stop had shaken me some and I wondered if it might have hurt her. Elizabeth answered, "I am okay, but what about the plane?" I knew the plane had suffered a lot of damage but did not want her to worry, so I told her that I would repair it and for her not to worry about it. By this time the villagers were all around the plane, and some of them were looking at the damaged wing. I told Elizabeth that we needed to go ahead and get her started treating the sick people. We unloaded the medical supplies and carried them to the village, setting them in order on a few tables furnished by the villagers. Many ill people were already there to be treated, so Elizabeth started treating them right away.

After I helped Elizabeth get set up, I walked back to the plane. During my short walk, I thought about how the pastor had promised me that they would remove the tree before I returned. I was quite upset with him for not removing it, but I determined not to embarrass him before the villagers. This would cause him to lose face in the village and would hurt his ministry.

Later I found out that some of the villagers did not want to remove the tree. It was very possible that the tree was used in devil worship. This was very common in the villages. I remembered that in one village there was a tree that was used in devil worship. Every time I saw the tree I thought about how the Devil Society had taken a little girl, broke both her arms and legs, and dug a shallow hole, and put her alive in the hole. Then they covered her up, planted a tree over top of her body, and made an offering of the child and the tree to the devil.

It was a horrible act, but in a Devil Society many terrible things take place. There was something special about the tree that I hit with the plane that caused some of the men not to want to cut it down. They were willing to cut the other trees down but not that one. Whatever it was, I determined to not show any anger at the pastor for the sake of the Gospel of Jesus Christ being preached in that village.

When I arrived back at the plane, there were about fifty African men, women, and children standing there looking at it. The plane sure looked sick sitting there slammed against that small tree. I asked the men to help me push the plane away so I could look it over. A limb of the tree had gone right through the leading edge of the right wing in one place, and the trunk of the tree had smashed the leading edge of the wing back almost to the front spar in another place. I examined the rest of the plane and found that the gas tank and the spar had not been damaged. The rest of the plane was fine. I had saved the propeller by quickly jamming the left rudder down to miss the tree trunk with the prop.

My big question then was, "How can I fly the plane out of the jungle airstrip with the damaged right wing?" If I did try to fly it out as it was, the 120-mile-per-hour wind, blowing through the large hole, would probably rip the metal right off of the ribs in that area, and then I would be in real trouble, because that wing would probably no longer fly. I had to get the plane back to my mission station where I could repair it, and it would be nearly impossible to carry the plane out of the jungle. I had to fly it out, but how could I do it with that big hole in the wing?

As I was thinking about this, the still, small voice of the Holy Spirit spoke to me and said, "You have the sheet metal screws in the plane." Then I remembered how the Lord had spoken to me a few days before this in His still, small voice telling me to put the screws in the plane and not in the hanger.

A plan started to form in my mind. I needed a piece of sheet metal to make it work. The Africans called sheet metal zinc, so I asked the pastor if there was any zinc in the village that I could have. He said there was a piece, and I asked him to bring it to me, as well as a hammer. One of the African men ran to the village and within fifteen minutes he brought back a small hammer and piece of sheet metal that was about eighteen inches square. I looked it over and noticed that it had a painting of the devil on it. Every village had a Devil Society that worshiped Satan, and this was probably a painting that had to do with their worship. I did not like having a picture of the devil on it, but I saw that it was the perfect size that I needed and was the right thickness, so I decided to use it anyway.

I had a nail in my toolbox, and I took the piece of sheet metal, laid it down, and used the hammer and nail to punch about six holes along the four sides of it. Then I laid it down above the hole in the wing and bent and formed it to fit almost perfectly the curve of the leading edge. I held it in place with one hand and used it as a template to mark the location of the nail holes on the wing. I took the nail and hammer again and punched small holes in the sheet metal of the wing. After that I took out the screws that I had in my toolbox and used them to screw the sheet metal over the hole in the wing. When I finished screwing it down, it looked very good. My repair would totally eliminate the problem of the hole in the wing even at 120 miles per hour. Also, the leading edge was so perfect that I would have excellent lift in that part of the wing.

I looked over the area of the wing that was smashed back nearly into the spar and did not see any holes in the area. I knew I would have very little lift from that area of the wing because of the large dent, but I also knew that I would have enough lift from the rest of the wing to get off the ground in time to clear the trees at the end of the strip if I flew out by myself. This meant that I could not take Elizabeth out with me.

Elizabeth had originally wanted to be in Nee-aa-ka Town two days, and I had planned to leave her and return for her. I still needed to get her back to the mission station, but I knew I could not have the Maule repaired in time to fly her out. I asked if she would mind if my friend with his Super Cub came and picked her up in two days, and of course she agreed to this. I knew the Piper Super Cub could easily land in the short airstrip. I also knew I would not be able to communicate with Elizabeth when I flew out, so I wanted to have a plan in place to get her out of the village before I left.

I got on my two-way radio and called my Baptist friend, asking if he would mind doing this for me. All of the missionary pilots had a good working relationship with each other, even though we were with different mission organizations. Each of us had flown for the other missions when their plane was down for repairs, etc., and we knew where each other's airstrips were. My Baptist friend agreed to get Elizabeth, so we had a plan and I was free to go.

I got into the mission plane, checked out the controls, etc., and started the engine. It fired up immediately and ran perfectly. Then I locked the brakes and gave it full power. Within two seconds the engine was putting out full rpm and full power. I pushed the yoke forward, raised the tail, and released the brakes. The plane shot forward at a tremendous acceleration, and within about four seconds I was flying. It came off the ground easily even with the large dent in the wing.

I climbed to about 250 feet above the trees and took a heading of about 260 degrees, and within ten minutes I was over my mission station. Due to the damaged wing, I had to increase my landing speed about ten miles per hour, but other than that I had no problem landing. I taxied it to a location on the strip where I could easily work on the wing but which would be out of the way enough that my Baptist friend could land with Elizabeth when she was finished with her medical work at Nee-aa-ka Town.

Shortly after I got back to my mission station, I started to repair the damaged wing. I had the needed supplies and equipment to make a professional repair to the wing and also knew exactly how to do it. Within three days the wing was professionally repaired, and it was almost impossible to tell that it had ever been damaged. Elizabeth Bowman had a very busy two days treating the sick people at Nee-aa-ka Town, and then my Baptist friend flew her back to our mission station.

I have often thought about walking out to our mission hangar with the box of sheet metal screws in my hand. I fully intended to put them in the hangar workshop where I stored my other screws, but as I walked by the plane, the Lord spoke to me in His still, small voice, "Put them in the airplane." I heard Him speak and I obeyed, even though I had no idea that within a few days I would desperately need them to repair a damaged wing in Nee-aa-ka Town. I know it was the Holy Spirit that spoke to me to put the screws in the plane. Otherwise they would not have been there when I needed them. Over thirty years have passed since that time, and I have never forgotten how God saved me from a lot of problems by just speaking to me in the still, small voice of the Holy Spirit and saying, "Put them in the airplane."

Ch. 13

THE PROUD AND ARROGANT DOCTOR

PROVERBS 16:18 says, *"Pride goeth before destruction, and an haughty spirit before a fall."*

For years I have guarded against pride coming into my life because I know it can bring about destruction and a fall. God hates it! Many times He has spoken to me through His still, small voice and also His Word about the dangers of pride. I have seen people that are prideful; they are proud of themselves and everything they have. I know they are in for destruction and a fall because God's Word tells us they are. I personally saw a very proud and arrogant man brought down to shame one day as I was flying.

I was asked to fly to an airstrip near a town in a very remote part of Liberia to get a doctor and fly him to a mission station on a certain day. I had flown to the remote airstrip about two years before this, so I knew exactly where it was. On this given day, I took off from my mission station at about 10:00 a.m. after the morning fog had lifted. It was a beautiful day with very few clouds in the sky, so my visibility was very good. About fifty miles after I took off, I saw the dirt road that headed directly toward the airstrip I was to land at. Since the road was going in my direction, I followed it. I always felt if the engine quit running in the jungle, it would be best if I could bring the plane down near a road. This would give me a chance to walk out and be picked up if I survived the crash, but it was not often that I found a road to follow.

My flight was during the dry season, which lasted from January to the end of March. During that time there is almost no rain in the jungle. In Liberia there are only two seasons, "The Rainy Season" and "The Dry Season." During the dry season, dust comes south from the Sahara Desert and at times is so thick that pilots can only see about a quarter of a mile. On this day the sky was very clear, and I could see for miles. The road below me was very dry and dusty. I could see that the dust from the few cars and trucks that traveled the road had left a brown covering on top of the trees. It looked like an ugly brown streak about a half a mile wide across the jungle.

Shortly after I landed at the airstrip, I met the doctor. Some missionaries brought him to the airfield where we were introduced. From the moment I first saw him, he was acting very arrogant to the people around him. He was rude and seemed to be filled with pride. He was in Liberia on some kind of medical mission, but he certainly did not make a good impression upon me. I had flown doctors many times in Liberia and personally worked with medical personnel in our medical evangelism. All the doctors I had flown were very fine people that treated those around them with respect and kindness. However, this man was different.

After meeting the people that brought the doctor to the airfield, the doctor and I got into the plane. He was somewhat sharp with me in our conversation, but I overlooked it and started the plane, had my prayer for God's protection, and took off. Shortly after takeoff, I put the plane on a heading for the mission station where I was to take the doctor. The weather was unusually clear for Liberia and we settled in for our hour-and-a-half ride over the African jungle. As far as I could see in every direction, it looked like we were flying over a carpet of green trees. There were no villages in the area, but I could see off to my distant left the dust from the road that I had followed to get to the airfield where I picked up the doctor.

The sound coming from the engine exhaust was so loud that normal conversation in the cockpit was very difficult. I always wore earplugs and my headphones to cut down on the noise and to protect my ears as much as possible. As a result the doctor and I were not engaging in conversation, which was alright with me as I was still disturbed by the way he had treated the missionaries. About a half an hour after we took off, the doctor leaned over and yelled at me in kind of a disgusted way, saying, "Do you know where you are?" He said it almost in an insulting way, which to me was suggesting that I didn't know where I was.

I knew we were on an exact heading for the mission station, and I could still see off to our far left the brown streak through the jungle, which was a landmark for me. After he asked me this question in a disrespectful way, I became more upset with him. I had watched him treat other people with disrespect back at the airstrip, and now he was treating me the same way. I gave him a very short answer, saying "Yes," which I knew gave him no confidence that I knew where we were.

We flew on, and I was relaxed and enjoying the view of the terrain below us. From the air, the jungle had a beauty all its own. As I flew over it, I tried to memorize every detail that I could about what was below me, but I also enjoyed the beauty of God's creation. He knew every detail of each plant that was below me. He knew how the vines grew in their own way, wrapping around the trees as they climbed toward the sky. He knew each insect that either flew or crawled in the thick undergrowth. He made the monkeys and their species and the jungle birds and their beauty, as well as the fish in the streams and rivers that we were passing over. Yes, I was looking at God's beautiful creation below us on this very clear day for jungle flying. This day was special to me because I could see so far.

About fifteen minutes after the doctor spoke to me, once again he asked, "Do you know where you are?" This time, however, he seemed even more arrogant and disrespectful, which irritated me even more. Again I gave him a very short answer, "Yes," with no details. I knew it upset him, but I felt he had it coming. I think the bad side of me was coming out, but at that time I just did not care. If he would have asked me nicely, I would have given him details on our heading and location, but that did not happen.

As we flew on, I could see out of the side of my eyes that the doctor was starting to get very upset. He appeared to be getting a frightened look in his eyes and on his face. It seemed like his cocky attitude was turning into fear. Again after about twenty minutes, he spoke to me in a disgusted way and said, "Are you sure you know where you are?" This time I felt that I should give him some details to settle him down so I said, "See those hills in the distance; the mission station we are going to is right on the other side of the hills."

I felt this would settle him down. He had something to look at, and we were headed right for those hills at about 130 miles per hour. I spoke with confidence, trying to give him assurance that I knew where we were. Within about twenty-five minutes, we flew right over the top of the hills and I knew the mission station was right in front of us. As always, however, a person cannot see a short narrow strip in the jungle until you are very close to it. As a result of this, the doctor could only see more trees below us and not the mission station.

Right after we passed over the tops of the hills, I could hardly believe what happened. Just as I glanced over to see how the doctor was doing, he threw up so forcefully that it hit the inside of the windshield and splattered all over me, the instrument panel, and back on him. I suddenly had a big part of my forward visibility reduced to nothing by vomit! It not only covered a big area of the windshield and the top of the dash, but it was running down over the instruments.

I had not only lost a big part of my forward visibility, but I also could not see many of my instruments. I could see out of a small area on the very left side of the windshield but nothing through the rest of it. The smell in the little cabin was atrocious. I did not say a word but just kept flying, and about ten minutes after this happened, I passed over the airstrip. I could see it out of the very left side of the windshield and my left window. I don't think the doctor could see it at all.

I glanced over at him and noticed that his arrogant look was no longer there; it had been replaced with a look of shame. At this point, I truly felt sorry for him. He was still gagging and seemed to be trying to throw up some more as I was maneuvering the plane to come in for a landing. This was hard to do as I only had a small area of the windshield to see out of. Even with the obstructed view and the terrible smell, I had to get my full concentration on the landing. The landing strip was only about seven hundred feet long, so I had to be careful. I made the turn on my final approach, slowed the plane, and brought it down for a perfect landing.

Once I landed, I taxied the plane to an area where I could park it off the runway. By the time I got there, a missionary man came out to the plane to greet us. The very embarrassed and still very ill doctor got out of the plane with vomit all over him. He smelled as bad as he looked, and his arrogant attitude was definitely gone. By this time he looked like he was the one who needed a doctor. He looked back inside the plane at how he had left it, and I could tell that he was very embarrassed. I also believe he could see by this time that I knew where we were at all times in our flight. He also knew by now that I had also known what time we would arrive.

I can't help but think of the times in our own lives when the Lord knows exactly where He is taking us, and yet we persist in asking Him if He knows what He is doing. When we see the end, we are humbled that we spent so much time in worry and stress. We actually make ourselves sick at times with our own lack of trust in the One who knows the way, and our arrival time to get there. PROVERBS 11:2 says, *"When pride cometh, then cometh shame: but with the lowly is wisdom."* I believe God humbled this man for his pride and arrogance toward God's servants in the jungles of Liberia. He certainly was brought to a place of shame. He probably had been prideful and arrogant with his staff back in the States and with most people he had been around for years.

Ironically, perhaps the Lord also humbled me a bit for getting so upset with the doctor. This thought occurred to me as I had to fly the rest of the day in a stinking cockpit and clothes saturated in vomit.

Ch. 14

A Needle in a Haystack

About thirty-five doctors from an organization called the World Doctors came to Liberia once a year and stayed for about two weeks administering medical treatment to those in need. The mission pilots banded together during that time, flying the doctors to various villages and towns to treat the sick people. One day I was asked to fly to a town on the very southern tip of Liberia, pick up some of the World Doctors, and fly them to another area. The flight to get them would take about two hours and would take me over some of the most remote jungle in all of Liberia.

I had never flown in this area before and that made this trip unique. The town was about 240 miles south of my mission station, and my flight navigation would be made strictly by visual and magnetic compass because we had very poor maps of the area, and no navigational radio beams in that part of the country. Approximately one hundred miles of my flight would be over what is called "The High Jungle" or "The Three-Canopy Jungle." These titles were established because the tallest trees in this area are about 150 feet high with one hundred-foot-high trees just below them. And just below the one hundred-foot trees are fifty-foot trees with an abundance of vines below them. At this point there is almost nothing growing on the jungle floor because of the lack of sunlight even during the brightest part of the day.

The two-hour flight there would use up about twenty gallons of gas, so I had to have both twenty-gallon wing tanks full. I also needed to carry about thirty gallons of gas in containers inside the cabin of the plane to use when I flew the doctors to their different locations. Most jungle pilots do not like to carry gas containers inside of their cabin due to the increased risk of fire and I was no exception to this. However, all of us had to do this occasionally because there were very few places in the country where we could get aviation fuel.

After getting the plane fueled up and doing my preflight check I took a little time to visit with my wife and family because I knew I would be gone for a few days and would miss them. By about ten o'clock the fog had lifted to about two hundred feet above the trees. I was now ready to take off. After I had climbed above the trees, I banked the plane and turned to a heading of about 190 degrees. My only way of knowing the wind direction and speed was to watch the small limbs and leaves on the trees along the way. This was not a very accurate way of navigating, but it was the best I had.

Within thirty minutes after takeoff, I was already in unfamiliar territory. About an hour after I took off, I was over the high jungle, which was so thick that there were hardly any villages in the area. It had probably been about fifty miles since I had seen my last village. In fact, all I had seen for some time were trees and more trees. Then all of a sudden, I saw a very small village. It really surprised me that a village would be in this location so far from any other civilization. As I got closer to the village, I saw what looked like a soccer field or a very short and wide landing strip. I was not sure which it was. The little field was almost square, so it looked more like a soccer field than it did an airstrip, but I was not sure.

The Holy Spirit then spoke to me in His still, small voice and said, "Study this field and remember it." I stared at it and tried to memorize every detail I could as I turned and made a circle around the village. The strip was very short, but it was an opening in the jungle that I thought I could get our plane down on. To do this, I saw that I would have to land coming in from the direction opposite of the village because the trees were shorter in that direction. After making the circle around the village, I put the plane back on the heading to my destination. I continued to think about what I had just seen even after I was long past it, just in case I should ever need a landing strip in this area.

I continued on my same heading for another hour, and sure enough, I came to the village along the ocean where the doctors were. I landed at the village airstrip, shut down my plane, and went to their location. For the next two days, I flew them to the villages that they wanted to go to in the area. After they treated the sick people in a village, I would fly them to the next place. I found the doctors to be very highly trained and qualified people that were using their profession to make a difference in other people's lives. I really enjoyed being around them and appreciated their dedication to helping the African people. After two days they were finished with my services, and I was free to continue my normal flying. I had to fly to another destination in the country, so I did not fly over the same remote area that I had on my way there.

About two years later, I was on a flight back to my mission from the Bassa tribal area. When I took off on that flight, the weather seemed to be good, but when

I got within one hundred miles of my mission station, the weather in front of me changed. There was a very black front coming in my direction from the north and east. I knew this type of storm contained high-speed winds along with up-and-down drafts that were capable of breaking up my plane if I would attempt to fly through it. There was no choice but to turn back, so I banked the plane and made a 180-degree turn. Once the turn was made I was startled at what I saw. The storm had formed in large U shape, with me in the middle of it. It was as black to the west as it was to the east and north. Both the east and the west sides of the U extended as far south as I could see.

Sometimes a black front has some lighter gray spots in it which a pilot can fly through. The gray areas indicate very high, rough winds, but they are not usually strong enough to bring a plane down. However, in this situation there were no gray areas to be seen. This left me with only one option, and that was to fly in a southerly direction. I quickly banked my plane and flew south between the two black sides of the front.

The winds in the jungle storms are usually very violent with speeds up to eighty miles per hour or more. It is hard to control a plane in this type of turbulent winds, much less the up-and-down drafts and the complete darkness. I had experienced these types of storms before and had barely survived them. As I looked and evaluated my situation, I knew that I was in serious trouble. I started to seriously pray for God's help because I was headed for the high jungle area.

I knew there were no places to land in the high jungle area except that small village that I had flown over about two years before. To find it again would be like trying to find a needle in a haystack. I was also coming in from a different direction than I had flown two years before when I had first seen it. If I missed the village by a quarter of a mile, I would never see it in the high jungle. It was like taking a one hundred-mile circle and trying to find a speck of a village in it. And then to add to the odds, the speck had to be found in the middle of a storm. At this point I saw the sides of the front coming closer together. Soon they would catch me, and I doubted the Maule could survive the turbulence. This was a time that God would have to deliver me, or I would soon be dead.

As I was flying, I could see that the space between the black walls of the fronts was getting narrower by the minute. After about forty minutes of flying between the fronts, I saw that I had to find the village quickly, because the black fronts were now only about one-half mile on either side of me. Soon I would be picking up the very violent winds and would not be able to land in them. Unbelievably, right at this point in my flight, I saw the village.

I was amazed, but had little time to even think about it. Both sides of the fronts now were less than one-quarter mile away from me, giving me only seconds to land before I would be in strong rain and wind, making it impossible to see well enough to land on this very short strip. Even though I had to get the plane on the ground quickly, I also had to land at a very slow speed to be able to stop the plane on this short field. I had to make a very good, low-speed landing with no bounce at all, or I would not get stopped in time, and I could destroy the plane and seriously hurt myself.

I passed over the village as I slowed my plane down. I had to cut my final approach very short to keep out of the front and strong rain. I slowed the Maule down to about an indicated forty miles per hour with full flaps and lowered my altitude to where I was just a few feet above the trees. I lined it up with the field coming in from the same direction that I had decided on two years earlier. Then I slowed it down as much as possible without stalling and started bringing the nose up very slowly, adding just enough power to keep the plane from dropping.

Soon I was flying very slow and right on the edge of the stall trimmer with a very high nose attitude and high power setting. The plane was hanging on the engine power at the prop. The nose was so high that I could no longer see the field by looking over the nose of the plane. In order to see my landing spot, I had to look out the left side of the windshield and the left side of the engine cowling.

I was no longer watching my airspeed; I was flying by the feel of my control yoke. My eyes were glued on the field, waiting for that last second before I cut my engine power. I wanted the plane as slow as possible, and hanging on the prop enough, that when I cut the power it would instantly stop flying and not float at all. I also had my toes on top of the rudder peddles with the brakes partly locked. Just as I passed over the edge of the strip, I yanked the throttle back, pulling the yoke back at the same time. The plane instantly stopped flying, settled to the ground, and rolled to a stop within about 150 feet.

At last I was safe on the ground. About ten seconds after I stopped the plane, the heavy rain hit. It was coming down so hard that I could hardly see outside. I just made it with no extra time! I sat there, knowing that God had delivered me from death again! He did it and He alone! He kept the storm back just long enough for me to get on the ground. To this day, I am still amazed at how I found the village. I know that I did not find it on my own, but that my God led me to it. He saved my life that day! Also, two years before this, the Holy Spirit spoke to me in His still, small voice telling me to look this landing strip over and remember it, which I did.

As I sat in the plane, I tried to call my wife on the radio, but I had little hope that the call would go that far, since my plane was sitting on the ground. However, this time the conditions must have been just right, because right after I called her, she answered. I was so glad to hear her voice, and she was just as happy to hear mine. I told her I was okay and safely in a village. I gave her the approximate location of where I was and told her I would be there for the night. I could rest much easier, knowing that Pat and the others would not be worrying about me now that they knew I was safe on the ground.

As I was passing over the village, the thought entered my mind that I didn't even know what tribe this was or if they were even friendly, but at the time, this was not a concern, compared to getting on the ground. I sat in the plane for a few minutes, reflecting on how hard it was raining and how close I came to not making it. To this day, I am not sure if the field I landed on was a village soccer field or a very small landing strip.

About five minutes after I landed, the villagers came running through the rain toward the plane. They were all excited to see a plane sitting on their field. As they gathered, I got out and greeted them. They led me to the center of the village, which was about 150 yards away, and had me sit down on a stool under a grass roof held up by four poles. As I sat there, I noticed the rain had lightened but was still coming down. After giving me a seat, they all left, and I found myself sitting there alone for about an hour. Although I was wet and a little chilly, I was thankful to be safe in the village. I knew I would be spending the night, but I had no idea of the surprise that the Lord had for me that evening.

About an hour later, a few men came walking toward me. The rain had nearly stopped by now, and I could also see a few people starting to come out of their huts. When the men got close to me, one of them spoke up in perfect English.

He greeted me and I greeted him, and then he said, "How do you like your chicken?" This was an unusual question for me, especially in this location. I answered, "I like it any way you cook it." He spoke back and said, "No, you see, I am the cook for the American Embassy in Monrovia, and I know Americans like chicken different ways. I will make you a meal this evening, and I will make the chicken any way you want it." He went on to tell me that this was his village, and he had returned here for a visit. As I remember, he gave me some different ways he could cook chicken, so I picked one. He and the other men left, and in about an hour, they appeared again with a very lovely meal. It was simply delicious—maybe the best tasting meal I have ever had.

After the meal, they showed me to a hut with a bed in it that I was to use. As usual, they gave me a bucket of hot water for a bath and showed me where the bathhouse was. Every village has a bathhouse, which is usually a small round hut with a layer of small stones covering the dirt floor. It is always refreshing after a hot day in the jungle to be able to get a hot bath before you go to bed.

I did not see the cook from the American Embassy again, but there was another man in the village who spoke some English. There were several Christians in the village, including this man. He became my interpreter, and I spent the evening with him and others teaching the Word of God.

The next morning the villagers gave me breakfast and asked if I would pray for some of their sick people. I gladly prayed for them to be healed and I also had the opportunity to talk to each of them about the Lord. They all seemed very happy that I was there to minister to them. It was such a refreshing experience to be able to minister to these lovely people that lived in this very remote place. Not only had I ministered to them but they had ministered to me, a complete stranger, dropping in on them as I had.

By about ten o'clock the weather cleared and, along with most of the villagers, I walked back out to the plane. I did a walk-around check of the plane, including checking the fuel in my wing tanks to make sure I had enough to get home. I thanked the villagers for their hospitality, climbed in, and did a preflight check. Everything checked out O.K. and the engine started immediately. After a few minutes it was warmed up enough for a takeoff.

The little field was almost square and it was too short in any one direction for a normal take off. When I landed the plane in the field the day before this, I was not thinking about how I would later make a takeoff. I was only thinking about saving my life in the storm. God had blessed and I was able to land and get stopped without a crash. Now I needed His help to fly out of the short field. By the time I climbed into the plane He had already spoken to me in His still small voice, giving me a plan on how to do this. It would be a very unconventional takeoff but it would work. I am always amazed at how God can make a way when there seems to be no way. He was doing it for me right at that time.

I would taxi the plane to one corner of the field and start my take off run along one end of the field. I could get about half of my needed take off speed along that end and then make a left ninety degree turn at that speed and get the rest of my needed speed heading along the other side. The main obstacle to my plan was keeping the right wing of the plane from tipping into the ground as I made my left hand turn. A plane has ailerons on each wing that are used to bank it to the left or right. When I made the left turn I would use my ailerons to help lift my right wing. There would not be a lot of lift but it should be enough to keep the right wing from tipping down into the ground. This type of take off run was not taught in the flight manuals but I had confidence it would work.

I made my take off exactly as I had planned and it worked perfectly. Thank you Lord! Just as soon as I cleared the trees, I made a turn to a heading of ten degrees and headed toward Bahn. I had enough gas to get there but not much extra. I leaned the engine out all I could without hurting it, then set the engine and prop control for a flight to use as little gas as possible. My heading worked out almost perfectly, and within about an hour and fifteen minutes I was back home safe and sound, ready for another day.

During those days of flying, I did not always tell my wife or children all the details about how close I came to not making it. They had enough worries about jungle flying without me adding to what they already knew. Usually I just acted like I had a normal day of being a jungle pilot, which in many cases, it was.

Ch. 15

A Beautiful Day Turned Ugly

One day Tony and I took off for a flight from Flumpa mission to deliver fifty-five gallons of kerosene to River Cess mission station. River Cess was in an area of the jungle where there were no roads, so all their supplies had to be delivered by plane. We were sitting in the front seats of the plane, and right behind us was the barrel of kerosene lying on its side in a cradle made just for this purpose. The plane was loaded to its maximum weight limit, but I knew we would still be able to get the weight off the ground due to the nine-hundred-foot-long airstrip at Flumpa.

When we got up to our altitude, I looked around to see if there were any storms in the area. There was not one cloud in the sky, which was very unusual for Liberia. All I could see was pure blue sky and the canopy of jungle trees below us. The day was beautiful! I told Tony that it was the best weather I had flown in since coming to Liberia. It looked like an easy day of flying.

Tony and I settled in for the hour and fifteen minute flight and engaged in some great father/son conversation. Since we were not pushed for time that day, I adjusted the engine controls to a conservative setting to save gas, and we flew across the jungle at about 120 miles per hour. About thirty minutes after we took off, the weather changed drastically. A jungle storm had formed very quickly, and we were encountering very high winds with strong turbulence that caused our plane to rock about radically. I thought about turning around to get out of the turbulence, but when I looked behind us, I saw we were surrounded by black storm fronts.

I looked in every direction for a way out of the storm fronts but found there was not a way out. We were right in the center of the very black fronts, and I knew from their dark color that they contained winds that were so violent they could tear the plane apart. As I scanned the area again, I saw there was no way out, and the fronts were closing in on us quickly. I could not help but remember a good pilot friend of mine who was killed in a storm very similar to the one that was bearing down on us at this moment. I had no other option; I had to get the plane on the ground right away.

One of our mission stations was about ten miles in front of us when I made the decision to get on the ground quickly. The weather was still clear there but their five hundred-foot-long runway was too short and hilly to land on with the weight we had in the plane. About twenty miles beyond them was a rubber plantation, and they had a runway that I could land on if I could get there in time. If I did land there, Tony and I would have to wait for the storm to pass, which could take the rest of the day and most of the night. I knew my radio would not transmit far enough on the ground to call my wife and tell her we were on the ground waiting for the storm to stop.

I also knew my wife and the others would be very concerned if they did not hear from us. They would most likely think we had crashed somewhere in the jungle. I was hoping I could call someone and tell them we would be landing at the rubber plantation, and that we were going to be okay. Then they could use their radios to let the rest of the missionaries know this information, so no one would have to worry through the night needlessly.

My wife was teaching school at that time, and I knew she would not be near the radio if I called her. I knew of no other mission station that would have their radio on and be able to hear our radio call. The mission station that was about ten miles in front of us normally did not leave their radio on because they did not have a generator to charge their battery. As a result, they only used their radio for fifteen minutes twice each day when all of our mission stations communicated at 8:00 a.m. and 5:00 p.m. My plan was to circle their station, rock my wings back and forth, and yell out the window to tell them to turn on their radio so I could call them. I was hoping they would realize that something was wrong and turn their radio on.

When we got to the mission station, I circled it at a very low altitude, rocking my wings back and forth as I had planned. The man at the station came outside the house when he heard us and looked up in our direction. I slowed the plane down as much as I could, cut the power on the engine to eliminate the noise and yelled, "Radio, radio, radio." He watched us do this but he evidently did not understand that I needed to talk to him. As a result, he did not go back in his house and turn on the radio.

I circled about three times, hoping he would know that I would not waste time on a flight doing this unless it was very serious. I could see the circle of weather closing in on us as I made each circle around the mission. I could also see it getting closer to the runway at the rubber plantation.

Finally I realized that he was not going to get on his radio to see if we were in trouble. I had to get to the runway at the rubber plantation in order to get the plane on the ground in time. By the time we got there, the weather was about a quarter of a mile away from the runway. However, I felt I had time to land before it hit us. The rubber plantation runway was level on the north end, but it had about a one hundred-foot-high incline on the south end. I would have to land the plane from the north and get it on the ground in the level area, and then let it roll up the hill as I stopped. There was no way a person could land coming in from the south due to the hill. I was flying very low when I reached the rubber plantation, so all I had to do was line the plane up with the runway, slow it down, and bring it in.

I slowed the plane down to about fifty miles an hour and lined it up with the dirt and gravel runway to make our landing. Everything was going well as we were coming in, but suddenly, as we were right above the trees at the end of the runway, we were hit with a very strong cross tailwind of about fifty to sixty miles per hour coming from our right rear side. We instantly lost most of our lift because the wind was coming at our wings from the back side. There was no doubt that we were in big trouble!

The right rear tailwind caused us to lose altitude quickly, and it pushed the plane to our left as it was coming down. Instantly I pushed the throttle in and the big IO-360A engine responded right away. I slowly raised my flaps back to the fifteen-degree setting in an effort to get more flying speed. My thoughts were totally on instant survival and not on the storm. To survive, I had to stop the plane from dropping any more, make a go-around, and try landing again. The heavy load we were carrying in the plane was making everything even worse.

I was able to keep the plane flying and out of the trees, but I was having a hard time getting it to climb due to the strong cross tailwind. I had to get the plane up enough to clear the hill, or else we would slam right into the side of it. I was holding enough back pressure on the control yoke to keep us in the air, but not so much as to cause the plane to stall.

We were climbing slightly and gained just enough altitude to clear the hill. That was a relief to me, but right after we cleared the hill, I saw a horrible sight in front of us. Someone had put a large electric power cable across the south end of the runway. It was about thirty feet high and we were headed right for it. Due to some small trees beyond the cable, I did not have enough space to go

99

under it, and the plane was not climbing enough to clear it! We were going to hit the cable, and that meant sure death for Tony and me!

I knew one last trick in flying that I was going to use in desperation to clear the cable. I reached down and grabbed the flap lever and pulled it up quickly, which lowered the flaps to the full landing position. This gave the wings a tremendous amount of additional lift, and the Maule plane rose almost instantly up about ten feet, giving us just enough extra altitude to clear the cable. The negative side of this maneuver was that the extra drag from the lowered flaps almost instantly reduced our airspeed. As a result of losing the airspeed, the plane's wings lost lift, and we started to lose altitude almost instantly after we cleared the cable.

The larger trees had been removed from the top of the hill, which helped us, but we still were only about forty feet above the ground when we started to drop after losing some airspeed. We were coming down fast, and I was still holding the flap lever and slowly pulling the flaps up in an effort to gain some flying speed. We were flying right on a stall now at about forty miles per hour, and the speed was still dropping off. Maule built this plane to fly at slow speeds, and we were testing it to the limit.

We were dangerously close to dropping out of the sky, and to make matters worse, we still had that strong cross tailwind. The crest of the hill was about 150 yards in front of us when we passed over the cable. I needed God's help to keep the plane in the air if we were to make it to that crest, because we were flying absolutely on a stall and just a few feet above the ground.

God blessed us, and we were able to continue flying at the stall airspeed until we came to the crest of the hill. The terrain dropped off at the crest into a fairly steep decline. To take advantage of this, I pushed the nose of the plane down slightly and followed the decline down the hill, staying just a few feet above the trees as we flew. When I was able to lower the nose of the plane, the airspeed increased, and within a few seconds we were flying back at about 120 miles per hour again.

God had delivered us from what could have been sure death. I was thankful for that, but we still had to get the plane on the ground quickly. I made a quick circle back to the north end of the runway. As I made the circle I was evaluating what I could do to land under the very adverse conditions. We still had the strong cross tailwind to contend with and I knew my ground speed would be at least forty miles per hour above my indicated airspeed. I also knew I needed to greatly increase my landing air speed in order that I could control the plane in the strong cross tail wind. This meant that our ground speed would be very fast, which would make it difficult to get stopped before we came to the end of the runway.

I was going to count on rolling up the hill to give us extra help in stopping. I knew that the narrow runway had tall trees on both sides and also had tall trees on the north end. The trees would help cut this wind down, so there would be little wind below the tree level. On the first approach we were hit by the strong wind when we were above the trees, so this time I wanted to have a high flying speed above the trees and slow the plane down when we were down below the trees.

This time I lined the Maule up on the runway and held it at about seventy miles per hour as we lowered it into the grove of trees. I could feel the strong tailwind as we flew, but at seventy miles per hour I had good control of the plane this time. I was watching the trees closely in anticipation of the coming wind changes, and almost instantly as we got below the tops of the trees, I could feel the cross tailwind drop off quickly. I pulled full flaps and lifted the nose as much as I could to lower our airspeed. With our extra weight of the fifty-five gallons of fuel in the barrel behind us, our airspeed dropped off quickly as I raised the nose. Within seconds we were on the ground, but at a very high ground speed. I pushed hard on the brakes and the plane slowed down. The hill then reduced our ground speed enough that we were able to stop by the time we came to the end of the runway.

We taxied the plane to an area where we could wait out the storm, and then I shut off the engine. The storm with its heavy rain hit us right after I turned the engine off. We had made it with only seconds to spare. The heavy rain was hitting the plane so hard that that the noise level inside the cockpit was unbelievable. Tony and I sat there listening to this as we thanked the Lord for His blessing in getting us down safely. Again God had saved our lives, and we thank Him for this even to this day.

We knew people would be wondering where we were, because they were expecting us to be at River Cess mission station, and we were sitting on the ground at the rubber plantation. We tried calling them on our radio but they did not respond, so there was nothing we could do to let them know we were okay.

As Tony and I sat in the plane waiting for the storm to stop, my thoughts were on how close we came to being killed and wondering why it all happened. Questions came into my mind, and I was looking for answers that only I could give. My son came close to dying that day and he knew it. Did I do anything wrong to cause this? The weather turned bad very quickly, and we were caught in it. I did nothing wrong that caused us to get caught in this storm.

If I did anything wrong, it was in being overly concerned about worrying Pat and the other missionaries as to where we were. I should not have circled the mission station trying to get them on the radio. This caused about a two-minute delay in getting to the rubber plantation. If I had arrived at the runway two minutes sooner, the violent cross tailwind would not have hit us because we would have been on the ground when it came. I clearly saw that this mistake could have cost Tony and me our lives.

The other thing I wondered about was why anyone would put a power cable thirty feet aboveground at the end of a runway. They should have known better than to do this, but there was nothing I could have done to stop them. I came to a final conclusion: I had made one mistake but God had delivered us, for which I thank Him.

I also knew I was where God had called me. I was flying in these conditions because of the call of God. He had spoken to me in the still, small voice of the Holy Spirit and told me to go to Liberia and preach His Word first and fly the plane second. I was doing exactly that, and even though it contained dangers, I was where He told me to go and doing what He told me to do. I knew this, and there was never one moment when I doubted my call of God to be flying in Liberia, even in the face of danger and possible death.

Other mission pilots were facing these same conditions daily. Occasionally we would see each other and talk about this among ourselves. One of the pilots told me that every day before he got in his plane the thought came to him, "Is this the day I get killed?" He knew he was where God had called him, but he also knew the dangers involved. I had three close pilot friends that were in jungle crashes but lived through them. One even came down upside down and survived. All of us knew that some of our friends who were very good pilots had been killed; yet God had delivered us from similar situations but had allowed them to be killed.

Why were they killed and we were not? None of us knew the answer, but we did know one thing. Our lives were in God's hands, and even if we were killed, we still won because we would be in heaven for eternity. As a result of knowing this, I was not going to be flying in fear but in victory, because God had called me there! As I sat there with these thoughts running through my mind, I had answered my own questions and was totally at peace with my conclusion and answers.

Tony and I sat in silence for a little bit as our minds went through the events that had just taken place, and then we started to talk, enjoying our conversation as father and son as we waited for the rain to stop. From my past experience, the weather looked like one of the jungle storms that could last for two or three days. Tony could see this also, so we both knew we might have to sleep in the plane for the night. At least we were safe on the ground. There were no people at all from the rubber plantation at the runway, so it was just Tony and me. Since we enjoyed each other's company, the time went quickly as we sat there conversing as the heavy jungle rain pounded down on the plane.

When it came time for all of the mission stations to get on the air at 5:00 p.m., we heard the missionaries at River Cess call the other mission stations and tell them that we did not arrive. They were all wondering where we were and if we had crashed. Pat was on the radio with them, and we could tell that she was concerned about both her husband and son. Since our mission had a pilot that was killed in a crash in the jungle there was always a concern that it could happen again. As our mission stations were talking, I tried to call them, but my plane radio signal was just not strong enough for them to hear me. When the plane was in the air, the radio signal could travel quite far, but when it was sitting on the ground, the signal would only travel about forty miles in most cases. We wanted to tell them we were okay, but there was no way to do it.

Not long after our mission stations started talking about where we were, the Baptist mission stations also got on the air and entered into the conversation. They had two planes, and I could clearly hear them say that they would start looking for us as soon as the storm cleared. From the conversations, I could tell that the storm was very widespread across Liberia. The Baptist mission stations reported that it was starting to show signs of letting up, so they were going to start looking for us as soon as it did. I could hear my Baptist friend, Abe Guenter, say to the other mission stations, "Bob knows the area well and knows where the landing strips are, so I believe he is somewhere waiting out the storm, but we will look for him anyway."

Abe was right; I was only about forty-five miles through the jungle from his mission station. I could hear his call clearly, and I decided to try to call him on my radio again. He heard me and called back, asking where I was. I told him that I was at the rubber plantation waiting out the storm. He knew my exact location and relayed my message to the rest of the mission stations, and they called off the search for us. Pat and all the other missionaries were very happy to hear that Tony and I were safe and on the ground.

About an hour after the radio call, the wind died down and the weather began to clear. By 6:00 p.m. it looked safe to fly again, and I decided to continue our flight to River Cess since we were only about twenty-five minutes from our destination. After our preflight checks, we were on our way, and within twenty minutes we could clearly see River Cess station. River Cess had a seven hundred-foot, level landing strip, so we had plenty of length to get the heavy load down and stopped.

It was late in the day when Tony and I climbed out of the plane at the end of the runway. We would be spending the night there. Tony liked the idea of staying at River Cess mission overnight because he had a friend there named Gordie Hodgson. That evening I had a good time visiting with Cecil and Margaret Hodgson, Marion and Ella Peterson, and Elizabeth Bauman, and Tony enjoyed his time with Gordie. The next day Tony and I continued on our way for more jungle flying.

I used to say when I was a bush pilot, "Each day of jungle flying is a 'happening'," and this day would probably fit into the same category. Many times our days just don't go the way we expect, or would like for them to. They start out beautiful and turn ugly. Sometimes we are disappointed in others. I was disappointed in the person that put the large cable thirty feet in the air right at the end of the runway.

If our day seems to go sour, does it mean we are out of God's will? No, of course not. It can be a time when we see the wonderful work of the Lord as He helps us get through some very serious situations as God did for Tony and me. It can also be a time of testing to see if we will go on with God regardless of the difficult time. During the difficult times, it is important that we know beyond any doubt that we are living for the Lord and doing what He wants us to do. Then, no matter how ugly the day gets, we know God is with us as we pass through it!

Even when we face a death situation, He is with us and we have nothing to fear. I have faced death many times. The times have included not only possible death from flying, but also possible death from terrorists as I was preaching in their area. Then there was the time I was dying and saw the Lord. I have also faced the possibility of prison because of where I was preaching. Through all these times, God has been with me and spoken to me in His still, small voice, giving me peace and comfort in the midst of difficult situations. The following verse almost brings tears to my eyes as I read it and know how close my God is and has been when I have faced near-death situations.

> *Yea, though I walk through the valley of the shadow of death, I will fear no evil: for thou art with me; thy rod and thy staff they comfort me.* (PSALMS 23:4)

Ch. 16

A MESSAGE FOR THE PRESIDENT

My family and I were spending two weeks at a mission station named Pillar of Fire, located about 150 miles south of Monrovia. The mission had a beautiful location right along the coast. They had a very sandy landing strip that was about one hundred yards inland from the beach. The strip was hazardous to land on because it was soft enough for a plane's wheels to sink into, causing the plane to tip over on its nose. This actually happened to one pilot, and he bent his prop badly.

The mission house sat about 120 feet back from the beach, and during the night you could hear the waves from the ocean coming in and out. It was so relaxing and pleasant to just sit and listen to the sound of the waves and see the ocean right beyond a line of coconut trees that lined the beach.

The missionaries at this station asked me to be the evangelist at a two-week revival meeting. During the day I did my regular job of flying, and in the evenings I preached at the revival meeting. The meetings were very successful with many people coming to the Lord.

This mission station, as did all of the others, had a two-way radio. One morning at about eight o'clock, a man named John Williams (not his real name) called me on the radio from Monrovia, saying he was from Israel and the Lord told him to come to Liberia. He went on to say that a person in Israel gave him my name, and he needed to see me. This surprised me as I did not know a single person in Israel. As we were talking, the Lord spoke to me in His still, small voice and told me that I was to see him. I told John to get a Liberian taxi and go to the airfield at a city named Buchanan. The drive would take him about one and one-half hours. I would leave my destination as soon as the fog lifted and be there around ten o'clock that morning.

By 9:30 a.m., the fog had lifted enough that I felt I could take off safely. I flew north, following the beach for about thirty minutes, and then landed on the dirt and gravel airfield just north of Buchanan. When I stopped the plane and got out, a man about forty years old, dressed in jeans and a light casual jacket, came walking toward me. He spoke right away, saying, "I assume you are Bob McCauley." I told him I was and he immediately said, "The Lord spoke to me in Israel that I was to come here and see you, and within three days I am to go back to Monrovia to make arrangements to see the president of Liberia. I am to give him a special message. Then I am to see the leaders of the next five countries south of Liberia."

I was very surprised at what he said and answered, saying, "John, it is very difficult to see the president of Liberia." I went on to tell him that sometimes people had to wait months to see him. John answered with confidence and said, "I am to go there in three days!" I invited John to stay with us until that time came.

On the third day after John came to Liberia, the Lord spoke to me in His still, small voice and told me to take him to Monrovia that day. John was already expecting to go that day, so we got into the plane at about 10:00 a.m., and headed for Monrovia. When we landed at Sprigs Payne airfield in Monrovia, I got a taxi and told him to take us to the president's mansion. When we got there, we walked into the lobby and up to the front desk. John told the receptionist that he came to Liberia from Israel, and he had a message for the president that needed to be addressed as soon as possible. The receptionist, a man, looked into his scheduling book and found that there was an opening in two weeks. John accepted the time and date that was suggested, and after completing a few details, we walked out, knowing he had a secure appointment with the president.

For the next two weeks, John stayed with us and helped in our ministry. When the day of John's appointment with the president came, we got into the plane, took off, and headed to Monrovia. During the flight I kept thinking about John talking to the president. I was very concerned about what could happen if he offended the president. I knew he could get into very serious trouble if the president did not like what he had to say. I was concerned that I could also get into trouble since I would be with him. I also was wondering how he was going to see the leaders from the five countries south of Liberia. This just seemed to be too big of a goal for me to believe in.

As I was continuing to fly the plane, I said, "John, what are you going to say to the president?" John answered, "I don't know. The Lord will give it to me when I need it." Then I was really concerned. Here we were, flying to see the president, and the guy I was going to go into the president's mansion with did not know what he was going to say. He told me, as well as the receptionist, that he had a special message for the president, but it seemed even he did not know what the message was. Now, without a doubt, I was very afraid for both John and myself. There was only one thing that kept me flying the plane toward Monrovia after that, and it was the fact that I had heard the still, small voice of the Lord tell me to take John to Monrovia that day.

I continued flying, but we had very little conversation for the rest of the trip. Inside I was very concerned, but I could not help but notice that John was quite relaxed and just seemed to be enjoying looking at the jungle view below us. About thirty minutes later, we were on the runway taxiing up to our parking area.

After parking the plane, we got a taxi and went to the president's mansion, which is called the White House. When our President Monroe sent the slaves back to Africa, they took them to the area that is now Monrovia, Liberia. The freed slaves so appreciated what President Monroe had done for them that they named the place Monrovia after him. Then they set up a government based upon the government of the United States and they even built the president's mansion much like our White House.

John and I walked into the White House lobby, and John presented himself to the man at the desk. He told John that he would be able to see the president within a few minutes. When the time came, an official took John into the room where the president met with his subjects. I waited in the lobby for about forty-five minutes while John was talking to the president. In my heart I knew God wanted me to bring John to see the president, but I did not know John that well, even after we had been together for the past two weeks. I was still concerned about how serious our situation could be if John offended the president.

As I waited for John in the lobby, my mind went back to about a year before this, to a village about 220 miles inland from Monrovia. This village rested in the deep part of the jungle. Another missionary and I were among some other special guests invited to have an evening meal with the president. We sat and talked to him for about two hours that evening. We found him to be very intelligent, and a man that one could not help but respect.

The president talked to me much like a loving grandfather would talk to his grandson. He took a special interest in me when he learned that I was a missionary pilot. It seemed that he wanted to make sure I knew how dangerous it was to be a jungle pilot in his country. He asked me to be very careful, because flying in the jungle was very dangerous. From the way he talked to me, I felt that he really wanted to do everything he could to keep me safe. His interest and special concern for me really impressed me.

As I was thinking about all of this, I was suddenly brought back to the present and began wondering how things were going for John as he was talking to the president at this very moment. Little did I know at the time that a young army sergeant, in the near future, would storm into the very lobby where I was standing and run into the president's bedroom and kill him. After about forty-five minutes of reminiscing concerning my jungle flying and also wondering and praying for John as he was talking to the president, John came out of his session. He had a calm look on his face, so I could tell that things had gone well.

I did not want to get into a conversation with John concerning his time with the president while we were in the lobby, so I waited until we were outside and about fifty yards away from the White House before asking how things went. As we walked, John told me that when he went into the room with the president, the Holy Spirit told him what to say. When John sat down in front of the president, he said, "Mr. President, the Lord says, if you will humble yourself, and pray, and seek God's face, and turn from your wicked ways, then God will hear from heaven and forgive your sin and will heal your land!"

I was rather shocked that someone would say that to the president so boldly. I immediately asked, "John, what did the president say?" He told me that the president slid his chair in front of him, took hold of both his hands, held them in his, then bowed his head and said, "Brother, pray for me." John said that he prayed for the president and that they talked after that for a time. He went on to say that the president had a very special dinner that evening with the representatives from five other African countries, and he wanted John to be his special guest at that meeting and to tell them exactly what he had told the Liberian president. John then named off the five countries that would have government officials at the dinner that night; they were the same ones that John had told me he was supposed to talk to.

That evening John went to the dinner as the president's special guest. When given the opportunity, he spoke to all of the officials, giving them the same message he had given to the president. The representatives of the five different African countries each invited John to come to their country, asking him to speak to their leaders. John set up dates to be at each one of the five countries.

John stayed with us a few days and then headed on to meet with the leaders of each of the five other countries. Even as I write this, I am still amazed at how John heard this prophecy from God and boldly followed it. Every bit of the prophecy came true exactly like John said it would.

It is also amazing how John heard my name in Israel. He told me another man gave him my name, and when he told me the man's name, I had never heard of him. The other man moved in prophecy also, so I wonder to this day if the Lord gave him my name and also told John to meet me in Liberia. If this is the way it happened, it would be much like what happened in Acts 10:1-5 when an angel told Cornelius to send men to Joppa to get a man named Peter.

I never saw John after that, but the memory of what happened when he came into my life has never left me. It gave me confidence in knowing how God can bless and use us if we hear and obey Him, letting Him guide us with His spiritual gifts in the direction He wants us to go. I probably was the only man in Liberia that could have helped John do what God wanted him to do. For one thing, I was moving in the gifts of the Holy Spirit myself and fully believed in prophecy. I also was a pilot and had the use of an airplane to get John around. Whatever it was, I believe God chose me to help John while he was in Liberia, and I am glad He did because this whole experience was a great encouragement to me. I know beyond any doubt that prophecy and the gifts of the Holy Spirit are for today, and I have moved in them and want to continue to do so.

About two years after John came to Liberia, a young army sergeant stormed into the president's mansion and killed him. The sergeant immediately declared himself the new president, and the country went into civil war that lasted for many years after that. It was an extremely tragic time for the country, and thousands of people died as a result of the war.

I am still amazed at how God spoke to John in a still, small voice and how John obeyed and came all the way from Israel to bring a message to the president. Then God spoke to me in a still, small voice to help John. God used the still, small voice of the Holy Spirit to not only bring a message to the president of Liberia, but also to the other five African nations through this obedient man.

Ch. 17

"Dad, You're Going the Wrong Way!"

L iving in the jungle as a family and being a bush pilot gave me lots of opportunities to spend quality time with my children. But as much as I loved this time, there were other times the same job required me to be away from them for days. For every night I got to spend at home, I would have to spend a night or two away. In an effort to spend more time with my children, I often took them with me, providing I had the extra room in the plane.

I wanted the boys to be good pilots but also to be aware that we were flying in some of the worst weather conditions in the world. I taught them the dangers of flying in this kind of weather and the best ways to avoid a storm or to get out of one when it was impossible to avoid. As the boys were flying with me, we often had conversations about some of the other missionary pilots that had been killed while flying. As the boys and I talked about the details of how each of them were killed, it helped them and myself to try to avoid, as much as possible, what went wrong that caused their plane to crash.

My intention in teaching the boys in this manner was not to cause the boys to have a fear of flying in the jungle, but to give them a healthy respect of the dangers it presented and the skills to overcome them. No doubt the firsthand experience did as much in teaching them what they could expect in jungle flying as anything I could have said.

I wanted to make sure the plane was in perfect condition at all times. All of our mission planes were required to have a major inspection after every one hundred hours of flying. To be extra safe, I decided to do a one hundred-hour inspection after every twenty-five hours of flying. It would usually take about eight hours to accomplish this task. It was a lot of labor to remove all the seats, floorboards, cowling, and inspection plates from the plane, and Mike and Tony were a big help. After I did the inspections, they would help me put everything back together again as well. Their work not only helped me, but it also taught them a lot about mechanics and the importance of keeping a plane in top condition at all times.

As the years passed, Mike finished his high school by correspondence and then returned to America to go to Purdue University. His parting was a very sad time for us, but we wanted him to complete his education. Not long after Mike left, Tony spent more time with his African friends. They all enjoyed going on hunting trips in the deep jungle. One day an African hunter came to our mission station and asked if I would buy his sawed-off shotgun; he only wanted twenty-five dollars for it, so I bought it from him and gave it to Tony as a present. Tony loved having his own shotgun and would take it with him as he and his African friends went on their hunting and exploring trips.

The jungle is intriguing to boys; it seems to draw them like a magnet. There seemed to always be something interesting for Tony and his friends to do in the jungle, and I usually let him go. Sometimes Tony would take a trip up the Cess River in a canoe for a week or two with a Lebanese trader; other times he would spend the night far out in the ocean in a dugout canoe, fishing with the Africans.

Tony also loved going long distances on the trails through the jungle with his motorbike. At times this included driving it down into the water and through the rivers in areas that were shallow enough to pass through, and other times he would take it across the large river in a dugout canoe. Throughout the years, he rode his motorbike about eleven thousand miles and learned the jungle very well. One day both he and I benefited from his knowledge of the jungle in a very unusual way that saved our lives.

The jungle has its own dangers such as wild animals, deadly snakes, etc., and there is also the possibility of getting lost, but none of the dangers seemed to bother Tony. I knew there were dangers in allowing him to go, but I felt the benefits far outweighed the dangers. If he could learn to face dangers in the jungle head-on and overcome them, I knew it would build strength into his character. Later this would help him face situations in the world in a very mature manner.

One day I had to make a flight from our mission station to another that was about one hundred miles south of us. We were living at River Cess mission station at that time, and our area as well as the area I was to fly over had an average of 180 inches of rain a year. Because of this, I was anticipating some rain as we made this flight. During my flying years in Africa, I had flown approximately two thousand hours over the African jungle and had made about four thousand takeoffs and landings in the jungle airstrips. Many of these flights had forced me into some very harsh flying situations and conditions. Tony and I were about to face this very thing on this day.

After Tony and I took off, I put the plane on a southerly heading toward the other mission station. When we got about fifty miles away from our station, we started to get into rain, which was fairly normal for the area. We continued on and I could still see fairly well. Then the rain suddenly increased, and the next thing we knew, we were in another one of those quick jungle weather changes. A minute or two later, the rain started coming down so hard that I could not see anything out of the front windshield of the plane. There was an extreme amount of water in the air. It was the most rain I had ever flown in, and I became very concerned about it.

The engine started to suck in so much water through the air intake that it started to misfire badly. It began making a loud backfiring noise. I knew the engine was sucking water into the cylinders and could stop running any second, which meant I had to get out of the rain as quickly as possible. I decided to head north, not really knowing if the weather would be any better, but I decided to take my chances. Not long after we reversed our course, the rain slowed down and the engine started running smoothly again.

It was a good feeling to hear the engine running well on all six cylinders again. However, we were not out of danger yet, because now we would soon be contending with the fast-approaching fog, which could be every bit as dangerous as the rain.

The fog continued getting thicker by the minute. This was causing a huge problem, because I needed to see the ground with its landmarks in order to get back to the mission station. I had no navigational aids and was solely relying on my magnetic compass to get us to the runway. The fog became so thick that I had to fly right above the treetops in an effort to stay in sight of the ground. Even at that, I could only see straight down and no more than two hundred feet in front of the plane.

After about thirty minutes of flying in these conditions, we were finally getting close to our mission station. At last I saw the jungle trail that led to and from our mission. I thought I was on the west side of our mission station, so I turned east and followed the trail, thinking it would lead us to our station and landing strip. The trail was very crooked as it went through the jungle, and I was trying to follow it at over one hundred miles per hour. The turns were coming at me very quickly, and I had to stay in sight of the trail. Since I could only see about two hundred feet in front of us, I had to bank sharply to my right and left in an effort to follow the trail.

I kept asking myself as I made the turns, "Am I going the right way?" I felt like I was going the wrong way, and maybe God was letting me know this, but I couldn't tell for sure. If I was going the wrong way, we were going to be in serious trouble soon because the fog was going to be too thick to see through in just a matter of minutes. Then, suddenly, I saw a large mud puddle on the trail, and I shouted, "Tony, which side of the mission is the mud puddle?" I was hoping that Tony's jungle exploring would pay off at this moment. I was thinking surely in all his jungle exploits he would have seen this mud puddle at some point. Not only was I desperately counting on his remembrance of it, but also as to where its relationship was to the mission.

Tony hesitated with his answer. I knew he was thinking at that time and trying to remember when he saw the mud puddle on the trail. He could see we were in trouble, and he knew his answer had to be right. I knew this was putting him under great pressure, but his answer was of utmost importance. If he waited too long to give his answer, we were in trouble, because the fog was setting in so quickly that I probably would lose sight of the trail. In this situation seconds were important! I am sure it wasn't helping to have me banking the plane sharply and quickly to the left and right to stay in sight of the trail. I could feel the strong gravitational pull on my body as I was making the sharp turns, and I knew Tony had to be feeling them also.

Suddenly, Tony shouted, "Dad, you're going the wrong way!" I totally believed him at that time. I knew Tony well enough to know that he would not have said this unless he was sure. At that instant, I was so close to the treetops trying to stay in sight of the ground that I had to climb up a few feet to keep my wing tip out of the trees as I made the sharp, 180-degree turn.

I followed the winding trail back for about a mile, and then, what a beautiful sight I saw. It was our mission station and runway below us. I was flying only about ten feet above the trees, so I cut the power, slowed the plane, and made a very sharp turn to my left at the end of the runway. The fog was so thick by this time that I could barely see enough to clear the trees and land the plane. God blessed, however, and we made it. It felt so good to feel the rumble of the wheels as they touched down on the ground as we landed. We taxied to the end of our strip, shut the engine off, and thanked God for getting us back safely.

When I first saw the trail and turned to the east, I was probably about one hundred yards east of our mission station rather than west. I was very close to being on course even though I was flying in the fog. Most days this wouldn't have made much difference, but that day it could have been tragic; I was close but I was still wrong, and it could have led to our death.

Proverbs 14:12 says, *"There is a way which seemeth right unto a man, but the end thereof are the ways of death."*

At first, my direction seemed right, but as I was twisting and turning the plane to stay in sight of the winding jungle trail, I know the still, small voice of the Lord was speaking to me, telling me I was wrong, but I was so busy trying to keep the trail in sight that I did not instantly respond.

Knowing the right direction in life can be extremely important. The Word of God tells us in Matthew 24 that in the last days there will be many false prophets that will lead many astray. We are seeing some of that today in churches where the "feel good Gospel" is being preached and many people are being led astray. When I turned the wrong direction, Tony and I faced physical death, but we were both ready to meet the Lord, and of course, that made all the difference. The people that follow the false preachers go in a way that seems right, but in the end it will lead them to eternal death in hell.

There is no escape from this death, and that is why it is so important that a person follows someone that knows the right way. When Tony said, "Dad, you're going the wrong way," I immediately made the turn because I knew he knew what he was talking about. The Word of God is our guidebook. If you are not living according to it, no matter what anyone tells you, you are going in the wrong direction, and it will lead you to an eternal hell. If you have any doubt about your direction, ask someone that knows, just as I asked Tony. If you are headed in the wrong direction, repent and turn around instantly, as I did, and you will escape certain eternal death and be in heaven forever.

Ch. 18

A Man and Beast Plane Ride

Two missionary women living in Liberia, West Africa, in the Bassa tribal area, had been praying for a man, with building skills, to come to their mission station and build a Bible school. Several years had passed and their prayers had not been answered. One day they agreed that they would both pray and trust God for an answer that very night.

The next morning they met for their morning prayers where they would share what they felt God had given them concerning the Bible. Both hated to be the first to speak because they felt God had given them something that seemed so strange. Finally one of them spoke out and said that God was saying that a man and a beast would come to the mission station, and this man would be the one that God had called to build the Bible school. The other missionary was surprised when she heard this, because the Lord had given her the same word. This encouraged them, and they continued running the station and waiting for God to fulfill the promise He gave them.

When Jim arrived in Liberia, a missionary couple from Saclapia Mission Station was ready to go on a furlough, but they needed someone to help on their station while they went home for the year. Jim and Mary went to Saclapia to help while the couple took their leave.

Before Jim and Mary came to Liberia. Jim was one of the largest pork producers in their area. Shortly after they came to Liberia, Jim had an opportunity to buy some hogs from a rubber plantation. He purchased about half a dozen and started raising them on the Saclapia mission station. There was a plant in the jungle that looked very much like a soybean plant. The plant's vines were extremely long and were loaded with pods that contained many beans. Hogs really liked the plant, and the beans had the protein in them that the hogs thrived on. These vines were plentiful and easy to pull out of the jungle. Jim's goal was to teach the Africans how they could easily raise hogs for their diet and also to sell them to get money for other necessities. The Africans caught on quickly, and the program was very successful.

Jim, also being the farmer that he was, decided to plant swamp rice on the mission station and to teach the African Christians how to grow it. The jungle was filled with swamps which could be converted into rice paddies. It took a lot of work, but they could grow rice in them year after year once the rice paddies were prepared. With the same effort, they could grow about four times as much swamp rice compared to the normal dry land rice that they planted. It was also a very successful program. The Africans caught on quickly to growing the swamp rice, just as they had to raising the hogs.

During the year, Jim had a dream in which he felt God showed him that He had called another man to build the Bible school in the Bassa tribal area, but the man had refused to obey the call, and now God was calling him to do this. Jim was very confident that God had called him to move to the Bassa mission station and build the Bible school. He told the mission field leader about this call and requested permission to move there after the missionaries from Saclapia mission station returned. The field leader then presented this request to the mission board.

For many years, the mission had a Bible school at Bahn mission station. Bahn was in the heart of the Gio tribal area. The students were all from the Mano and Gio tribes. These two tribes were located side by side in the jungle, and most of the Gio and Mano people could speak or understand both languages. The mission also had a large work in the Bassa tribal area, but it was about a hundred miles away through the jungle, and they had a totally different language. The Bassa could not understand the Mano or Gio, and the Mano and Gio could not understand the Bassa.

Years before we came to Liberia, some Bassa students attended the Bible school, but it was very difficult for them. Each weekend the Mano and Gio students would go into the villages and preach the Gospel. Since the Bassa could not speak the language, it was impossible to preach in the villages to the Gio or Mano people, and it was too far away for them to go to the Bassa villages. In addition to the language problem, many of the non-Christian Gio and Mano treated the Bassa students very harshly. This made living in the Gio and Mano area very hard for the Bassa students. As a result, no Bassa students were attending the Bible school.

When the field leader and the mission board talked about Jim and Mary moving to the Bassa mission station to build the Bible school, major problems arose.

Some missionaries felt strongly that they should not have two Bible schools because they felt it would split the church. Others felt that it would not hurt the church at all, and that they should have a Bassa Bible school in their own area. The students could go out every weekend, teaching and preaching in the Bassa villages in their own language.

There was a lot of discussion on whether or not to allow Jim to build the Bible school. It seemed to me and also to Jim that the decision should be made on what God was saying, and we felt He was saying to build it. What we did not know at the time, but God did, was that in a few years nearly all of the Christians in the Bahn area—men, women, and children—would be lined up and shot on the mission station where the Bahn Bible school was located. A few days after this tragic event, some of the missionaries would be shot. This would be the end of the Bahn Bible School making the new Bible school extremely important.

God's plan did eventually prevail after several difficult and lengthy discussions. The final decision was that Jim could build the Bible school if they called it an Agriculture Bible school, and if Jim would teach raising hogs and growing swamp rice as part of the curriculum.

Jim agreed to this, and he and Mary made plans and preparations to move to the Bassa mission station. Jim planned to take half of his hogs to the Bassa mission station with him and leave the rest of them with the Christians in Saclapia, so they could start raising their own hogs. To do this, he loaded half of the hogs, with the exception of one sow, into his pickup truck and drove them three hundred miles through the jungle to the Bassa station.

The sow he kept back was nearly ready to have pigs and was a very prime animal. Jim hoped to use her pigs primarily to get the Bassa started on a new venture of raising hogs. He was very concerned though that the long, rough ride in the back of the pickup truck could cause the sow to lose her pigs. He began to wonder if flying her there might be a better option, so he asked me what I thought of the idea of flying her to the station in the plane. Thinking only of the weight of the sow, which was about four hundred pounds, I didn't see any problem with the idea.

Jim and I talked about the details of how we could best accomplish our task. First we would need to remove the back seat from the plane and use the empty area for the sow. Next we needed to build a crate out of very heavy boards in order to secure her. I told Jim that I had just the right type of boards at my station and could make the crate that same evening. He thought that would be great and proceeded to give me the length and the width the crate should be made. We agreed we would have to fly out of the Flumpa mission station, which was about an hour drive away from Saclapia, and that we would meet there and leave the following morning.

When I got back to my station and started to build the crate, I realized that the crate would still fit in the plane if I made it wider than Jim's instructions. Jim had said to make it twenty inches wide, which seemed to me like it would really restrict the sow a lot. I decided to give the sow plenty of room, so I made the crate as wide as would fit in the back of the plane. I thought this was a great idea, and the trip would be lot easier for the sow if she had room to move about. However, what seemed like a good idea now would turn into a bad idea the next day.

The following morning I flew the plane to Flumpa and met Jim, who arrived about the same time with the sow in the back of his pickup. The mission plane had double doors on the side, so I opened both doors and showed Jim the crate. Jim's reaction was not what I had expected; he was alarmed that I had made the crate so wide. He wanted it built about twenty inches wide so the sow would be restricted from moving, and I had made it about twice that width.

Jim explained to me that he wanted the crate narrow so the sow could not jump around during the flight. I now understood the importance of the crate being built the size Jim had requested; however, I also knew it would take a whole extra day for me to get back to my station and build a new one. The sow was very close to having her pigs, and we wanted to get her to the Bassa station before she started birthing. If we waited the extra day, it would require Jim to drive the sow back to Saclapia and then back the next day on the rough roads, which would definitely be a risk to her and her pigs.

We talked this over and decided that since it was so important not to lose the sow or her pigs, we would go ahead and fly out as planned despite the size of the crate. We also reasoned that if the sow reacted badly when I started the engine, we would not go, and if she did move about and get really excited as we took off, we would simply turn around and land the plane. It seemed to us we had it all figured out, and so we proceeded with what we thought at the time was a good plan.

119

We unloaded the sow from the pickup and drove her up a ramp that Jim had brought along for loading her into the plane. The sow walked up the ramp and turned with her head facing the back of the seat just like this was a normal everyday occurrence for her. It sure was a funny-looking sight, a four hundred-pound sow standing in the back of the plane in a crate with her head directly behind the front seats. We both looked at her for a bit and even took a picture of her standing there. She was as calm as could be! I had made a large door on the side of the crate for the sow to go through; we closed and secured it, and got ready for takeoff.

I started the engine, and it roared to life with its very loud noise level. We were watching the sow to see how she reacted, and to our delight she did not act as if the noise bothered her at all. I felt confident that things were going well. We taxied to the end of the mission runway and turned around, and still the sow did not move or react. Things looked good and we took off. The sow acted like an old pro at flying. She was just standing there motionless with her nose right behind our seats. She was not excited at all.

We continued to watch the sow for any reaction that would lead us to feel we would need to turn around. After about fifteen minutes of flying, we were starting to relax and feel more confident that she would stay calm. It was a very clear day, making it easy to see my landmarks along the way. The flight was smooth, and the dense jungle looked like a green carpet about five hundred feet below us. We were still about an hour from our destination, so Jim and I began having light conversation.

Our smooth, relaxing flight suddenly came to an abrupt end at about the halfway mark of our trip. The sow suddenly became very violent, ramming as hard as she could against the sides, front, and rear of the crate. I could hear the boards cracking as she hit them with her four hundred pounds. She tried to jump over the top of the crate, also hitting the top or the cockpit as she did. We were at what some call the point of no return when this happened. It meant that we were just as far from our takeoff point as we were our destination. It was useless to turn around, so we had to continue on our flight. We were in the worst possible location for this to happen.

The boards were made of a very strong wood from the jungle, but I could hear them cracking every time she rammed them. She continued ramming the front and back of the crate and also throwing her full weight against both sides. Her four hundred pounds were like a heavy battering ram hitting the crate. It was like the demons themselves were causing her to do this. Today I believe that is exactly what happened. Somehow we had to stop her.

Jim unbuckled his seat belt and turned around with his knees in the seat, grabbing the sow by her ears. She was trying to turn around, and we were afraid if she did get turned around, she might bust out the back of the crate and lunge to the rear of the plane. If she did, the weight and balance of the plane would be off and I would not be able to control the plane, causing us to crash. Jim was holding her ears with all his strength, but she was fighting him with all her strength. She was extremely strong, and I could see the desperation in Jim's face as he fought to hold her from turning around.

We realized we might have to actually kill the sow in order to survive. The question was how to accomplish it. I had a flare gun in my survival kit, but if I shot her with it, there was a good possibility it would set the plane on fire. Ruling that plan out, I knew I had a hunting knife in my survival kit that we might use to kill the sow with, but if we didn't accomplish her death on the first try, she would become even more violent. Both plans were too dangerous, so if we were to be saved, God would have to do it.

Jim kept fighting to keep the sow from turning around but after only ten minutes of holding on to her, he was looking extremely tired and sweat was pouring off his face. The sow, on the other hand, looked just as strong after ten minutes of wrestling with Jim as she had in the very beginning. I felt badly that I couldn't help him. The plane was rocking so badly, as the sow moved her 400 pounds of weight around that I had my hands full just trying to keep it level. Later, Jim told me that he was so tired that he could hardly hold on, but he knew that he could not give up.

There was only a half hour of flying time left from the time the sow went berserk until we saw the landing strip just ahead. However, it was one of the longest half hours of our lives. As all of this was going on, Jim and I were praying. God answered our prayers by not letting the sow break out of the crate or letting Jim run out of strength while holding her back.

Now that the landing strip was in sight, it would be another adventure to land. I would be able to make a straight-in approach on the six hundred-foot landing strip. This was good because I would not have to spend any extra time in a landing pattern.

The first three hundred feet of this strip were fairly level, but the last three hundred feet were sloped downhill quite a bit. This would make stopping on the latter three hundred feet very difficult if we had much speed at all when we passed the halfway mark. I would have to land the plane and get slowed down almost to a stop on the first three hundred feet in order to get our heavy load completely stopped in time. One problem with this plan was that I had to slow the plane down to forty miles per hour. At that low speed and with the violent rocking of the plane, I would have to be extremely careful that I did not stall the plane and kill us.

As I slowed down my airspeed and lined up for a landing, Jim continued holding the sow's ears and doing all he could to keep her from rocking the plane. I knew he was putting all his effort into keeping her from moving back and forth. I also knew he could not keep it up long, as his strength would not continue to last. His efforts did help, and for the last one hundred yards before we touched down, the sow was not able to move as much, which greatly helped me. I was able to touch down right at the beginning of the airstrip and stop the plane in three hundred feet.

We were so relieved to be on the ground at last and we thanked God for His protection. We wasted no time getting out, opening the side doors of the plane, and getting the sow out. Unbelievably, the sow instantly became quiet and peaceful as she jumped out of the plane and onto the ground. Jim and the sow quietly started walking up the path from the airstrip toward the missionary houses.

The two missionary women looked out the window of their home and said to each other, "Man and beast." Here it was before their eyes, a man and a beast walking to the mission station just as the Lord had shown them three years earlier. The message seemed strange to them at the time, but now they were seeing it with their own eyes. A man and a beast were walking up the path of their mission station. There was no doubt God was in this, and something good was about to happen.

Over thirty years have passed since I flew the sow to this mission station. It seems only like yesterday, and the details are still very clear in my mind. Having Jim and Mary at the mission station along with the sow was a very important part of building and starting a Bible school. Without Jim and the sow at this mission station, the Bible school would not have started. The mission board had refused to let Jim build the Bible school unless they called it an Agriculture Bible school, and Jim would teach raising hogs and growing swamp rice as part of the curriculum. As a result of their decision, the sow had to be there and have her pigs in that location for Jim to teach the people how to raise them.

Satan knew this, and I believe with all my heart that his demons caused the sow to react as she did right at the point of no return in our flight. He was trying to kill us and the sow to stop the Bible school from being built, but God intervened and we made it safely there. A few days after the flight, the sow had a large litter of pigs, and Jim used them to teach the people how to raise hogs. It also gave the African people a good source of meat. The descendents of that sow are still going on today, and the people are raising them. In addition to that, the Bible school was built and is still going on today.

Jim knew exactly what he wanted in a crate for the sow. I, on the other hand, thought my idea to build the crate larger was better, so I did. My actions got us in big trouble. Was I right to do what I did? The answer is clearly, "No." I did not know hogs that well and I disobeyed the directions from a person that did. Could Jim have explained why he wanted the crate a certain size? Yes, he could have but even with this answer in mind, I should not have gone against his directions. Esther has used this story many times when she talked to children about obeying their parents. She tells them how they can get themselves in trouble by not doing what they are told, just like I got Jim and me in trouble by not doing what I was told. I did what I thought was right, but I disobeyed. God wants us to obey Him at all cost; even when we don't always understand His ways.

Ch. 19

A Plane Crash and a New Bible School

Jim, Mary, and their three children moved to the Bassa station, and Jim quickly got into the preparations for building the Bible school. During this same time period, God spoke to me in His still, small voice, telling me to go to our mission board and request that they allow me to go to the Bassa mission station for four months to physically help Jim with the building project. I did this at my first opportunity, and in my request I assured them I would continue to do my regular flying, but from the Bassa station rather than from Bahn mission.

After I presented my request, I felt the Lord wanted me to leave it in their hands and not push the idea. The mission board said I was needed more at the Bahn station when I wasn't flying so I could not go help build the Bible school. I could totally understand their reasoning and probably would have said the same thing if I had been in their place. After they turned down my request, I prayed and said, "God, I did what You said and they turned it down, so it is up to You to do what You want." I was completely at peace with this and went on with my daily flying.

A few days later, I flew from Monrovia to River Cess to drop off some supplies. I planned to fly on to the Bassa station, which was about fifty miles north of River Cess. While I was there, I gave the missionaries my flight plan and approximate arrival time at the Bassa mission station. If I did crash, the people would know in what direction to look for me. Right after unloading the supplies, I took off and headed for the Bassa station.

Shortly after I took off, I looked at my watch and realized I was running ahead of the arrival time I had given the missionaries at the Bassa station. The missionary ladies at the Bassa station had asked me to fly four one hundred-pound bags of rice from a village called Gaguya Town to their station. They wanted the rice for a scheduled conference that would be held within a week. I had not been able to fly the rice to them yet, but since I was ahead of schedule, this seemed like the perfect opportunity. Gaguya Town was only forty miles out of my way, so I decided to change my flight plan and take the forty-mile jog to pick up the rice. Even with the extra stop, I should get to the Bassa mission station near my estimated time of arrival. There was no one manning the radio at River Cess or the Bassa station, so I could not tell them about my change in plans.

I made a turn toward my new destination, found the village, and came in for a landing. To my surprise, the grass on the strip was very high, and the plane slowed to a stop very quickly. Normally the villagers keep the grass on the little airstrips cut very short, but it was quite tall and that concerned me. I knew the high grass would slow me down on my takeoff roll, so I would have to be very careful when I took off. I taxied to the end of the strip and shut the plane off. I had to decide what to do about the grass and wondered if I should not take all of the rice at one time. I decided to load the four bags of rice in the plane and see how quickly it accelerated when I gave the engine full power. If it did not pick up speed quickly, I would shut if off and remove some of the rice.

The African Christians loaded the rice for me; I started the engine and did my preflight check, gave it full power, and let off on the brakes. It started to roll, but I quickly saw that the tall grass was giving the plane too much resistance, and it was not accelerating as it should. There was no choice but to cut the power. As I was coming to a complete stop near the far end of the runway, I hit a very rough area that I did not know existed.

This rough area was caused by water which, at some point, flowed across the runway. When I hit it, the shocks and springs bottomed out, the landing gear tubes bent badly, and one steel tube on each gear broke in two. The fuselage of the plane dropped to the ground, tearing a large hole in the bottom right under where I sat. The propeller was still turning when the plane dropped, and one blade was bent back under the front of the plane. When the fuselage dropped, one of the wheels came up into one of the struts and bent it. Even though I was not moving fast, the damage to the plane was immense.

I quickly got out of the plane and looked at the wreckage. The once-beautiful airplane looked terrible. I was so devastated that I dropped to my knees, put my head on the ground, and started to weep. I said out loud, "Bob, you just tore up the mission's thirty thousand-dollar airplane." I felt terrible! Not only had I torn up the plane, but I had violated my own procedure by not letting anyone know where I was flying to. No one knew where I was, and that was going to be a big problem. I also knew I probably would not be able to radio out to let people know where I was or that I was okay. I knew that my wife and children and the other missionaries would be devastated when they found out that I did not arrive at the Bassa station. They would be certain that I had crashed and was probably hurt badly or dead. I did not want to put them through this pain, so I desperately wanted to be able to call them on my radio.

I finally got up from my knees and tried to evaluate my situation. The first thing I needed to know was if my radio worked. I began trying to call out, but I could not get an answer. With the body of the plane flat on the ground, my antenna was too low to get a signal out. I knew that the missionaries at the Bassa station would be wondering what happened to me since I was not there. Even though I could not use my radio to get a call out, I did keep it on, and after about an hour and a half I heard the Bassa mission station calling the River Cess mission to see where I was. I could hear the missionary at River Cess say, "He left here two hours ago and it is only a twenty-minute flight to your station. He said he was on his way there. Something has to have happened."

After hearing their conversation, I knew they were very concerned about me, and I continued trying to call them, but to no avail. The only thing they knew to do at this point was to wait until our mission stations came on the air at our 5:00 p.m. radio broadcast; they would then tell the other stations that I had not arrived at the Bassa station. Then all of the WEC mission stations would decide what action to take. They tried to call my wife, Pat, but could not get her because she was teaching at the mission school and would not be on the radio until 5:00 p.m.

While I was waiting for all of the mission stations to get on their radios at 5:00 p.m., I decided to evaluate the airplane condition some more. The first thing I was concerned about was getting the plane out of the deep jungle to a mission station where I could rebuild it. I thought about carrying it out, but quickly gave up on that idea. There was no way to hand-carry a plane through jungle paths and over rivers, etc. This plane would have to be flown out; there was no other way. It was too valuable to just leave there. I had to figure out a way to repair it right where it was, and then to fly it out.

My concern then centered on the crankshaft flange that the propeller bolts to. Sometimes they bend and sometimes they don't when a propeller is bent. The condition of the crankshaft flange was extremely important to me at this time. I always carried a toolbox with me in the plane, and I was sure thankful this was part of my routine. I used the tools to remove the bolts that held the prop to the engine flange and lifted the bent prop out of the way.

I looked the flange over closely. It looked okay, but it was hard to tell by sight alone. I had a piece of sheet metal about one inch wide and four inches long in my toolbox. I loosened a bolt on the front of the engine, put the end of the sheet metal under the bolt head, and tightened it to hold the sheet metal firm. I had a feeler gage in my toolbox and I got it out. I bent the sheet metal so that the end of it was exactly .010 of an inch from the engine flange.

Next I hit the starter and rotated the flange a little and rechecked it. The edge of the flange was still exactly .010 of an inch from the sheet metal. I did this numerous times until I was convinced that the flange was still perfectly straight. That meant that the engine was capable of flying the plane out of the jungle if I could get the rest of it repaired. I was really relieved, but the relief did not take away the feeling of depression I had over the whole ordeal.

Two years before, I purchased a new propeller and put it on the plane while I was in Monrovia. The old propeller was still usable, so I put it in the plane with the intention of flying it back to my mission. I also had a full load of supplies for the different stations along my way. I landed at the Bassa station first and unloaded their supplies, but I felt the plane was too heavy to take off from their short airfield, so to lighten my load, I took the old propeller out of the plane and left it there. I knew I would need another propeller to fly the Maule again, and it was a comfort to know that I could use the old one that was only forty miles away at the Bassa station where Jim and Mary lived. I would not have to order a new one and wait months for it to arrive. I am sure that it was of God that I left that old prop at the Bassa station two years earlier.

I closely evaluated the fuselage. It had a large hole in the bottom side of it and some of the ribbing was bent; also a support tube that went between the landing gear mounts for each wheel was cracked about half way into. There were some very small cracks around the landing gear mounting brackets also. The bent strut had not changed the wing angle at all, I knew it would hold in a flight out. I looked closely at the cracked support tube and determined that I could fly out with it cracked as long as I had a very light load.

As a result of my evaluation, I came to the conclusion that I needed to repair the landing gears, make a temporary repair to cover the hole in the bottom of the fuselage, and put the old propeller on the plane. I also would need dependable help, and I knew my brother was that person. I knew he would come to the village airstrip and help me, and he was an excellent welder, so he could also help me, using his welding skills to make the repairs.

After my evaluation, I formed a plan in my mind on how we could lift the front of the plane about five feet off the ground so we could work under it to repair the hole in the fuselage, remove and mount the landing gears, and mount the propeller. We would have to lift about five hundred pounds, so we would need a very sturdy framework to hook a hoist to. My plan to do this included the materials I would need. If I could get a radio signal out, I knew exactly what I was going to request from whomever I talked to.

Even with this plan in mind, I was still very depressed over what I had done to the mission plane. I desperately wanted to let my wife and the other missionaries know that I was okay and where I was, but I could not figure how to get a radio signal to them. The Bassa station was the closest one to me; they were only forty miles away and could not hear my radio signal, so there was no way I could get a signal to the other stations that were farther away. My wife and family were one hundred miles away, so it would be nearly impossible to get a signal to them.

There was no shade around the plane because it was lying on its belly near the end of the bush airstrip, so I was working in the direct African sun checking the plane's damage. I had no water with me, and after about three hours I was getting very thirsty. By this time many people from the village had come out to watch me; they were standing in sort of a circle around the plane just watching and hardly speaking a word. It was like they were intensely studying my every move. This did not bother me at all as I was sure they had never seen anyone work on a damaged airplane before.

The hot African sun was taking its toll on me, and I was perspiring tremendously. I must have looked like I needed a drink, because a little girl that looked to be about ten or eleven years old came up to me with a pleasant smile on her face and said, "Do you want some water?" I said, "Yes, little girl, please get me some water." I so appreciated her thoughtfulness. In about fifteen minutes she came back with the smile still on her face, carrying a jug on her head. I took it from her, lifted it to my lips, and drank a tremendous amount before I tasted it. After I finished drinking, I had a terrible taste in my mouth. It tasted like the smell of stagnant water and something rotten.

I looked into the water jug and saw thousands of swamp water worms swimming around in the water. The water looked like it was alive with all the half inch-long worms rapidly swimming in circles. I probably drank thousands of them in the half jug of water I had just downed. For a moment I just stood there shocked because I knew the dangers of drinking worm-infested water, but there was nothing I could do to undo the damage. I asked the little girl where she got the water, and she sweetly said, "From the swamp." How I hated to hear those words, but I knew they were true because I saw the evidence of it in the water.

I really started to berate myself at this point. I had not only crashed the plane, but I had overlooked obvious precautions in drinking water that had been offered to me. I carried a survival kit with me at all times that had water purification pills in it just for this kind of situation. I could not believe I drank the water without even checking it out first. Usually the people at the villages give missionaries boiled water, and maybe I had expected this from the little girl. Whatever it was, I was very unwise to have drunk the water, so it was my fault.

I knew all kind of things could be in that water besides just the worms. Swamps not only have dead animals in them, but also have human and animal waste that washes in from the jungle rains. The swamp water also contains dangerous parasites that eat holes in your liver. I had just exposed myself to all kinds of possible sicknesses. The knowledge that I possibly could be in the village for a long time added to my concern. If I did get very ill from the water, there might be no way I could get proper medical help. The results could be very serious.

Thankfully I was able to keep in perspective that this was just a little girl trying to help a man in distress in her little way. I was not angry with her, and I thanked her for the water, which caused her to walk away with a smile on her face, obviously thinking she had done me a great favor. Despite its taste and the water worms, etc., it did help my thirst, and I decided to think of the verse in Mark that says if they drink any deadly thing it will not harm them. Once I began thinking in this manner, the Lord gave me peace, and I really did have the faith that God was indeed going to protect me in this situation. Now that I had that settled in my mind, it was time to get back to my problems with the plane.

I knew that if I could not get a radio signal out, it could be a long time before I got back to any mission station. This would especially be true if a search party could not find me. Since I had changed my mind and flew out of my way to go to Gaguya Town, the search party would not be looking in my direction. Instead they would be spending a lot of their time searching on a straight line between the two mission stations. There were no roads out of Gaguya Town, and it would take days to walk through the jungle to any mission station. I kept desperately hoping I could get a radio signal out soon so that I could get help from some other mission pilot.

Finally 5:00 p.m. came and our mission stations started talking to each other over their two-way radios. I had my radio turned on and could hear them tell Pat that I was probably down in the jungle somewhere. They told her that I had left River Cess at 11:00 a.m. and that I should have been at the Bassa station by 11:20 a.m. but never arrived. I could hear Pat's reaction, and I knew this news had shaken her up. Although she was trying to stay strong, I could hear the sadness in her voice. I so much wanted to tell her I was okay.

The Baptist mission station had their radio broadcast at 5:15 p.m. right after our fifteen minutes. Each mission organization had a fifteen-minute allotted segment of time for their radio broadcast. We all would turn our radios on before our fifteen-minute segment of time so we could be ready at the exact time of our broadcast. As a result, the Baptists had their radios turned on during part of our broadcast. They could not help but overhear that I was down, so they entered in on the conversation with our missionaries in an effort to help find me. They had two planes and wanted to start searching for me right away. As they talked to our missionaries, I could hear them forming a search party for me. You can imagine what a strange feeling this was to have so many people talking about me so seriously when I was just fine, but had no way to tell them.

Suddenly God, in His still, small voice, gave me an idea. My antenna was a wire that went from the top of the cockpit back to the tail and then out to one wing tip. As they were discussing the details of the search party, I grabbed a set of wire cutters from my toolbox, cut the wire off of the insulator at the wing tip, and slid it through the insulator on the tail. This gave me a straight wire that was about thirty feet long. I had a long rope in the plane; I tied it to one end of the wire and asked the tallest boy standing near me to pull the wire straight with the rope and hold it as high as he could. The radio signal would not be reduced as long as he was holding onto the wire with the rope, and he would not get shocked by the radio signal.

I also knew that the strongest radio signal goes out at a right angle from a straight wire antenna. I knew the direction to my mission station where Pat was, so I chose a location for the boy to stand while holding the rope. The antenna wire would then be perpendicular to the direction of Bahn mission station, which was about one hundred miles away. Since God had given me this plan, I felt the radio signal would go one hundred miles where Pat was.

I put the plan into action and then keyed my mike and called, "Bahn, this is Bob McCauley," but I received no reply. I could not get through because the missionaries kept talking and I could not override their more powerful signals. I kept trying, however, hoping to find a break in their conversation. Finally Pat called to everyone and said, "I think I hear something." She called out and said, "Bob, is that you? If it is, I think I can understand a yes or a no. Just answer me with a yes or a no. Is that you?" I answered, "Yes." Pat said, "I heard the yes. Are you okay?" I answered, "Yes." She then said, "Is the plane okay?" I answered, "No." I wanted to give her details, but she could not hear me well enough and neither could any of our other mission stations.

There was a Baptist mission station located about forty miles perpendicular to my wire antenna but in the opposite direction as Pat. I had a very close friend at that station, and he interrupted the conversation, saying that he was just now able to hear me with great clarity. The change in the antenna had worked. I could not talk clearly to Pat, but since he was also perpendicular to my wire antenna but in the opposite direction, I could easily talk to him. It felt so good to just be able to talk to someone on my radio. I was able to tell him where I was and to give him details of my situation. He then relayed the details on to the other mission stations.

After everyone was satisfied that I was fine, they started asking me what I needed them to do to help. I asked the Baptist pilot if he would fly my brother to me the following morning. I also asked him to have Jim bring enough food and water to last for three days, a shovel, a hoist, a heavy rope, a hammer, and an ax. He relayed this information on to my brother, who was also on his radio at the time but could not hear me. Jim and my pilot friend agreed to be there the next morning with the food and equipment, so I felt better knowing we had a plan in place to start repairing the plane.

It was a good feeling to know that everyone was happy that I was safe, and I was also relieved to know that no one seemed overly concerned about the plane. It was a relief to know that my wife and children would not have to worry that I was out in the jungle alone and maybe hurt or dead. I was so happy that God had spoken to me in His still, small voice and given me a way to get a radio signal out.

I also knew my Baptist friend completely understood my situation, as he and his father had both crashed a plane in the jungle. My friend actually came in upside down in his plane and lived through it. His father crashed in the jungle as the result of a faulty fuel valve in a Maule plane exactly like I was flying. He also had his Super Cub torn up as the result of a bull running in front of him as he was landing on a village airstrip. He lived through both crashes.

One of their other mission pilots was flying a load of school children from Liberia to their boarding school in the Ivory Coast and was missing for three days. He had to come down in the jungle due to an engine failure, but was able to land on a jungle road. He made a repair on the plane's engine and was able to fly it out. There were a lot of happy parents and missionaries when he showed up three days later. Almost every jungle pilot that had flown very long had some kind of accident with their plane because the flying conditions and landing strips were so bad. Never once did I hear a negative thing said by a mission pilot about some other mission pilot who had an accident, because they all knew it might be them the next time.

Shortly before darkness set in that evening, some of the people from the village took me to a small mud hut where I would stay for the night. My small room had a bed, a small table, and one chair in it. Sitting on top of the table was a very small, teacup-sized pot filled with some kind of oil. It had a small hole in the top of it with a piece of string sticking out of the hole. One of the men lit the string for me before they left the room.

I sat down on the chair and looked around the room. The little lamp put out a flame that was about the size of a match, so everything in the room looked dingy and dark. I had stayed in such rooms many times before so I was some-what used to them, but this time it was different. I was feeling very low and drained emotionally. I was extremely tired, and my clothes were soaked with sweat. I felt sticky and very uncomfortable, and I had no dry clothes to change into. I knew the nights in the jungle got very cool, and since I was very wet, I knew I would be quite cold during the night.

In addition the insects and mosquitoes are usually very bad at night, and I had no mosquito netting, which I normally took with me if I planned to stay overnight in the villages. The thought of spending a chilly night with mosquitoes and other insects did not bother me much, but thinking of the plane and knowing it was lying out there on its belly, all busted up, was breaking my heart, and I was blaming myself for the accident.

If there was any humor in the evening, it was this: the village people asked the same little girl that had given me the swamp water to make supper for me. I was very hungry because I had not eaten since breakfast, and after about half an hour of sitting in the room by myself, the little girl came to the door of the hut and brought a bowl into my room. She had the same big smile on her face as she had when she gave me the swamp water.

I knew what happened the last time she came with her sweet little smile, but I thought surely it would be different this time. However, I was wrong, and again she had a nasty surprise in store for me. She sat the bowl down on the little table in the room and gave me a very large spoon to eat my meal with. I thanked her for the food, and she was very happy as she walked out of the room.

I picked up the little lamp and held it close to the bowl to see what she had made for me. It was bitter ball soup! My first thoughts were, "Oh no, not bitter ball soup!" This soup consists of hot water with about six bitter balls in it. Bitter balls are about the size of golf balls and taste extremely bitter, or like something that a person occasionally belches up from their stomach. They are extremely nasty! I have had to eat a lot of unpleasant things in the jungle, including a rat, and have found myself capable of eating about anything. But bitter ball soup is definitely one of the worst.

I knew it would be considered an insult to the villagers if I did not eat what they had given me, so I forced myself, although it was extremely difficult, to eat the entire bowl. About half an hour after I finished the bitter balls, the smiling little girl returned to get her bowl. Once again, I thanked her simply out of courtesy, and she left with her bowl, still smiling. After she left, I sat there in the nearly dark room and thought about the day. I told myself, "Bob, you crashed the plane, drank swamp water, and now you finish off the day with bitter ball soup. It has been quite a day." I was trying to make a joke out of it for myself, but somehow it was not all that funny.

I did, however, get a little humor out of the smiling little Bassa girl with her swamp water filled with worms and her bitter ball soup. Could she have been smiling because she was playing a joke on me? No, I don't think so! Regardless of this, I prayed and asked God for His blessings and help through it all. He was the Almighty God and I was His servant. I knew He could take the most impossible situation and make something good out of it, but at the time I was so depressed that it was difficult for me to see what good could come out of wrecking the mission plane.

I blew out the little lamp, lay down on the grass-filled mattress in the room, and tried to sleep. I was exhausted by this time and should have fallen asleep right away, but sleep just did not come. Within minutes the mosquitoes and other insects started biting me, and soon I itched all over, was sticky from sweat, and chilled to the bone as a result of being so wet. I slept very little through the night and could hardly wait until daylight. Finally it came, and I got out of bed even though I was still very tired and depressed over what I did to the plane. Through the night, my clothes and I dried out some, so that was a help.

Right after I got up, I started walking to the airstrip. I was hungry, thirsty, and somewhat dehydrated, but I needed to keep going. As I was walking down the jungle path that led from the town to the airstrip, I was surprised to hear my Baptist friend coming across the jungle in his Super Cub. I knew he had to have started his flying at the crack of dawn and was trying to get aid to me as soon as possible. I appreciated his effort and also that of my brother. It felt so good to hear the drone of the Super Cub's engine, knowing they were coming to my aid, and it lifted my spirit also, which I needed at the time.

The Super Cub was the only plane I knew of that could land over the top of the Maule on the short runway and still get stopped. Before they even landed I saw my friend and Jim in the plane, and that was a welcome sight. I was sure looking forward to their help and to having a way to communicate with the outside world again. I was also looking forward to having food and water, because I had not had anything to eat or drink for twenty-four hours except swamp water and bitter ball soup.

I was standing off to the side of the runway as the Super Cub passed over the Maule and landed. When they stopped, Jim and my friend jumped out and unloaded the tools and the food. My friend said he had a lot of flying to do for the next few days, but he would be available to pick us up at any time that we called him on the radio. We assured him we would, but not to expect to hear from us for about three days. In a matter of minutes he was off and flying again. Jim had all the tools I had requested plus the food and water for three days. The first thing I did was to get a drink of water and eat some of the food. I felt a little weak before this, but shortly after getting the food and water my strength came back, and I felt physically good again.

We started the job by cutting down three trees that were about six inches in diameter. We used these to build a support for the hoist. Then, using the hoist, we lifted the front of the plane off of the ground high enough to remove the landing gears and to make temporary repairs to cover the large hole in the bottom side of the fuselage. We removed the bent and broken landing gears from the plane and evaluated what we needed to make the temporary repairs to the bottom side of the plane. To my surprise, the work only took us about five hours instead of three days. We were ready to fly out, so we called my Baptist pilot friend on our radio and asked him to come and get us. He was very surprised to hear from us so soon, but within a short time he arrived and flew us and the broken landing gears to the Bassa mission station.

It was so good to get back to Jim and Mary's mission station, and I was able to use their radio to call my wife and children and tell them personally about my adventures in Gaguya Town. They were as happy to hear my voice as I was theirs. After that I took a much needed bath. I was covered with insect bites, especially around my head and ears. Jim loaned me some clean clothes while mine were being laundered, and Mary made us the most wonderful supper. Later that evening we joined together for prayer, thanking God that I was out of the village and at Jim and Mary's home. Then we asked God to help us get the plane repaired so we would be able to fly it out of the village.

The next day Jim and I took the landing gears to a rubber plantation, which was about a thirty-minute drive away. When we got there, we asked them if we could use their machine shop and welder to repair the gears. They were agreeable and we were so thankful. We needed some tubular steel to repair the landing gear steel tubes, so we looked in a scrap iron pile they had.

We found some old shock absorbers that had the exact tube diameter we needed to slide over the gear tubes. The fit could not have been more perfect. We were able to cut them into tubes and slide them over the landing gear tubes, and then weld them in place. I could hardly believe how well the shock absorber tubes fit, and I am sure that it was God that gave them to us. Within four hours we had made very good repairs to the landing gears, and they were actually stronger after the repairs than they were when they were new. We were ready to go back to Gaguya Town with landing gears that were very serviceable, and we were so thankful.

We called my pilot friend on the radio that evening and asked him to fly us back the next morning to Gaguya Town. He was glad to, and the following morning we headed back with the repaired landing gears, the old propeller, and sheet metal to make some temporary repairs to the bottom of the fuselage. Our friend left us there so he could go on about his work. We told him we would call him when we were finished, but not to expect a call before the next day. The reason we wanted him to come back was to pick up Jim, because I wanted to fly the Maule out by myself for two reasons. One, I wanted the weight to be as light as possible because of the broken frame brace, and two, I didn't want to put Jim in any danger if something should go wrong.

We began work on the plane right away. Jim started working on making temporary repairs to the hole in the fuselage, and I worked on mounting the propeller and the landing gears. By about three o'clock that afternoon we had the Maule sitting on the repaired landing gears. That was sure a good sight to me after seeing it lying broken on the ground just three days before this. The old propeller was mounted; I had checked it to see if it rotated without any wobble, and it was perfect. The flange was not bent at all. Jim had repaired the hole in the bottom side so that it would not catch the wind while flying at over one hundred miles per hour.

I started the Maule and it fired to life with its normal roar. I checked the propeller again when the engine was running; it had no vibration at all and the propeller control was working perfectly. Next I checked the controls to see if they were working correctly and was thrilled to find out they were. The plane was ready to fly even though it had the bent strut and a few cracks in the frame.

I taxied the Maule to the edge of the landing strip and shut it off. We called our pilot friend, and within a very short time we could hear his Super Cub flying in our direction. Within minutes he was landing back at Gaguya Town to get Jim. I climbed into the Maule, started the engine again, did my preflight check, and it still checked out okay. While I was doing all of this, Jim and my friend loaded the tools into the Super Cub and he did his preflight check. Now that we were both ready to go, I went ahead and gave the Maule full power. With the light load, I was off the ground and flying in seconds with excellent control; the bent strut was not changing the wing's lift at all.

My friend was flying a short distance behind me and to my left. I decided to slow the Maule down to ninety miles per hour instead of the normal speed of about 130, because I felt the slower speed would help keep excess pressure off the cracked frame. Since part of the frame was cracked and we only had temporary repairs on the bottom of the fuselage, I felt that it was only fair to me and my family that I fly the plane to the closet mission station, which was where my brother and his wife lived. I reached the station in about fifteen minutes and was able to make a normal landing. I taxied the plane up near the house where Jim and Mary and their family lived. Within seconds the Super Cub touched down as well. My friend and Jim unloaded the tools, and he flew back to his mission station.

Now we could restore the Maule to be completely flight worthy. I had worked and rebuilt engines and airframes for years when I flew as a hobby. I was confident that with my skills and with Jim's welding and tinsmith skills, we could rebuild the plane to its original condition. First I would need to order a new propeller, landing gears, and a new support brace to replace the one that was cracked. We could repair the bent strut, so it wouldn't need to be replaced. Fortunately, I already had materials at Bahn mission to repair the hole in the fuselage. We knew all this was going to take a lot of work, but we also knew God would be with us, helping us all the way. I was so thankful and felt so blessed that the plane was repairable and sitting at Jim and Mary's mission station.

There was a road from the Bassa mission station to Monrovia. The next day I made the two-hour drive into Monrovia and reported the accident. Just as I had expected, the aviation authorities said that I had to have the plane completely inspected after all the repairs were made.

I had previously thought about making some better temporary repairs and then flying the Maule back to my own mission station to complete the job. However, the aviation authorities would not go along with this plan and insisted I make all the repairs at the Bassa station. Once the repairs were made, I could fly it to Monrovia for a final inspection. Since I could not make a temporary repair and fly it back to Bahn, it meant that I was going to be at the Bassa mission station for a long time, and there was nothing I could do to change it. I would have to be separated from my family for an unknown length of time while the plane was being repaired. I always hated being separated from them but there was no one else to repair the plane so I had to do it. They would have loved to come and be with me, but Pat had to stay in Bahn because of her teaching job at the Bible school and mission grade school.

I ordered the new landing gears, new support brace, and a new propeller. I also made the long trip to Bahn mission station by road and got the supplies that I needed for the rest of the repairs. As soon as I returned with all the supplies, we began the repairs on the strut and the fuselage. The strut was finished fairly quickly, but the fuselage was covered with fiberglass cloth, and it had to be completely dry when we worked with it. Keeping it dry was quite a challenge, as we didn't have a building to put the plane in. To make matters worse, it was the early part of the rainy season, and the rain caused us to miss many days of work.

When the first day of rain came, it kept us from working on the plane, so we decided to start working on the Bible school. There was one large existing building on the mission station that was in the location where we wanted a dormitory. The building was made out of mud blocks with a tin roof. It was about forty feet long and twenty feet wide with no walls or rooms on the inside. It had only one door, which was in the front, and it needed to have a back door. After deciding where we wanted to put the back door, we used Jim's hand wood saw and sawed a door opening in the mud blocks. This worked great, and we were on our way to building the Bible school that many had been praying for. God blessed from that time, and the work progressed wonderfully.

As the rain continued, we kept working on the school. Besides putting in the door, we also made rooms by adding walls. This was a big job that took us a few weeks to complete, but we ended up with a very nice dorm for single students. We also started making individual huts for those who had families. The African Christians were very good at making huts, so they did most of the work on these. Jim and I also changed another unused building into classrooms. We worked on the plane when it was dry and the school buildings when it was raining. During this time, the new landing gears, propeller, and landing gear

A PLANE CRASH AND A NEW BIBLE SCHOOL

brace arrived at about the time we needed them. With a lot of very hard work, both projects were finished in about four months.

The Bible school with all of the living quarters looked wonderful. To say the least, the Bassa Christians were elated at having it, and they rejoiced before the Lord over their prayers being answered. We rejoiced with them, in addition to being very happy at how well the plane looked inside and out. In fact, no one would be able to tell it was ever in an accident. I would even go so far as to say that with the paint job we put on the repaired area, it looked nearly new.

In addition to working on the Bible school and the plane during the daytime, Jim and I spent nearly every evening going to a local rubber plantation to preach and teach the Word of God to the Bassa workers. Nearly every evening after hearing the Word of God, people would make a decision to accept Jesus Christ as their Savior and be born again. We had about 250 people give their hearts to Jesus Christ. The four months were a very productive time in our ministry!

The day after we finished the plane, I flew it to the aviation inspector in Monrovia to schedule an inspection. Surprisingly, he was able to do it right away. I had to prepare the plane for his inspection by removing the seats, the cowling, the floorboards, the inspection plates, and a few other odds and ends. Once I had it all finished, I notified him that I was ready. Liberia had recently hired a very strict airplane inspector from England. I was aware of many other repair jobs that he had rejected, so I knew our repair job would have to be almost perfect in order to get his approval. His general appearance reminded me of the pictures I had seen of Sherlock Holmes. He not only dressed like him, but even wore a hat and carried a magnifying glass with a handle on it, which he used for long stretches of time looking at Jim's welding job.

Finally he stood up, looked at me, and said, "I see that you have kept up your welding skills very well." That was music to my ears, because it told me he approved of the work. I did not want to get into details by telling him my brother did the welding, so I just kept quiet. Finally, he let me know he was very pleased with the repairs and signed my maintenance logbook as acceptable. As soon as I got the plane put back together, I was ready to get back to my job as a missionary pilot, and I was very thankful to God for all He had done.

It didn't occur to me until after the inspector signed my paperwork that it had been four months to the day since I had the accident. This was exactly the amount of time that God wanted me to request from the mission board to go and help Jim build the Bible school. It was amazing to think about how the Lord had managed to put me exactly where He wanted me, for the amount of time He wanted me to be there, even when the mission board had turned down my request.

About a year before this, my friend, Bill Kimbery, noticed that I was spending a great deal of time repairing the plane and he shared with me that he wanted me to pray with him for a new airplane. I told Bill that I did not have the faith to pray for a thirty thousand dollar airplane. Bill told me that he did. I then said, "Bill, I will pray with you on your faith." We then prayed and left it in God's hands to furnish the new airplane. Our mission, WEC, had a policy that we were not allowed to let our needs be known to anyone but God. After the accident, several missionaries wrote home, telling of the accident, and as a result, several churches in Switzerland went together and collected money to purchase a new airplane for the mission. God used this one incident not only to get me to the Bassa mission station for four months to help Jim build the Bible school, but He also used it to answer our prayer for a new airplane.

Thirty five-years have passed since we built the Bassa Bible School. Many students have graduated and gone out to peach the Gospel, and as a result, hundreds have come to know Jesus Christ as their Lord and Savior. About eight years after we built the Bible school, many people in the area were killed or persecuted due to a civil war in the country. The Bassa mission houses, clinic, church, and a lot of the original Bible school buildings were completely destroyed in that war. Many Bassa Christians were scattered, and the Bible school was relocated for a time in a safer location.

A few years later, it was back up and running at its original location and is still continuing as of this writing. During the civil war, two of our missionaries were killed, and seventy of our Gio and Mano Christians were lined up and shot at Bahn mission station where Pat and I lived when I crashed the plane. The Bible school there was stopped and has never started again.

In chapter three I told how we are often tested before God uses us. Two people in the Bible that I gave as examples were Jesus and Joseph. Abraham was also tested when God asked him to sacrifice his son. I am sure that it would have been easy for him to have said "No" when God asked him to sacrifice Isaac.

I did not realize that I was being tested when I was depressed after tearing up the mission plane, drinking swamp water, eating bitter ball soup, and spending a bitter cold, itchy night after it all happened. Neither did I think about it while I was away from my family for so long, but now I know, beyond any doubt, that God was testing me to see if I would continue to obey Him, regardless of how bad things were. Now, I believe the key word here is, "continue." It is easy to follow what we feel God has told us to do when things are going great. What about when they turn bitter? It is then that we, and even others, can find our true strengths and weaknesses. Will we continue to serve God or will we give up and quit after hard times come?

The day I tore up the plane in Gaguya Town was the worst day I ever had in my life, up until then. I could have thrown in the towel, quit, and went back to America, saying it was not worth it. When the bitter time came after I crashed the plane, I continued with what I knew God had spoken to me through His still small voice, and helped build the Bible school, and repaired the plane while we were doing it.

I have known some people that quit when things became difficult. Some have had a good job and after a few difficult days, they quit, saying it was not worth it. I have also seen this weakness with some people in the ministry. I would like to tell the younger generation, who are living for the Lord, "Life is full of days when you may drink swamp water, eat bitter ball soup, and have chilly nights with the insects biting you. You may even crash your plane. What do you do when this happens? You pray, commit it to God, and keep on going, and He will work it out for good in your life." Praise His Name for He can do this!

Also as a point of interest, I never did get sick from drinking the swamp water that was loaded with all of those swamp water worms and other terrible things.

Ch. 20

A TABLE IN THE WILDERNESS

Can God furnish a table in the wilderness today as He did in the wilderness with the Israelites? In PSALMS 78:19 we see that the Israelites made this statement — "*Can God spread a table in the desert?*" (NIV) I know He can and will do it because I have seen Him provide things for us that were absolute miracles. There was no way they could have come about except by His hand. We have seen God provide for us so many times that I cannot write them all down in this book, but I do want to share a few stories with you of events that happened when we lived in the jungle. First of all, I want to do it for God's glory, and second, that it might build up your faith.

1) BUSH FLYING COST FOR EVANGELISM

When we first arrived in Liberia, very few missionaries were using the mission plane for evangelism because of the cost. It was the mission's policy that if a missionary wanted to fly to a jungle village for evangelism, they had to pay the cost per hour to fly to and from the village. This cost not only included the gasoline, but also the maintenance to fly the plane. It is expensive to fly a plane anyplace, but it is especially expensive to fly in the jungle, due to the high cost of gasoline and maintenance. The cost to fly was more than most of our missionaries felt they could afford.

As I have stated before in chapter ten, part of my flying ministry was called medical evangelism. Using the airplane in this type of ministry was very successful, but unfortunately the plane was not being used much due to the flying cost. It would take hours to walk to some of the villages, but I could fly to the same village in one minute for each hour it took to walk. If it took ten hours to walk to the village, I could fly there in about ten minutes or less. I really felt badly about the cost of flying the plane, but there was nothing I could do about it. The mission board had determined the price per hour to fly the plane before I got there, and I had to abide by what they had established.

I prayed desperately about this problem, and the Holy Spirit spoke to me very clearly in His still, small voice, saying, "I will provide the money to pay for the cost of flying the airplane for evangelism. If the missionaries want to use the plane for evangelism, do not charge them. If they do want to pay some, only allow them to pay for the gasoline and no more."

I knew what God said to me in His still, small voice, but I had one problem with what the Lord told me. Thinking of this problem, I prayed and said, "Lord, you know the mission has the policy that the cost to fly the airplane cannot operate in the red. I cannot fly the plane without having the money in advance. If I am hearing Your voice correctly, have someone send one hundred dollars to the mission plane for evangelism within two months, and I will put it in a special fund to use for evangelism."

I finished that prayer and dropped the issue at that time. I knew that the possibility of somebody sending one hundred dollars to the mission plane within two months for evangelism was highly unlikely unless God did it. WEC's policy was not to make our needs known. They said that if God wanted it, He would provide, and we were not to ask for money. As a result of this, I did not even let my wife know about my prayer, and I did not write or tell anyone about it. It was between God and me.

During the next two months, I almost forgot about the prayer. One day I flew into Monrovia, the capital city, to get supplies and pick up the mail for the different mission stations. The business agent, a missionary from British Columbia, Canada, would put the mail for each mission station in a large plastic bag with the name of the mission station marked on each bag. It was my job to get the mail to each station. He had one letter that was addressed to the mission airplane.

I was standing about five feet away from him when he flipped it to me through the air and said in a joking way, "Since the airplane cannot read, maybe the pilot can." It was his little joke toward me, suggesting I might not be able to read the letter. His little joke had some substance to it, however, because I was not able to read everything that was in the envelope.

I looked at the envelope and it was from Denmark. I knew no one in Denmark, but I opened the envelope. It had a note in it that was handwritten in English, and it also contained a check. The note simply said, "To be used for evangelism with the mission airplane." I could read the note, but I was completely unable to read the check. From some markings on it, I thought it was in Danish marks, but I was not sure, nor did I know how much it was. I gave it back to the business agent and asked him how much it was. He quickly saw that the check was in Danish marks and figured out that it was for $100.03.

I suddenly remembered my prayer concerning the one hundred dollars and how the Holy Spirit had spoken to me in His still, small voice concerning the evangelism ministry. I knew the date of my prayer and quickly realized that it was exactly two months before this one hundred dollars came addressed to the mission airplane as I had prayed. I had told no one about the prayer, or how I felt God was leading me to fly the plane for evangelism, but here in my hand, exactly two months later, was the $100.

I was extremely surprised in a way, but in other ways I was not. I clearly had heard God's voice on how the plane was to be used, and I felt that He was going to bless the use of the plane. I asked the business agent to put the one hundred dollars in a special account and told him that I would use it only for evangelism with the airplane. This gave me a very small nest egg to start flying evangelism, but it was a start.

I flew back to our mission station, which was two hundred miles back in the jungle from Monrovia, and told the mission nurses about the one hundred dollars. They wanted to do more evangelism with the plane, but had not been using it much, due to the cost. They were excited to have a little money in the fund and decided to use the plane shortly after that for medical evangelism. A few days later, we flew to a village called Sea-app-lee; I preached the Word of God, and then we treated the sick people. I was able to pay for that flight exactly as God had spoken to me through His still, small voice. This was the first flight of many through the next years of using the plane for evangelism. Everyone involved was very happy about this new financial policy of using the mission plane.

One hundred dollars does not last long flying a plane in the jungle. I knew it would not last long, but I was not concerned about it. I knew how God had provided, and I knew He would continue to provide. From the time I received the one hundred-dollar check until the day I made my last flight, I was never able to use up the evangelism fund. I never wrote one letter or asked anyone for money for the fund, but it always had money in it.

Sometimes it had only enough money for one more flight, but before I needed money for the next flight, I had it. This went on for five years and hundreds of flights; thousands of dollars came in to pay for every one of them in advance.

At times I wondered if I would be able to break the fund if I really tried, and flew even more than I had before, using the plane for evangelism. After doing this for a while, I realized that it was impossible to break the fund; that would only happen when God was through using the plane.

After that first letter to the mission plane, funds to be used for evangelism with the plane came in from many countries of the world and from various sources. At times I would receive special requests from business people who wanted flights back into the jungle villages. The mahogany trees in Liberia were in great demand at that time, and many people wanted to go into the deep jungle to locate the trees; the village strips were so short that the charter planes could not go into them, but the missionary planes could, and they would ask us to take them.

When one of the business people wanted to fly into some of the small airstrips and asked me to fly them, I would pray and the Lord would speak to my heart about how much to charge them. Usually it was a lot, but when I would tell them I would fly them in for that amount, they always seemed more than willing to pay it. I knew that God wanted me to put the extra money into the evangelism fund. At times some of the nurses wanted to help out on a flight, but I only let them give for the gasoline. It was like a continuous happening to see how God supplied for the evangelism flying through those years.

God can set a table in the wilderness! God can provide our needs to do His will. He is still in that business, and I am still amazed at how He provided the funds for evangelism exactly as He told me He would do. Going from an engineer to a missionary pilot was a big change, but it was exciting to see God take my life and the lives of my family to make a difference.

I kept a logbook of every one of my flights, and approximately 350 lives were saved from a physical death as a result of our medical evangelism. In addition, a vast number of people accepted Jesus Christ as their Savior, making a difference in their lives for eternity. Through this ministry, God was able to use us to make a tremendous difference in the lives of many people that lived in the deep jungle. Many lives were saved physically, and many souls were saved from hell.

2) God Fed My Family in the Wilderness

A few months after we arrived in Liberia, West Africa, our family ran out of money. We received no money from home, and within a short time we used what money we had on hand to purchase food. As we said before, we lived near a large village of about ten thousand people, called Bahn, where we bought most of our food. Women would sit on the ground or on a small stool near the center of the village with difference kinds of produce on a cloth in front of them. Their produce consisted of vegetables, fruits, rice grown in the jungle, and there was a man in the village that sold meat. It usually was goat meat, but occasionally he had some deer or beef hanging out in the open, covered with flies. We ate what the Africans ate, but it did take money to purchase it.

When we ran out of money, we had a little food on hand but soon used it up. It would have been easy for my wife and me to get discouraged because we had our family in the deep jungle with nothing to eat, but we didn't get discouraged, and we didn't share our problem with the children. And of course we could tell no one of our needs, due to the mission policy. We did, however, go to prayer about our problem. We had seen our God provide many times before and knew that He would provide, but we wondered how He would provide food for us back in the jungle with no one knowing our need.

After we ate our last meal with the food we had on hand, we prayed and told the Lord about our need. My wife told the Lord that we needed some meat, and that she would like some deer meat and rice, etc. Well, before it was time to prepare the next meal, a little old lady who looked very poor showed up at our door with some rice rolled up in a piece of cloth. She said she felt that she should bring it to us. Then another old lady showed up with a piece of deer meat. Some more ladies brought some vegetables, and we had enough for a very good meal. We thanked God for that meal and prayed for the next one. Before the next meal needed to be prepared, more old ladies or men came with more food, and we had another good meal.

This was very good, but how long would it continue? Our funds came to Africa from America once a month. We felt that we would receive money when the transfer of funds came for the next month, but they did not come. This went on for four months. We had no money for all of this time and yet we did not write about it or tell anyone, including the other missionaries or the Africans. Every day for all of the four months, Africans came by with food. Many times they looked so poor and like they had very little themselves, but they gave food to us in our need. They were God's servants feeding us. We never missed a single meal. We always had a good balanced meal, and the food was very good.

Four months later we received money, and right after this, the Africans stopped bringing food to our door. This happened exactly to the day when we received money to buy our own food. Never again did the Africans bring us food as they had. God used them to spread a table before us in the wilderness. It was very humbling to accept food from people that looked so poor, but we knew that it was God that had sent them to provide for our needs. We brought our needs to God in prayer, and He answered and provided. We learned a tremendous lesson: our God can provide for us in any situation! We praise Him and know that He can provide for us as we step out to obey Him. Praise His holy Name!

God provided for us through the poor Africans, and this made a difference in our lives. He provided during our great time of need, and He can do the same for you. Bless His holy Name!

3) Two Bolts in the Wilderness

When we first arrived at the mission station in Liberia, I was told that the mission Volkswagen van had been wrecked. The engine had been torn out of its mounts, making the van useless. The missionaries needed the van for the ministry and were anxious for it to be repaired. They knew I could do some mechanic work and wanted me to look at it. The engine was mounted in the rear of the van. When the accident happened, the van went over a large tree stump, which tore the engine away from the mounts. Two large bolts that held the top of the engine in place had been stripped right out of the engine block. There was a lot of other damage also.

I worked on the van in all my spare time for two months. The main problem was caused when the two bolts were torn out of the engine block. The threads were all stripped out, and the bolts were missing. I would have to put in larger bolts. This would require that I tap new, larger threads in the engine block, and I would have to drill out the engine block to the exact diameter to fit the larger tap size. Then I would have to find two bolts with the exact diameter and threads per inch and length that I needed. This problem was complicated because of the van being back in the jungle two hundred miles with no hardware store where I could purchase the bolts, drill bit, and tap.

For years I have had the policy that when God gives you a job, you start on it, doing everything you can, and let Him furnish what you need! Several things had either been broken or bent badly when the van went over the stump.

I repaired everything I could find that was damaged around the engine area. After finishing those repairs, I looked around the mission station for an old junk box. Usually there is a junk box someplace, and I found one.

I dug around in the box, found an old drill bit, and also an old 5/8-11 tap. I checked the drill bit size, and it was the exact size I needed for the 5/8-11 tap. This drill and tap size would work perfectly to repair the stripped-out holes in the engine block. Somehow, I was not really surprised. I just felt that God would provide, and He did to this point. I also knew that all the equipment, cars, trucks etc., in Liberia used metric bolts, and the 5/8-11 tap was English, so the chances of finding two 5/8-11 bolts two and one-half inches long two hundred miles back in the jungle in Liberia would be nearly impossible.

I found an old pair of vice grips and used them to hold the drill bit, since I did not have an electric drill. I was able to hold the drill bit with the vice grips and rotate it well enough that I got each hole drilled out just as I needed. Then I used the vice grips and tapped each hole. This took several days but it worked great. After I got the other repairs made and the new bolt holes tapped, I lifted the engine in place under the van. I had it sitting on pieces of wood and located in the exact location so that the bolts would line up perfectly. After two months of work, I was ready for the bolts. As I was still lying on my back after adjusting the engine block to the exact location that I needed to slide in the bolts, I said, "God, I am ready for the bolts now."

I started to slide out from under the van, and as I did, I saw an old, rusty, beat-up pickup truck pull up. The driver was out of the truck and at the van before I had a chance to slide out. I stood up, and he looked at the back of the van and said, "Do you need those bolts?" I was shocked when he said this. How did he know to even ask me about the bolts? A person could hardly see under the van, let alone see that I needed two bolts. I said, "Yes, I do, but I need English and not metric, and they have to be 5/8-11 thread and two and one-half inches long." He quickly answered, "I know, and I have them."

Again I tried to tell him that they were English and not metric, but he insisted that he had them. He led me over to his pickup and pulled out an old, small tool box. It was completely filled with dirt. He dug down into the dirt and pulled out three bolts. I looked at them; they looked to be the right size, but I was not sure the thread was 5/8-11. I still thought they might be metric and would not work. The man seemed to be in a hurry. I wanted to pay him for them, but he would not take anything, and he got in his truck and left.

I slid back under the van, put the first bolt in place, and rotated it to see if the thread would engage the threads I had tapped in the engine block. The bolt thread engaged the engine block threads as I hoped it would. I knew that if the bolt had a metric thread, it would lock up and not continue to turn into the English-threaded hole. My heart was almost in my mouth as I slowly rotated the bolt. I was very happy as it continued to rotate all the way in. Then I did the same thing with the second bolt. They were perfect! The bolts had 5/8-11 threads and were two and one-half inches long, exactly as I needed. I already had a wrench lying under the van, and I tightened them up. After this, I slid out from under the van and said, "If God could furnish three (even one extra) 5/8-11 bolts two and one-half inches long at the exact time that I needed them, then He can truly furnish a table in the wilderness."

Over thirty-five years later, I am still amazed at God's provision of the two bolts. To me it was a miracle of God's provision. I don't know what the odds are that a man I had never met would drive up right when I was ready for the bolts, have the ones that I needed, and give them to me. Then add in the fact that this was two hundred miles back in the jungle; this even ups the odds. Then add on top of that the fact that everything in the country was metric and these bolts were English. I figured those were probably the only 5/8-11 bolts two and one-half inches long in all of Liberia, and I got them exactly on time. It was within seconds of the time I said, "God, I am ready for the bolts now." The odds of this happening two hundred miles back in the jungle are so great that it makes it impossible for it to have happened on its own.

I have done mechanical work at my home in Indiana and needed bolts to continue the job. Even in Indiana where there are all kinds of bolts, what are the chances of a complete stranger walking into my garage where I do most of my work and then hardly looking at what I was doing and for him to say, "I have those bolts," and then give them to me and drive off? This just would not happen in Indiana, but it happened two hundred miles back in the African jungle, and I witnessed this miracle of God's provision.

I know that it was God and that He and He alone did this miracle of provision. Did God's provision make a difference in our lives? Yes, it did. It encouraged our faith and also gave us the use of the van for His ministry.

Ch. 21

SKILLS GIVEN BY GOD'S STILL SMALL VOICE

God is multifaceted—He can and usually does many things at the same time. He has all of the skills in the world, and He gives skills to His people. I know He has done this for me. I have been absolutely amazed at times when God has given me the knowledge of how to do something that I would not have thought of on my own. He gave skills to people in the Bible days also.

> *And the LORD spake unto Moses, saying, See, I have called by name Bezaleel the son of Uri, the son of Hur, of the tribe of Judah: And I have filled him with the spirit of God, in wisdom, and in understanding, and in knowledge, and in all manner of workmanship, To devise cunning works, to work in gold, and in silver, and in brass, And in cutting of stones, to set them, and in carving of timber, to work in all manner of workmanship.* (EXODUS 31:1-5)

In this passage we see that God said He was the one who filled Bezaleel with the spirit of God in wisdom, understanding, knowledge, and in all manner of workmanship; God helped him to devise cunning works in gold, silver, and brass; to cut and set stones, to carve timber, and to work in all manner of workmanship.

I grew up as a farm boy who had very little special training in industrial skills, yet I have been able to do things far above what I could have thought of on my own. I have been able to do mechanic, carpentry, brick work, electrical, plumbing, farming, and engineering jobs. In addition to these, He has helped me be a husband, father, missionary, preacher, Bible teacher, and jungle pilot. There have been many times when I have needed a special skill at a specific time that I did not have on my own. Sometimes I did not have the equipment to accomplish what needed to be done. It is at these times that the Lord has given me special insight on how to fix something without the proper tools or the proper training. It gives me great joy to bring honor to God's Name by telling you some specific times this has taken place in my life.

1) Straightening a Bent Van Frame in the Jungle

In the chapter "A Table in the Wilderness" and part 1) "Two Bolts in the Wilderness," I told the story about how God provided two bolts right when I needed them to repair the mission van. This was a miracle of God's provision that I am still amazed about. As great as this miracle was, there is more to this story that I want to tell you about.

As I said above, my first job after I arrived in Liberia was to repair a van that had been in a wreck. The repair could not be completed without two special bolts that the Lord provided right at the time I needed them. After I got the engine mounted in the van, I got into the driver's seat to start the motor and quickly discovered I could not move the gearshift lever. I got under the van and started looking at the gearshift linkage to see what was wrong. It didn't take long to find that the A-frame between the front wheels was bent badly back into the gearshift linkage. Up to this point, I had only looked for damage in the back of the van around the engine area. For some reason it had not occurred to me to look at the A-frame. However, it was evident now that the very heavy piece of steel had been bent badly as the van went over the stump.

It was obvious there would be no way we could use the gearshift without straightening the A-frame. Since the A-frame steel was very thick and strong, it would take close to one thousand pounds of pressure to straighten it. I certainly didn't have anything on the mission station to put that much pressure in the right location to do the job. God was going to have to come to my aid once more if this van was ever to become useful again.

I did what I always do in this kind of situation—I prayed and asked God for the wisdom to fix it. Almost instantly, the Lord spoke to me in His still, small voice and showed me how to get enough pressure in the right location to straighten the A-frame. It was so simple that I laughed out loud when the Lord showed me how easy it would be to do this job. I could never have thought of this on my own, but God gave me a word of wisdom just when I needed it. Without His help, this would have been an impossible job to tackle two hundred miles back in the jungle.

We had a very long log chain on the mission station. I don't know where it came from, but it was there when we arrived. There was a high hill leading up to the mission station houses from the road that led to the mission station. Near the top of the hill was a tree that was about three feet in diameter. I wrapped one end of the log chain around the base of the tree and hooked it there. Then I had the schoolboys help me push the van up the hill to the tree. Next we put pieces of wood behind the back wheels to keep the van from rolling backward down the hill. I hooked the other end of the log chain to the A-frame in the exact location where I needed the one thousand pounds of pressure to straighten it out.

I got in the van, and the boys removed the wooden pieces while I held my foot on the brake. After making sure the boys were out of the way, I braced myself securely, trying to make sure my head was not going to get snapped backward by the sudden stop. Then I quickly took my foot off the brake and the van rapidly rolled backward down the hill. When it came to the end of the chain hooked to the A-frame, the van stopped instantly. All the pressure to stop the van had put tremendous pressure on one point on the A-frame.

I got out of the van and looked at the A-frame. It was bent back to within about an inch of being perfect. We repeated the same process, but this time we only pushed the van up about ten feet and let it roll backward. This time the A-frame was bent back to the perfect position. The three thousand pounds rolling downhill had generated enough speed that it took about one thousand pounds to stop it instantly and this was what I needed to straighten the A-frame.

What had seemed to me to be impossible was taken care of within one hour as the result of a word of wisdom from the Lord. Again the still, small voice of the Lord helped me tremendously. I gave Him credit for this then and still do.

2) Jungle Repair on Plane's Starter

It was customary for pilots from different mission stations to help each other when needed. On this particular day, one pilot needed me to fly five men to a remote village. I was glad to help, and since there were five men and their baggage, I knew it would take two trips to accomplish the task. During the second flight, I saw a very strong storm front coming straight toward the village I was flying to. I estimated that I had just enough time to land, let my passengers off, and quickly take off again before the storm got there. I had a lot of things to do this particular day, so I was sure hoping my estimate on time was correct. If it wasn't, and I did have to wait for the storm to pass, it would definitely mean spending the night since it was already late afternoon.

I landed the plane, shut off the engine, and let the men out. They took off walking fast to the village to beat the rain as they also saw it coming. I jumped back into the plane and yelled, "Clear prop," even though there was no one in sight. I turned the key, expecting to hear the engine roar to life as it normally did. Nothing happened! There was no starter noise at all except a "click." Something had happened to the starter. I looked in the direction of the storm, and it was coming fast.

I jumped back out of the plane, grabbed a screwdriver out of my toolbox, and quickly took the top cover of the cowling off. I loosened the band around the starter and slid it back so I could look inside, in an effort to evaluate what was wrong. I saw it right away. One of the starter brushes was not down because of a broken spring. The engine starter would never work without that brush in place. My first thoughts were, "How can I fix it quickly." I no sooner thought this when a clear answer came to me through the still, small voice of the Holy Spirit. I immediately knew what to do.

I quickly opened my survival kit, pulled out my big knife, and yanked it out of its scabbard. Then I ran to the edge of the airstrip and cut a branch from a small tree. I quickly whittled a small wedge from the branch and placed it between the top of the brush and the small metal bracket that keeps the spring in place. Next, I took the back of my knife and gave it a few light taps, which forced the brush down in place. There was not enough time to test it, so I slid the starter cover back in place and screwed the cowling back on. The whole thing only took me about three minutes. I jumped in the plane, turned the key, and the engine instantly roared to life.

As I took off, I found myself flying along the very edge of the storm, with rain pounding down on my windshield. If I would have had to work on the plane for even thirty more seconds, I would not have been able to get out in time. I was very thankful that God gave me wisdom on how to temporarily fix the plane in such a quick and efficient manner.

> ——*For your Father knoweth what things ye have need of, before ye ask him.* (MATTHEW 6:8B)

God knew I needed to make a quick repair on the starter, and even before I asked Him, He answered and showed me how to do it. Praise His holy Name!

With that one idea, the Lord saved me a huge amount of time and energy. If I had been unable to fix the plane, I would have had more problems on my hands, such as the worry I would have put on my family and friends, who would not have known where I was. I would not have been able to contact with them because I was too far from a mission station to send out a radio signal. Another challenge would have been to get back to my mission station at all, as it was two hundred and twenty miles away. Once I finally found a way home, I would have needed to find the part for the starter and then come back again to fix it. All of this would have taken an unknown amount of time that I sure did not have to spare during this very busy flying time.

> *God is our refuge and strength, a very present help in trouble.*
> (PSALMS 46:1)

I was in trouble with a broken starter and a storm coming, and God was my help during this time.

3) JUNGLE REPAIR ON PLANE'S BRAKES

One time I flew into a village airstrip knowing I would be spending the night. The next day I noticed some brake fluid on my left tire during my preflight inspection. I closely examined the left brake cylinder and found that brake fluid was slowly leaking past the seals of that cylinder. I got into the plane and pushed down on the top of the left rudder pedal to activate the brake on that side. The pedal went almost all the way down before it set the brake. I quickly realized I did not have enough brake on the left side to stop the plane. I was in trouble! I had brake seals at the mission station, but not with me in the plane. The leak was so slow that it would have been possible for me to get to my mission station if I had some brake fluid to fill up with. But since I didn't have any with me, I again looked to God for a solution. That's when He spoke to me again in His still, small voice and showed me how to temporarily fix the problem.

Water is about the same density as brake fluid, and would not hurt the seals on the master cylinder. I could fill the left reservoir with water, and it would work as brake fluid. It would not all leak out in my twenty-minute flight back to my mission. Then I could drain the water from the left brake cylinder, master cylinder, and the brake line. Since I was flying in the jungle, I did not have to worry about it freezing. I got clean water from the village and filled the left reservoir. Then I checked it for air in the line or cylinders, and it worked fine. Right after I filled the reservoir with water, I got in the plane, started the engine, checked it out, and took off. Twenty minutes later I was landing at my mission station. Right after I touched down, I pushed down on both of my brake pedals, and they worked fine. The plane stopped easily, and no one would ever have known that I was using water as brake fluid.

I have said for years that God is the best engineer ever and knows how things can be fixed. We certainly need to remember to ask for His wisdom and never forget that we serve a mighty God who is at the same time personal and interested in our problems.

4) Mission Generator Repair without Proper Tools

One evening I flew into Bahn mission station with the intent of staying all night. I barely got out of the plane when Bill Kimbery, who was the mission station's leader, told me they had no electric lights because he had failed to put new brushes in the generator, and the spring steel that pushes down on the brushes had came into contact with the rotating commentator.

This caused an electrical short that burnt deep pits in the commentator. It also left the commentator very rough, and it needed to be smooth in order that the brushes could slide easily on it as it rotated at high speeds. If it were rough, it would wear out the carbon brushes within minutes. The generator was worth several thousand dollars, and Bill felt very badly because he thought he had totally ruined it and blamed himself for failing to replace the brushes. He knew that the mission station did not have funds to purchase a new generator, but at the same time they needed it to run the mission station.

Bill and another missionary, Dwight Land, asked me to look at the generator. As I walked over to look at it, they walked beside me, telling me they didn't really have any hope that it could be repaired, and as I looked at it, I found myself agreeing with them. It looked like it was totally ruined. The pits were deeper and the roughness was rougher than I expected it to be. My first thought was, "There is no way to repair the commentator without dismantling the generator and mounting the commentator on a very large lathe to cut away all of the pits and the roughness."

I knew of no place in all of Liberia where this repair could be done. Repairing the generator looked pretty hopeless without shipping it out of the country. If the generator had to be shipped back to the United States or to England, the cost would be tremendous. The cost was not the only problem. It would take at least six months to get the generator back, and they would be without power all this time. Without sharing any of these thoughts with the others, I just continued staring at the damaged equipment.

As I stood there looking at it, God spoke to me in His still, small voice, and a plan formed in my mind on how to do the repair right there where the generator was sitting. I asked if they had a sharp wood chisel. Dwight spoke up right away and said he had brought a new one with him when he came to Liberia a few weeks before. I also asked them to find a short two by four that was about twelve inches long. I knew there were some on the mission station. I also knew there were some very good C-clamps on the station, and I asked Bill and Dwight to get them for me.

Then I asked if they had a pair of micrometers that I could use to measure the diameter of the commentator, and Dwight said he had also brought some from America. On top of that, I asked for a fine file and some fine sandpaper, which they had. Bill and Dwight gathered these items together and brought them to the generator building as I stood there looking at the generator and forming the plan in my mind.

I was planning on making a lathe right where the generator sat. Rather than rotating the commentator on a large lathe, I was going to rotate it using its own bearings and drive it by running its own large engine. I planned to use the chisel as a type of lathe-cutting tool. I would clamp the two by four about one-sixteenth of an inch away from the commentator. I would then, very carefully, lay the chisel on the two by four and hold it very tightly in both hands at about a forty-five-degree angle with the face of the commentator. Then I would very slowly move the chisel's point into the rotating commentator. By holding the chisel on a forty-five-degree angle, just the point of one side of the blade would touch the commentator.

The chisel point would be like the point of a lathe tool bit coming into contact with the material it was to cut. If this worked okay, the point of the chisel should cut into the rotating commentator a few thousandths of an inch. Then I would very slowly pull the chisel across the two by four letting the point cut the rotating brass on the commentator. This would cut away the rough and pitted surface of the commentator if it all went according to the plan in my mind that God had given me.

I had to be very careful in doing this, otherwise I could get hurt badly. The engine was very large with a flywheel that was about three feet in diameter and probably weighed about five hundred pounds. The engine drove three large V belts, and they drove the generator. I would have to work in a space right beside those belts. If I accidentally rubbed against them, they could pull me into the pulleys and could cut my arms or legs off in an instant. I also had to be very careful not to get into the spokes of the flywheel, as it could also very seriously hurt me.

The other possible danger would come from the generator itself, because it would be running at full speed when we started the engine. As a result, it would be producing a very high amount of voltage and amperage. When I touched the rotating commentator with a steel chisel, that I was holding, a high amount of voltage would flow through the chisel to me. That could seriously hurt me and it would blow another hole in the commentator just as the springs did when they touched it. To eliminate this danger, I had to disconnect the right wiring from the generator armature so that it did not produce electricity.

By this time the sun was setting, and it was becoming very dark. Bill brought a kerosene lamp and lit it so I could continue to work. The light was dim, but it was sufficient for me to see well enough to continue on with my plan. I clamped the two by four in place and disconnected the wires on the armature. Then Bill and Dwight hand-cranked the large engine and got it running up to speed. With great care, I slowly moved myself into the cramped space between the engine and generator and carefully got down on my knees. With the large belts running at a high speed right beside me, I moved my left arm into place very carefully, as it was only inches away from the belts.

Next, I took the wood chisel, very carefully placed it on top of the two by four and slid it against the rotating commentator, just as I had planned. As I held the chisel very tightly in my hands and slowly pulled it to my left across the rotating commentator, a very thin ring of about ten one-thousandths of an inch per side of shavings came off of the commentator surface just as I planned. I was amazed at how well it worked. In fact, it worked about as well as if I had cut the commentator surface on a proper lathe. When I finished making this cut, the commentator surface looked very good. I took the file and very lightly filed the rotating surface to remove my tool marks. Next, I took the fine sandpaper and lightly sanded the rotating surface until it was extremely smooth.

After this we turned off the engine and let it stop rotating. When it stopped, I took the micrometers and measured the diameter to make sure it was perfectly round. It was as perfect as if I had done it on a lathe. Then I measured the amount of taper on the surface of the commentator from one end to the other. To my surprise it only had .001 of an inch taper per side from one side to the other. A piece of normal paper is .004 of an inch, so the taper was only one-fourth of the thickness of a piece of paper from one side to the other. I was simply amazed at how accurately it came out. After that I took new brushes that Bill had on hand, mounted them, and reconnected the wires that I had previously disconnected. Then Bill and Dwight restarted the engine, and the whole mission station came to light. The generator worked perfectly, and every missionary on the station rejoiced and thanked God that once again they had electric lights.

I heard the still, small voice of the Holy Spirit as He showed me how to repair the generator right where it sat. God had given me the plan and the ability to cut the brass on the commentator very accurately. I want to look again at Exodus. 31:4-5 and see how this is stated in the scripture.

> *To devise cunning works, to work in gold, and in silver, and in brass, And in cutting of stones, to set them, and in carving of timber, to work in all manner of workmanship.* (Exodus 31:4-5)

The commentator was brass. I needed to cut it to make it usable. God had given Bezaleel skills in working with brass and also in cutting stones as we see in Exodus. 31:4-5. He needed to cut stones to make them usable. God had given me a skill and a plan on how to cut brass to make it usable. I did not have the proper equipment to do this in the country where the generator was located. Bezaleel also did not have the tools we have today for cutting brass and stones. They had not yet developed the materials that we have today for doing this. They also did not have the equipment that we have today for getting the stone out of the stone quarries. Even without what we would call proper tools for cutting and shaping stone, they built what was probably the most beautiful building the world has ever seen. How did they do it? God gave them the skills to do it with the tools they had, just as He gave me the plan and skill to cut the commentator on Bahn mission's generator with the tools we had on hand!

5) A Toyota Land Cruiser That No One Could Repair

After my brother and his family moved to the Bassa mission station, they purchased a Toyota Land Cruiser. The vehicle was purchased at a fraction of the normal cost because the motor misfired badly, but it was nice looking and well built for the rough African roads. Jim knew it was running badly when he purchased it, but the cost was so cheap that he took it anyway, hoping it could be fixed. It sounded terrible and used a lot of gas due to the fact that it was only running on about half of its six cylinders.

The Land Cruiser was originally purchased from a Toyota dealership in one of the larger cities in Liberia. Normally they have good mechanics, but we were told they were not able to find the problem with this particular vehicle. My brother asked me to look it over to see if I could fix it. I had never worked on a Toyota, but I agreed to give it a try. At first I thought it might be an ignition problem, so I checked out the ignition, and found it was working well. After that I decided to check the carburetor for problems. I was used to working on American-made engines, and the Toyota carburetor was different than any I had ever seen; however, I managed to take it apart but could find nothing wrong with it.

It looked like it should work fine, but when I put it back on the engine and started it up, it ran just the same as it had before I worked on it. I checked the compression, valve timing, spark timing, spark plugs, and spark plug wires. All of them looked perfect to me, so I decided to take the carburetor off again and look at it more closely. Again I could see nothing wrong. I was totally at my wits end as to what was causing the engine to run that badly.

After exhausting all of my knowledge, the Lord took over with His knowledge, showing me a problem that no one else who had worked on the vehicle had noticed. As I was looking at the inside of the carburetor, a clear thought came to my mind. I know it was the still, small voice of the Holy Spirit saying, "Look at the two jets in the very bottom of the carburetor." As I did this, another thought came to my mind, indicating one of the jets was set for high-speed driving and the other for low-speed driving. I looked very closely at the jets; one had a very small hole in it, and the other one had a hole in it that was about twice as large in diameter.

Suddenly it all became clear to me; I was able to see that the low-speed jet was mounted in the location of the carburetor that takes over when the vehicle is at high speed. I simply took out each jet and mounted them in their proper locations. Then I put the carburetor back together and remounted it back on the engine, reconnected the gas line, etc. You can imagine my excitement when I started the engine, and it purred like a kitten.

My guess was that someone in Japan had reversed the two jets accidentally, and no one had ever been able to find the problem. Whatever happened, Jim was able to purchase the Toyota at a great price, and the whole thing certainly worked in his favor. He could never have purchased it at the normal price, but now that he had it, he used it to get to many places where hundreds were won to Christ. We praise the Lord again for His faithfulness and wise council that He gave me through His still, small voice.

6) REPAIRING A THREE-CYLINDER DIESEL

One day Wesley Bell, who was the field leader of the Liberia Inland Mission, asked me to look at his diesel engine tractor. I knew very little about diesel engines, but I agreed to look at it. He said it got very hot every time he tried to mow the grass on the mission runway. I was surprised to find that it had a three-cylinder diesel engine in it that came from Europe. It was about the size of a Ford tractor that many farmers used in America in the fifties. I had never heard of a three-cylinder engine. If it would have had a gas engine, I would have looked at the cooling system to see if it was plugged or had something restricting its flow of water. If that was okay, then I would have looked at the spark timing to see if it was advanced too much, and next I would have checked out the gas mixture to see if it was too lean. The only thing in common between the gas and diesel engines that could make them both run hot, that I was aware of, was the coolant system. Wesley's tractor's cooling system seemed to be working very well, so I was stumped as to what was wrong.

Wesley and his wife, Molly, were both from Ireland and were missionaries with WEC just as we were; in Liberia, however, the mission was called Liberia Inland Mission. Like many missionaries, Wesley and Molly received very little support and did not have money for another tractor. If I could not fix it, it would be of little value to them. I knew how badly they needed the tractor, and I sure wanted to fix it for them. I would definitely need the knowledge of the Lord to accomplish it, because I did not know what to do.

Once again I called upon God for His knowledge concerning this issue, and once again He shared His wisdom with me. It was like He was leading me step by step with His still, small voice, giving me the answer. I disconnected one of the fuel lines that went from the diesel pump to one of the cylinders. The diesel did not have spark plugs, but it did have glow plugs for heating up the fuel in cold weather. I took the glow plug out for the cylinder that the fuel line went to, and using a piece of clean wire, I was able to establish top dead center for the piston travel. Slowly I turned the engine until the fuel line ejected out diesel fuel. I figured it should eject out fuel about one-sixteenth of an inch before top dead center, because that is about where a gas engine fires. To my surprise, it ejected out fuel about one-sixteenth of an inch before bottom dead center.

This meant that the diesel fuel would be in the cylinder all the way up on the compression stroke. It would fire anywhere up on the compression stroke when the compressed air reached seven hundred degrees. Since Liberia is near the equator, it is very hot there. This meant that the explosion in the cylinder would be much sooner than it should be, because the hot African air would reach seven hundred degrees much sooner than air from a northern country. This made the diesel engine act the same as a gas engine when the spark is too advanced. This is why it was overheating; it was actually working against itself. In fact, I was surprised it even ran at all.

Now that I knew what was causing the engine to run hot, I needed to know how to fix it. I did not know how the fuel injector pump was made or how it could get this far out of time. So I did the only thing I knew to do, and that was to take the pump off of the tractor. Amazingly, as soon as I got the pump off, I was able to see the problem. I could see that there were two ways the fuel pump could go back together, and that the two ways were 180 degrees different. Whoever had mounted the pump on the engine had assembled it exactly 180 degrees wrong. I simply rotated the keyway on the pump shaft 180 degrees and remounted the pump on the engine block. Next, I reconnected the fuel line and put the glow plug back in. Wesley started it, and it ran great with no more problems.

I was blessed in knowing that Wesley could now use his tractor. And I was doubly blessed in knowing that once again God gave me the ability to get the work done. He had spoken to me in His still, small voice and showed me where to start on the diesel problem. Then He just brought to my mind, step by step, what to do. As I followed His voice, the problem was fixed, and His servant had the use of the tractor without the problem of overheating.

Bob, Pat, Tony, Tanya and Mike McCauley, 1972

Bob flying three world Doctors to treat sick Africans

Jim McCauley family in Liberia: Mary, Belinda, Debbie, Mark and Jim

Jim and Bob McCauley by Maule airplane

Mark, Tony, Tanya, Bob and Pat in Liberia

Africans helping Jim build student dorm at Bassa Bible School

August wedding: Tanya, Miriam, Esther, Bob, Kevin, Tony and Mike

Esther and Bonnie Sparling helping load semi-truck for Moscow

Bob, Esther, and Lena Zdor

Esther going into Russian sewer in St. Petersburg

Inside Russian sewer where street children sleep

Vera, Sasha, Bob and Esther beside Hermitage Museum

Feeding street children

Children enjoying a good meal

Vera 'loving' the children

Bob teaching math to boys in prison

Esther giving bananas to youth in prison

Esther, using a Russian Bible, to teach English to youth in prison

Esther and Vera enjoying children at Children's Ark Orphanage

Bob and Esther McCauley - January 2011

Ch. 22

THE DEVIL SOCIETY ENCOUNTER

One Christmas while we were in Liberia, Jim and Mary and their children, Belinda, Debbie, and Mark, came to our mission station at River Cess to spend a few days. Our two children, Tony and Tanya, were really excited they had come. Our son Mike, by this time, was back in America going to college.

Tony and Mark were nearly the same age and both loved spending time together exploring the jungle. They both had motorbikes that they rode down the jungle roads and on the footpaths. They became very good at controlling their bikes as they rode through the rough trails and rivers. Tanya enjoyed having her older cousins with her, and both Belinda and Debbie seemed to love being with their younger cousin. Christmas Eve was a joyful time as we had our meal and exchanged a few presents.

Later that evening, Jim and I went out to our mission carpenter shop to have prayer together. The shop had a small second floor, and Jim and I went up there for our prayer. The room was not clean at all, and the floor was covered with dust from different building projects, but it was a place where we could go and not be disturbed. As we started to pray, I heard the still, small voice of the Holy Spirit tell me to lie down on the floor and pray in that position. I was wearing my only good white shirt at the time. The first thought that came to my mind was, "If I get on that dirty floor, it could ruin my only white shirt." I hesitated for a short time, and again I heard God tell me to get down on the floor. This time I went face down on the floor and started to pray.

Jim was feeling that the Lord was leading him to leave Liberia and go on to Swaziland, and he wanted me to pray with him concerning this. A few years before this, God had given him a dream in which he saw the words, "Move to Swazi and preach." Jim did not know what it meant and had no idea what the word "Swazi" was. After praying about this, he felt the Holy Spirit lead him to look in the encyclopedia for the word Swazi, and he saw that the Swazi were a tribe in a country called Swaziland located in southeast Africa.

From that time on, Jim knew that God was calling him to go Swaziland and preach, and he started to pray and seek God about doing it. One evening the Holy Spirit spoke to him through His still, small voice, giving directions for selling most of his land. He was to keep the home and fifty acres of land where he lived and to give the profit from the rest of the land to God's work. Then he was to go to Swaziland. Jim did not hesitate to tell the Lord he would obey and put his property for sale. This was a major sacrifice financially on their part.

It was a cold winter evening when God gave Jim this word. Later that very evening he noticed that there was no light under one of the water fountains for his hogs' water. That meant that the heater flame had blown out and that the fountain would freeze, which would cause the hogs to have no water within a short amount of time. Immediately he went out to the barn lot to light the flame.

Suddenly the eastern sky lit up with the brightest white light that Jim had ever seen. It looked like many angels standing in the sky. The brightness was intense, yet he could clearly see them. They stood there for a little time and then moved and formed a very large triangle. To Jim, the triangle represented the Trinity of the Father, Son, and the Holy Spirit. He watched the angels for a time, and then they formed an arrow that shot southeast toward Africa. Jim stood in his barn lot, amazed at what he had just seen. He had witnessed something divine. He would never forget this time, and his life would never be the same after it. Few people have ever seen an angel, but Jim had just seen many. God had given him a confirmation on his call to sell his land and to move to Swaziland and preach.

From this time on, Jim knew that God wanted him and Mary in Swaziland, but he also felt that first the Lord wanted them to come to Liberia, where he built the Bible school. By this Christmas Eve, the Bible school had been built. Many African students had come to get an education in Bible, and the other missionaries on Jim's mission station were teaching the Bible classes. Jim had also taught the Africans how to raise hogs and swamp rice. He had fulfilled what he felt the Lord had called him to Liberia to do, and he wanted us to have prayer together for guidance concerning him going on to Swaziland.

Right after I started to pray with my face to the floor, the Lord spoke to me in His still, small voice and gave me a word for Jim. It was, "Set your face toward the south and follow me." Since Jim was already in Africa, Swaziland was south from Liberia. The Lord also made it clear to Jim that he was to leave Mary and the children in Liberia and fly to Swaziland on March 15 (as I remember the date). Swaziland was about three thousand miles away. It seemed that the date to leave Liberia was very important, but we did not know why. Later we would find out just how important this date was. Jim received no other word as what to do or who to see when he got to Swaziland. He was just to go there on that date.

Our time in prayer was not long, but the Lord gave direction to Jim that would result in thousands of people coming to Jesus Christ. Fourteen churches would be established, and church buildings and parsonages would be built for those congregations. Jim and Mary would spend the next twenty-two years in Swaziland. We had no way of knowing all of this as we prayed on the floor of that dirty carpenter shop that Christmas Eve, but now, forty years later, we can see the wonderful results of what happened as we heard the still, small voice of the Lord and obeyed what He said.

Right after the prayer and words from the Lord, Jim said, "I will plan on going to Swaziland on March 15 just as the Lord told us." Jim was simply going to obey what the Lord said. He was not planning on going there to see if he liked it or if he found something that suited him and Mary. He was not going there to test or spy out the land to see if it was a desirable place to live. He was going there for one reason only, and that was because God had spoken to him in His still, small voice.

After our families had our Christmas together, I flew Jim, Mary, and their children back to their mission station. Immediately Jim and Mary started preparing for Jim to go to Swaziland on March 15. We did not know it, but Satan was going to strongly oppose Jim's going on this date. A major problem was on the way that was going to make it very difficult for him to obey God.

The preparations to go to Swaziland seemed to be going well through January and February, but things suddenly changed around the first of March. One day Mark was riding his motorbike down a jungle trail when he saw a very small path that led off the main trail. Mark was seventeen years old at the time and, as many boys of that age, he liked to explore new things and places. He decided to leave the main trail and see what was down this small path. There were signs along the way that showed the local Bassa people that they were forbidden to travel down that path unless they were members of the Devil Society. Most of these signs consisted of branches broken from the trees in a certain way that were a warning to the Bassa, but not to a seventeen-year-old from America.

174

Mark headed down the path on his motorbike, and after a while he came to an opening in the jungle. In the center of the opening was a building with a very large grass roof that was supported by wooden poles. The sides were open, and Mark could see many African men doing something in the building. He was curious as to what was going on, so he slowly road his motorbike up to the side of the building and looked inside. All of a sudden the men started running toward Mark. They were shouting and very angry. His motor was still running, and he quickly put the bike in low gear, gave it gas, let out on the clutch, and got out of there before the men caught him. He then headed back to the mission station as fast as he could.

That same day, I had been doing some flying in the Bassa area and was on my way back home. My flight took me right by Jim and Mary's station, and since it was getting late in the afternoon, I decided to stop at Jim and Mary's station and spend the night with them.

Very early the next morning, we heard a great commotion outside, and when we looked out the window, we saw many angry men walking toward the house. The men were so loud that it alerted the whole mission station, and everyone came out to see what was going on, including Jim and me.

The men were from the local Devil Society, and they were demanding that Jim hand Mark over to them immediately. They said that Mark had violated one of their most sacred devil worship rites. He had seen the "host," and if anyone that was not a member of the Devil Society saw the host, they had to go through the devil rites within twenty-four hours. This meant that Mark would be forced to worship the devil and make a sacrifice to him. The men would cut Mark and get some of his blood and sacrifice it to the devil. They also could cut off a finger or some skin, and sacrifice it to the devil. Mark was in serious trouble, and the missionaries knew it. What made it more serious was the fact that the Devil Society was a strong part of the law in the jungle.

Each Devil Society in the jungle sacrifices a human being, which they call a "host," to the devil once a year. The Devil Society was in the process of sacrificing a human to the devil when Mark rode his motorbike up to the large building. Because Mark had looked into the building, the Devil Society members felt he had seen the host that they were sacrificing, and because of this, it was their strong law that Mark had to go through the devil rites and join the Devil Society within twenty-four hours. In their law, they were to make no exceptions to this regardless of who the person was-including Mark.

Jim refused to turn Mark over to them, and the Devil Society men threatened to take Mark by force. The missionary women tried to help out and talked to the angry men, asking to take the case to the government officials, and the Devil Society men agreed. All of the men and the missionaries walked to the local government office in the village to talk to the highest official, who was in charge over several villages in the area. The Devil Society and the missionaries talked to this official about two hours.

During this time Jim and I were very concerned, because we knew that most of the high officials in the country belonged to the Devil Society, so this made things worse. So far we had seen no evidence that the official was going to stop the Devil Society from getting what they wanted. It did not look good, and we were praying that God would intervene for Mark. We knew that one of the highest sacrifices that could be made in the Devil Society was for a member to sacrifice one of their children or a wife to the devil, and some of these men had done just that. If they would do such a heinous thing, then they would not hesitate in forcing Mark to go through the devil rites.

After loudly discussing what to do with Mark, the Devil Society finally agreed to let Mark go if Jim would give them one thousand dollars. However, Jim did not have one-thousand dollars and neither did all of the missionaries put together. He would gladly have given them the money, but he didn't have it. Jim told them he did not have that much money and finally they said that since Mark was an unintelligent American boy that did not know their ways, they would let him off if Jim would give them a large hog, (Jim had a few of them on the mission station), two hundred pounds of rice, and two hundred dollars.

Jim agreed and was able to come up with the two hundred dollars, the rice and one of his hogs. The Devil Society took the hog, the rice, and the two hundred dollars and left. They still, however, did not seem happy, but all of the missionaries were glad that Mark was still with them. It had been a hard day, but things were looking better, or at least we thought they were.

Jim and Mary continued to make plans for Jim to go to Swaziland, but one problem remained: Jim did not have the money for the plane ticket. After praying about this problem, it came to his mind that he still had all of his tinsmith tools. When Jim sold his farming equipment before he and Mary went to Africa, he kept his tinsmith tools and took them to Liberia. Jim really loved those tools and could make almost anything out of sheet metal with them. He hated to sell the tools, but if that was what it took to obey God and go to Swaziland, then he would do it.

God spoke to Jim through his son Mark as to how much to ask for the tools. Mark said. "Dad, I think you should ask seven hundred dollars for the tools." Mark did not know it, but Jim needed exactly that much money to go to Swaziland. Seven hundred dollars sounded like a lot of money for the tools, especially since they were in Africa. Who in Africa would buy the tools for such a high price? Selling them for that seemed impossible but Jim continued to make arrangements to go to Swaziland in spite of not having the money, and God started to do His miracle of provision.

A man from a rubber plantation (located about twenty miles from the mission station) heard that Jim had tools for sale. He drove to the mission station and asked to see them, and after looking at them, he offered Jim three hundred dollars for the lot. Jim told him that he wanted seven hundred dollars for them. The man laughed and said that he would not pay that much for them, and then he left. Things didn't look very good as far as selling those tools for that much money.

Jim continued to get things organized on the mission station in preparation to go to Swaziland even though he did not have the funds. He had to purchase the ticket in advance of his flight. That date was getting closer, and still there were no funds. All the things he had to do to leave were nearly finished, and still no money came in. Then the day before he had to purchase the ticket, the man from the rubber plantation returned to Jim and Mary's house and said that he would pay the seven hundred dollars for the tools if Jim still had them. Jim sold him the tools, which gave enough money to purchase the ticket.

Jim needed to purchase the ticket for his flight to Swaziland right away, and I was making a flight into Monrovia to get some supplies for the mission stations the next day, so he asked me to purchase the ticket for him. That morning just as soon as the fog lifted I got into the Maule airplane and made the flight over the jungle to Monrovia.

The fog had delayed my flight and I was unable to get to the ticket office before it closed at noon. It opened again at two o'clock in the afternoon, but if no one was in line to purchase tickets, they usually didn't stay open very long. I needed to be there right at 2:00 p.m. to make sure I got the ticket before they closed. Since the money for the ticket was not available sooner, Jim could not purchase the ticket in advance, but it was now March 13 and I was going to be asking them for a flight to Swaziland on the fifteenth in order that Jim could depart on the day that God had told him to leave. There were only a few flights out of Monrovia each day, so I was really pushing it to get a ticket out of there in two days. The timing was very close.

Since I missed getting to the ticket office before noon, I went to the mission headquarters in Monrovia. The missionaries in Monrovia were just getting ready to have their lunch when I arrived, so they invited me to eat with them. About halfway through the lunch there was a noise at the door. The weather was very hot and they had the door open to get a breeze, but there was a full-length screen door that was closed but not locked.

Everyone looked up at the door, and there stood a witch doctor. We could tell he was a witch doctor from his dress and markings on his body. He looked demonic as he stood there, staring at me sitting at the table along with about six other missionaries. He looked at no one else but glared at me. Then, in a voice that sounded like the devil himself, he spoke in long, drawn-out words, "I want that man." He was pointing directly at me as he spoke. The words were so demonic sounding that I will never forget them.

It was like Satan himself knew that I was there, and he sent this witch doctor to hinder me. I did not know what was happening in the demonic world at that time, but today I know that Satan was trying to stop me from getting to the ticket office that day. God had a series of events lined up in Liberia and South Africa, and getting to the ticket office that day was very important to God's plan. When the other missionaries heard this witch doctor saying that he wanted that man and pointing to me, they encouraged me to go out and minister to him.

This was an immense delaying trick by Satan, and I made the mistake of falling into the trap. God wanted me to purchase a ticket and not to do anything else. However, as a result of the coaxing by the missionaries, I excused myself from the table and followed the witch doctor up a small hill about one hundred feet from the mission house. I thought I could minister to him, but God was not in it and it did not work. God had called me to purchase a ticket, and here I was standing at the top of this hill facing this witch doctor.

I had allowed myself to be sidetracked from doing what God had called me to do. Even though I was out of God's will, I had to prove to the witch doctor that the power in me was greater than the power in him. I had the conviction in my heart that I must not run or walk away but that I had to just stand there and trust God for the rest. I obeyed my convictions and just stood there, looking at the witch doctor.

The other missionaries did not come outside but stood in the doorway watching through the screen door. The witch doctor walked under a tree and picked up a limb that was about six or seven feet long—strong enough to do terrible damage against a human being if it was used as a club. I stood watching and did not move. I knew that the witch doctor was probably going to try to hit me with the club, but I stood firm, not moving a foot.

The witch doctor walked toward me, his eyes glaring with an evil, demonic look. When he got within about six feet of me, he drew back his club and swung it as fast as he could to hit me in my left midsection. The witch doctor was an extremely strong man, and the speed of the blow was so fast that I could hardly see the club as it swung toward my left side. I never flinched or moved in any way.

When the club came close to my left side, it went up and over my head and down at the same level as it was in the original swing. The club was moving so fast that it rotated the witch doctor around at the end of the blow. By this time, his eyes were glaring at me with hate as he was preparing for his next blow. He pulled his club way back and swung with what seemed like even more force, this time at my right side. The club's speed was extremely fast as it headed for my right midsection. Once again, I did not move but stood firmly there. The second blow did exactly as the first and didn't touch me.

Then the witch doctor lifted the club over the top of his head and swung it straight down in a very fast blow aimed at the top of my head. Right before it hit my head, it veered off to my left and hit the ground so hard that a large piece was broken off of the end of the club. With even more hate in his eyes, he lifted the club and made another blow to hit me on the top of my head. This time the club veered off to my right and hit the ground so hard that the club was broken into many pieces. After the fourth blow failed to hit me, the witch doctor was so confused that he walked away, talking or mumbling something that I could not understand.

Who caused the club to veer off like it did on each swing? There was no way the witch doctor could have caused it to veer off on each blow. The club was long and moving very fast and he could not have controlled it like that with such a rapid swing. It was only the Lord that did it, and He probably had an angel deflecting each blow so that I would not be diverted from getting that ticket. If any of the blows had hit me, I could have been severely injured or killed and would not have been able to get the ticket, which was so important to what God had in mind for Jim. By just standing there and letting God deliver me, I proved to the witch doctor that the power in me was greater than the power in him. He knew it, and it left him very confused.

As the witch doctor was walking around mumbling and looking confused, I looked at my wristwatch and suddenly realized that I had wasted precious time in doing this. I felt that God was telling me that this was a delay trick and that I was to get to the ticket office as quickly as I could. Ministering to a witch doctor like this had little value if God had directed me to do something else.

Even though it might have sounded like a good ministry, it was not what God had directed me to do at the time. The missionaries expressed their disappointment that I was not staying to minister to this witch doctor, but I ignored them and headed for the ticket office. It would take me a half hour to get there, and I did everything I could to make up for the wasted time. I prayed that God would help me get there in time and that I would be able to get the ticket at this late date.

When I got to the ticket office, the doors were still open. I walked in and sat down in front of the ticket agent's desk. The agent had no idea that just minutes before a witch doctor had tried to kill me. As professionally as I could, I asked for a ticket to fly out of Monrovia to Swaziland, South Africa, in two days. The agent acted like it was impossible to get on that flight due to the short notice, but he did some checking and said that he would be able to book the last seat on that plane. I took the ticket and gave him the money Jim had received for his tools.

There had been much opposition to get Jim on that flight, but the worst was yet to come. Shortly before Jim was to leave the mission station and fly to Swaziland, some of the Bassa Christian men came to him with a warning concerning Mark. They said it had been reported to them that when the Devil Society men returned back to their village without Mark, the rest of the members were very angry. The members said that under no circumstances should the men have let Mark off, and they demanded that he be forced to take the Devil Society rites just as their law stated. The Christian men reported to Jim that the Devil Society was going to capture Mark, and if he would not join the Devil Society, they were going to kill him.

If they captured Mark, they would take him to their jungle headquarters and require that he worship Satan. If he refused to do this, they would kill him and sacrifice his body to Satan. Mark was in extreme danger.

Jim was faced with a terrible situation. His son was faced with either death or sacrificing his blood to Satan if captured by these terrible people. The Devil Society was very large, so there were hundreds of them. They were scattered throughout the area, and it would be easy for them to capture Mark. It was no small matter. Jim knew that these men would do this if they could, and he knew that God had given him a date to leave Liberia and go to Swaziland.

Jim had been willing to give up his land, income, retirement, medical insurance, and leave the home he loved in order that he might obey God. Now it seemed that he was even being asked to leave his son in one of the worst situations that he could imagine. Jim's pain over this was almost unbearable. With this extreme pain in his heart, he said, "I must obey God, and I will go as He has directed." I told my brother that I would watch after Mark, but I had no idea what to do." Knowing that I was going to help his son made Jim feel a little better, but he was still very concerned.

On March 15, Jim and his family and I drove their Land Cruiser to the airport in Monrovia. Mary had tears in her eyes as she said good-by to her husband, and all three children were weeping as they said good-by to their father. I even had tears in my eyes as I said good-by to my brother, not knowing what lay ahead for him in Swaziland. Jim, with tears in his eyes, walked across the tarmac, climbed the stairs leading up into the plane, and took his seat for the long flight to South Africa. The planes engines started up, and soon it was in the air. We all watched the plane as long as we could see it and then made the long drive back to the mission station. None of us knew what lay ahead for Jim.

Everyone was sad as we drove back to the mission station. It was a two-hour drive and there was little talk along the way. I was thinking about how difficult it was for my brother to leave his family; I could see the pain in his face as he said his good-bys, walked across that tarmac, and got into the plane. I did not know it at the time, but Jim wept almost the whole time he was on the flight, getting farther and farther away from his beloved family.

As I was driving, I was also praying about what to do concerning Mark. I told Jim that I would take care of things with Mark, but I just did not know what to do. I felt a huge responsibility with this situation. I felt sure that the Devil Society would try to capture Mark, and force him to worship the devil, or kill him, and sacrifice his body to the devil, as they said they would do. Almost every village had a Devil Society, so they were a very widespread and strong organization in the jungle. Since they were such a large organization, I did not know how I could stop them from finding and capturing Mark.

All of a sudden, as I was still driving down the road through the jungle, the Holy Spirit spoke to me in His still, small voice that I recognized and said, "You have an airplane, don't you?" I almost laughed at the simplicity of the answer that I received from the Holy Spirit. I did not laugh out loud, but I am sure I got a smile on my face when the Holy Spirit spoke those words to me. God can take something that is so serious to us, which seems to have no answer, and make it so simple! This was one of those times. I immediately knew what the Lord was saying. I wished I could tell Jim how simple the answer was, but there was no way for that as he was hundreds of miles away on his way to South Africa and Swaziland.

I then said, "Mary, just as soon as we get back to the mission, get a bag of clothes packed for Mark as quickly as you can. I will get the plane ready to fly as you do it. Then I will fly Mark out to my mission station. We won't tell anyone where Mark is, so if the Devil Society tries to find out where he is, no one at your mission station will be able to tell them." Mary fully understood this plan and was happy about it.

I knew that our mission station was so far away that the Devil Society would not get word to that area concerning Mark. They also would not have any communications through the jungle that far away, nor would they travel that far looking for Mark. I knew that the Devil Society would not hurt Mary or the girls, so they would be in no danger. It would be only Mark that they would try to capture and they would not find him.

About one hour later we arrived back at Mary's mission station. All of us already had a long day and were tired, but we had important things to do quickly. I wanted to get them done so quickly that if some of the Devil Society men were near the mission station, they would not have time to capture Mark. Just as soon as we drove into the mission station and up to Jim and Mary's house, I ran to the airplane. As I was checking the plane out and getting it ready to fly, Mary, Mark, and the girls were getting Mark's things ready to leave. This took about fifteen minutes. By this time I had the Maule Rocket mission plane ready to fly except for starting it and checking out the engine before takeoff. I did not want to start the engine until the very last minute so as not to attract attention in case some of the Devil Society men were nearby.

Just as soon as Mark's things were ready, he ran to the plane, said good-by to his mother and sisters, and quickly got into the right front seat. This would be his last time on this mission station. I was already in the plane and ready to start the engine. I shouted the normal, "Clear prop," and turned the starter switch. Almost immediately the engine started with a roar. I quickly checked out the mags and controls and got my concentration fully on the takeoff. I applied full power, released the brakes, and the plane shot down the little runway. In about four seconds it came off the ground and we were in the air and over the trees.

I kept the plane on a straight-out heading at an altitude just above the trees until we got out of sight. In case any of the Devil Society men were around, I did not want them to see which way I turned after my takeoff. Right after we were out of sight from those on the mission station, I turned the Maule to a two hundred-degree heading toward River Cess. Feeling good about what we had just done and the simplicity of it all, I settled in for the flight.

We were flying over very high jungle, and I was closely watching the compass to keep us on a course to River Cess mission station. Shortly before we reached the mission station, we flew over the Cess River. The river was very wide and there were no bridges that crossed it. There were a few dugout canoes that were used by some of the Africans to cross the river, but in general, people did not go from one side of the river to the other.

My mission station was about twenty miles south of the Cess River, and the jungle in that area was extremely dense. This made travel by foot in that area very difficult. I was confident that Mark would be very safe living with my family in River Cess until Mary and the girls had things ready to return back to Indiana. When we landed the plane at our mission station, Tony was there, and he was very happy to see his cousin Mark get out of the plane. The two boys would have a wonderful time together in the jungle.

When Jim's flight arrived in Johannesburg, South Africa, he was to catch another plane from there to Swaziland. As he was walking up to the ticket counter to check in for his flight to Swaziland, a young man stepped in front of him and got the last ticket out that day for the Swaziland flight. There was nothing Jim could do, so he would have to wait twenty-four hours for the next flight. Jim knew nobody in Johannesburg, but through a strange set of circumstances of meeting someone in the airport, he was invited to spend the night with a white South African Christian couple that he did not know.

Early the next morning, Jim went out to the kitchen, where he met a man and woman that had just dropped in for a quick visit. They were passing through Johannesburg on their way back home to Cape Town, which was about one thousand miles away, and they stopped in that morning for a very short visit. This couple had already talked to the couple that lived in the home where Jim had spent the night, and they were told that Jim was on his way to Swaziland. The first thing they said to him was, "We hear that you are on your way to Swaziland." Jim affirmed that he was. Then they said, "About two years ago we met some old missionary ladies from Swaziland, and they gave us a map to their mission station." They pulled out a handwritten map drawn on a small piece of paper that they had been carrying all this time and gave it to Jim, suggesting that he might want to visit them sometime. This couple was in the home with Jim for only a short time, before they headed on to Cape Town.

The timing of this meeting was very critical for what God had in store for Jim concerning his direction. The couple with the map had been on a long trip. If they had stopped at their friend's home the day before, Jim would not have been there; if the young man had not stepped in front of him at the ticket counter and gotten the last ticket to Swaziland, Jim would not have met these people. If Jim had not been invited to stay all night with this Christian couple, neither of them would have met him. And if the couple would have stopped to see their friends later in the morning, Jim would have already been gone.

If I had spent even a few more minutes with the witch doctor, I would have missed getting the ticket, and Jim would have missed these people. And most important of all, if Jim had refused to go on the flight the day God told him because of the situation with Mark and the Devil Society, he would have missed these people with the map. The meeting with these people was critical to everything that would happen for the next twenty-two years and beyond.

Before Jim left Johannesburg, he met another man named Eddie Cain. When Eddie found out that Jim was going to Swaziland, he gave him an old Citron car that had about five hundred thousand kilometers on it. The floor boards were so rusted that you could see the ground through the holes! Even though it looked terrible, it ran well and Jim took it. Rather than flying the 250 miles on to Swaziland, he drove there in his car that God provided.

When Jim arrived in Swaziland, he followed the map that the couple had given him to a very remote mission in a semi-desert area of the country. The mission was so remote that Jim would never have found it without the map. The drive there took him over many miles of very rough dirt and gravel roads. When he finally came to the mission station and turned in, Jim saw about fifty buildings that were very run-down and looked like they had not been repaired in years. His first thought was, "I hope this is not where God has called me."

Jim drove up a driveway which was about a quarter of a mile long and up to one of the houses. An elderly lady was outside when he pulled his old car up near where she was standing. She stepped over to the car before he had time to get out and asked, "Have you come to stay?" The lady's words seemed to be prophetic, as Jim would be staying there for the next twenty-two years.

The Holy Spirit through the spiritual gifts and through circumstances took Jim to the exact location where two missionary women were praying for a man to come and help them. They lived on a run-down mission station in a very dry and poor area of Swaziland. Many Swazi people lived in the area, and most of them lived in poverty conditions. This would be Jim and Mary's home for twenty-two years.

Three weeks after I flew Mark out of his mission station, Mary, Belinda, and Debbie went to Monrovia. I then flew Mark to Monrovia from River Cess mission station where we had been hiding him from the Devil Society, and Mary and her children returned to Indiana. After Jim got things established in Swaziland on the mission station where the two elderly women were living, Mary went to Swaziland and ministered with him. By this time the children were old enough to stay in Indiana on their own, so they were never with Jim and Mary in Swaziland during their twenty-two years.

A book could be written about all of the ministry and miracles that happened with Jim and Mary's ministry in Swaziland. It took the hand of God leading and directing all of us to get Jim at the exact location to get the handwritten map that these people had been carrying for two years. The map was critical to get Jim to the right location. Jim and Mary's ministry made a tremendous difference to thousands of people in Swaziland. They also raised five Swazi children while they were there, and made a tremendous difference in their lives.

What made the difference in bringing about Jim and Mary's ministry in Swaziland? It was obedience to the call of God no matter what the cost, and it was also knowing and hearing the still, small voice of God and then obeying it. I firmly believe a person can miss what God has for them in life. I also believe there are things in the ministry that go undone because a person refuses to obey God. Jim could have refused to go on to Swaziland because Mark was in serious trouble.

I almost caused Jim to miss going on the exact day that God told us he should go by getting involved with the witch doctor. I did this because of pressure from the older missionaries, but it was the wrong thing to do. Finally, in the midst of getting sidetracked, I got back to what God was telling me to do and got the last ticket out of Monrovia to Swaziland.

My disobedience could have cost me my life, but out of God's mercy He delivered me. My story of the witch doctor reminds me about the actions of the young prophet and the old prophet in 1 Kings 13. The young prophet was given specific directions from God on what to do, and as a result of pressure from the older prophet, he disobeyed those directions, which cost him his life.

There was a lot of pain that went into obeying God, but in the end, God, in his love and might, worked everything out. If a man or a woman obeys the call of God no matter what the cost, they will make a difference in this world. Our sacrifice in obeying God is nothing compared to the great sacrifice God made in allowing His beloved Son to be a sacrifice for all our sins.

As C.T. Studd said, "If Jesus Christ be God and died for me, then no sacrifice can be too great for me to make for Him." C.T. Studd was a famous cricket player in England who was also a very wealthy man. When he became a Christian, he gave away all of his millions and spent the rest of his life in China and Africa making a difference in other people's lives. He was also the founder of WEC International Mission.

Obedience coupled with our willingness to make sacrifices for the service of our Lord will always bring us to the place of making a difference in this world and in our own lives. We can have the fullest life when we live it for our Lord Jesus Christ.

Ch. 23

GOD BLESSED OUR CHILDREN IN AMERICA

Michael, our oldest son, was back in America, attending Purdue University when Pat started to have some health problems in Africa. She had pain in her lower abdomen area and was tired all the time, plus she looked very pale. Our nurses could not help her, so I took her to the Methodist hospital in Liberia. The hospital was about two hundred miles back in the jungle and had very little equipment compared to hospitals in America. The African doctor took blood samples, examined them, and then reported that she had a major health problem but he did not know what it was, so he recommended that she return to America for treatment. Both Pat and I decided that she should return to the States right away and that I would stay with our children in Africa for the time being.

We were encouraged by our mission for her to fly home as soon as possible. Soon she was back in America, and after her arrival in Indiana she stayed with our friends David and Mary Ann Long. Our son, Michael, was also staying there, so it was a special time for Pat and Michael to be together again. Within a few days of her arrival, she went to the doctor and was scheduled for an examination.

After the test results were in, the doctor told Pat that her problem was simply a bladder and kidney infection. He added that the tube between her bladder and kidneys was too short, and that this was a contributing factor to the infection passing from her kidneys to her bladder. To correct this problem, the doctor wanted Pat to get her weight down very low. He recommended that she go on a strict no-carbohydrate diet. He mentioned that there was a very small chance she could get colon cancer from this diet, but that the chances were so small that she need not worry. He then prescribed antibiotics for the infection, which Pat took for a few weeks. She started to feel much better, and when the doctor released her, she said good-by to Michael and her friends and returned to Africa. The doctor wanted Pat to stay on the protein diet even when she returned to Africa, which she did.

After her return to Africa, she still remained tired and run down and was never able to get her normal strength back again. We remained in Liberia another year and one half, which made our stay there a total of five and one half years. Before we left, another pilot came to take over my job as the mission pilot for that area. I trained him for about six months before we felt free to return to America.

When Pat and I told Tony and Tanya that we were going back to America, Tony became very upset. He did not want to leave the jungle; it had become his home and he loved it. His everyday life consisted of taking long trips on his motorbike to different places in the jungle. Some of these places were very remote, but Tony knew them well. He also spent a lot of time getting to know the people and the chiefs of many different villages. He had even become the mechanic for many of the chiefs that had motorbikes. They themselves became very concerned about Tony leaving, so they came to me asking if he could stay in the jungle instead of going home with us. Tony hoped I would agree to their plan, but in the end he realized we could not, so he reluctantly left the jungle with us as we returned to America.

When we left Liberia, it never entered our minds that in a short time the president would be shot, the country would have a long civil war, and almost all of our Liberian Christians that we loved and worshiped with at Bahn mission would be lined up and shot. Neither did it enter our minds that some of our missionaries would be shot also, and that the entire mission work would be stopped in the country for years to come.

When we arrived back in Indiana, the first thing on our agenda was to see our son Michael. Our reunion with him was grand; he was no longer a boy but a mature young man. By this time he had taken the test for an apprenticeship as an electrician and had passed with very high marks. A company had hired him, and he was working as an apprentice making good money. We were all very happy for him and proud of his accomplishments.

We rented a small house, and soon our family all moved in and we were ready for a normal life. Jim and Mary had finished their time in Liberia, and Mary and their children were back in Indiana while Jim was in Swaziland.

Two days after we returned home, Tony went to the high school graduation of the class of students that he was with before he went to Africa. He had already graduated from his correspondence school, and we had given him a celebration while in Africa. Tony watched his class graduate with their caps and gowns and all of the speeches, etc., and he felt left out and somewhat depressed. When he came home that evening, with tears in his eyes, he told his mother and me that those kids got a first-rate education while he felt he only got a third-rate education. He was certain he would never be able to get a good job.

I felt like crying with him, but I also knew that God had spoken to me in His still, small voice and said that He would bless my children if I obeyed Him. I hardly knew what to say to Tony as he was weeping, so I simply told him what God had told me. I don't think he fully understood it at the time, but I think it gave him some encouragement.

The very next day when all the students with their new high school diplomas had the opportunity to go out and look for jobs, Tony also went looking for a job. That evening he came home somewhat depressed and told us that the only job he was able to find was a janitor job at a tool and die shop, sweeping the floors and cleaning the toilets. He felt that this was not a good job, but I was elated.

I said, "Tony, that is wonderful. Get to work fifteen minutes early every day and start working as soon as you arrive. Make the toilets shine and keep the floor very clean. Listen to the people over you and do everything they tell you the very best you can. Then some day they will get behind in cutting steel and will need someone to run a milling machine. Listen to them very carefully and cut the steel just like they say, and I believe they will take you on as an apprentice tool and die maker. The job is a wonderful opportunity to advance."

Tony did exactly as I told him, and things worked out exactly like I told him they would. Soon he was cutting steel and helping build tools and dies. The shop owners later sold out and closed the shop, but not before Tony received some very valuable experience. Soon he got an apprenticeship as a mold maker in another tool and die shop called Hewitt Tool and Die.

From there Tony kept advancing until one day he became an engineer for General Motors, and now he is a purchasing agent for the company. Michael also finished his apprenticeship and became an electrician for General Motors, making very good money. Tanya works for a large financial firm, and she makes very good money also. God truly did bless my children financially, and I believe it is because I obeyed His still, small voice.

About three weeks after we returned to Indiana from Liberia, Jim came back home. I was very surprised when he and Mary walked into our little house. We had no idea that he was back in America. Jim had gotten situated in Swaziland and was now ready for Mary to come down and be with him. He had not been back in Indiana for about four years, so he had returned home for a three-week visit before Mary went to Swaziland to be with him.

Shortly after Jim came home, the Holy Spirit spoke to me in that precious still, small voice, telling me that I was to return to Swaziland with Jim in three weeks. Little did I know at the time that the results of hearing and obeying this still, small voice would lead to miracles beyond anything I had ever experienced. I would see hundreds of people come to Jesus Christ. I would hear God speak to me audibly and see a vision that was like looking at a television set. I would hear Him speak to me many times, giving specific directions for us in His still, small voice. I would preach the blood of Jesus Christ and repentance many times in an area where terrorists were training people to kill whites! Also, within days, I would be the shop foreman of a very large machine shop in Swaziland.

Immediately Pat and I started to make arrangements for me to go to Swaziland with Jim. The airplane ticket was going to cost eighteen hundred dollars and I did not have it, but it was not a worry for us because we had learned that God would provide finances when we needed them. A few days before I had to have the money for the ticket, a church that I had never heard of had their Wednesday evening prayer meeting. There were thirty-four people at the prayer meeting that night, and our pastor was one of the thirty-four attending. During the meeting, he mentioned my name and requested prayer for me.

The church's pastor then announced that God had spoken to him that day, telling him that he was to take up a collection for someone whose name would be mentioned during the meeting. When our pastor asked for prayer for me, the minister said that I was the person he was to take a collection for. He also said that before the meeting he had already placed envelopes in the pews for the collection. He asked the people to put money in the envelopes for me at the end of the service. They had never met me, nor had I ever been in their church. When the money was counted, it came to exactly eight hundred dollars. This was a lot of money for only thirty-four people to give. They made out a check to me for that amount, and our pastor gave it to Pat and me. How did God speak to the pastor to take up this collection? It was by the still, small voice of the Holy Spirit.

190

The next day after this God again did something special for us through His still, small voice, speaking to someone else. I went with our pastor to visit one of his farmer friends. We had a nice visit with the farmer, and he asked me a few questions about missions. As we left he gave our pastor an envelope, which our pastor gave to me as we were driving away. It had a check in it to me for one thousand dollars. God knew I needed one thousand dollars more to have enough to buy the ticket to Swaziland. He had spoken to the farmer in His still, small voice to give me the exact funds I needed. God provided the exact amount of money I needed for my ticket within less than twenty-four hours. I thanked Him for it and also thanked the people that gave it.

About a week later Jim and I boarded an airplane headed for Johannesburg, South Africa. Shortly after we arrived in Johannesburg, Jim purchased a new pickup truck which we drove to Swaziland. I got a job as a foreman in a large machine shop in order that I could stay in the country, and within a couple of months, Pat, Tanya, and Mary joined Jim and I. Through the week I would work in the machine shop, and on weekends we would make the two-hour drive to where Jim and Mary lived on the mission station. Jim and I would go into the villages and preach the Word of God.

Ch. 24

A Pomeranian Puppy and a Swimming Pool

" $\mathbf{D}$ ear God, when we go to Africa this time, please give me a Pomeranian puppy and a swimming pool." Tanya and her mother were having their evening prayers in America before they came to Swaziland when our nine-year-old Tanya prayed this prayer. Her mother, Pat, did not know Tanya was going to ask God for this special puppy and a swimming pool when they came to Swaziland in South Africa to join me.

My brother and I had left our wives in America and went to Swaziland to get settled. Two months later they flew there to join us, so we had time to write back and forth. It was during this time that I received a letter from Pat telling me about Tanya's prayer. Pat said she guessed this would be one prayer that would not get answered. When I read her letter, I felt the same way. There was just no way for Tanya to have a swimming pool and Pomeranian puppy in Africa.

We had lived in Liberia, Africa, for years and knew there were no Pomeranian dogs there, nor were there any swimming pools that we would have access to. There was no way this could happen. At least that is the way both Pat and I looked at it. We felt badly for Tanya because we knew she would be terribly hurt when she did not get her prayers answered. There was nothing we could do about it, however. We just did not want it to take away our little girl's faith.

Jim had been in Swaziland before and had gotten settled on a mission station in a very remote semi-desert area. When we arrived in Swaziland, Jim was already registered in a leadership position with his mission station, so he was cleared right away through customs to go on to his mission station, but I was only given three weeks to stay in the country. I could not get permission to stay in the country as a missionary, so I had to come up with some kind of job that would permit me to stay there and still be able to work as a missionary!

Jim had talked to a man that owned an airplane spraying business about my flight experience, and the man told Jim that he would hire me as a sprayer plane pilot.

My salary would be good, and with my hundreds of hours flying in all kinds of conditions, I knew I could fly a sprayer plane. I also had a commercial license and a multi-engine rating, so I was qualified this way also. This seemed like it would be a very good job for me, and I could work with Jim as a missionary in my extra time. Jim and I went to the airport and talked to the owner of the sprayer business. He was a German pilot that had moved to Swaziland. After a short interview, he said he would hire me, and he told me what to do with the Swaziland government to stay in the country. I was happy about the job and was looking forward to flying a twin engine 310 Cessna as a sprayer plane.

Jim found me a place to stay with a pastor and his wife, who lived in the city of Mbabane. After seeing the owner of the flight spraying business, Jim went on to his mission station, which was about a two-hour drive away from Mbabane, and I stayed with the pastor. That night as I was praying, the Lord spoke to me in His still, small voice that I knew so well and said, "You are not to take the flying job, but rather you will receive an opening for a job that will come through the pastor. The job will be related to your tooling and engineering profession." I wanted the flying job and figured I would make very good money at it, but now I knew that God was not leading me that way. I wanted God's will more than anything, so I rejected the flying job and decided to wait on what would happen with the pastor I was staying with.

The next day the pastor talked to me about my background, and when he heard about my tool and die experience and my engineering job, he said that he wanted to introduce me to a man that owned a machine shop. To my surprise, there was a very large and fairly modern machine shop not far from the pastor's home. He took me to the shop, introduced me to the owner, and asked him if he had any jobs available. The man told me to come back the next day, and he would give me a test to determine if he would hire me.

The next morning when I went to the shop, I had no idea what kind of test he was going to give me, but I went with a fair amount of confidence, knowing my extensive background in machine shop tools and engineering. The owner of the shop greeted me in a friendly but businesslike manner. He took a piece of paper and drew a bolt and a nut. The bolt was ten millimeters in diameter with a special type of square thread. Then he gave me a bar of steel, a blank tool bit, and a pair of vernier calipers, and told me to make the bolt and nut. The owner took me to a very large old lathe and told me that I was to use it to make the bolt and nut. Then he walked away and left me standing there.

As I looked at the lathe, I saw that all of the graduations were marked in millimeters, and I was not familiar with the gearbox at all. The calipers were in millimeters and the print was in millimeters, and I had never worked in millimeters before. I had only worked in inches, so I had no idea how big a millimeter was. I looked and looked at the calipers but just could not figure out which graduation on them was a millimeter. If the test had been in English and inches, it would have been simple for me, but I was stumped on this one. I just did not know where to start! I prayed and asked God to help me.

A German young man had been at the lathe when the owner took me there. He walked away and started doing something else at the time, but I had noticed him looking at me every few minutes. He looked as if he was not happy with me being at his lathe. Finally I walked over to him and asked him a question. I did not know if he would answer me or not, but I asked, "How many millimeters in an inch?" The young German snapped back in a very sharp reply, "25.4." I thanked him for this answer and walked back to the lathe. Then I took the calipers and moved them out to about an inch and counted the little marks. When I got to the size that had 25.4 graduations on it, I saw that it was about the size of an inch. I then knew which graduation was a millimeter. Then I moved the calipers out to ten millimeters and I knew how large my bolt was to be.

I took the blank tool bit and ground one end of it to make a lathe-cutting tool. From there, I practiced with the lathe enough to get it to turn the right rpm and travel the right cutting speed. Then, I cut the steel bar down to the ten millimeters in diameter and to the right length; I ground the other end of the tool bit to make an external thread-cutting tool to cut a square thread according to the print. Once again I asked the young German a question about the lathe gearbox, and he showed me how to set the gearbox to cut the right threads. This was a big help, especially since I could not read the markings on the lathe. I cut the threads on the bolt and then reground the tool bit to cut internal threads. Then I set up the lathe for internal threads and cut them.

When I got done, the nut and bolt fit perfectly. I took them into the owner's office and he looked them over really well. He tried the nut on the bolt both ways, and he got a very pleased expression on his face. His first words were, "Good job, I will hire you as my shop foreman. I will give you six hundred rand-a-month wages, and you will work forty hours a week." This was a very good wage for South Africa, but it was very little compared to what I had made in America.

I felt the Lord had told me that my opening into the country would be related to my tooling background and that it would come through the pastor, and this job fit both of these conditions. I could hardly believe it. Within a very short time I had walked into this machine shop and had become the foreman over seventy men. I was even foreman over the young German that had helped me with my questions on millimeters and on how to set up the gearbox on the lathe. Later he and I became good friends.

Even though I had desired the job of flying more than the job of being a foreman in a large machine shop, the latter proved out to be by far the best choice for my employment in the years to come. By following God's leading and turning down the flying job that I wanted, I had the opportunity to learn skills that would be a great financial blessing to me and my family in the future. For one thing, it got me started into learning plastic molding, which I later would use in my occupation as an engineer for General Motors. I also learned leadership skills in working with skilled tradesmen from different cross-cultural backgrounds. This would be a great help to me in the future. Unknown to me at the time, I would later become shop foreman in a large plastic molding business called Hewitt Tool and Die. This employment would end up being a great blessing to me also.

God spoke to me in His still, small voice; I heard Him and obeyed, and I am so glad I did. Later I found out that the owner of the flight spraying business did not pay his pilots, and great problems arose as a result. God knew this, and He also knew the direction He was going to take me years later.

How does this all fit into the prayers of a little girl who prayed for a Pomeranian puppy and a swimming pool when she got to Africa? Let me tell you how. I started my new job right away, and in the evenings I looked for a place for Pat, Tanya, and I to live. I looked for several weeks but was not having any success. Then someone told me about a house that was for rent. I went to see it, and it was small but very nice and clean, so I told the man that I would rent it; I signed the papers and put some money down on it.

I made arrangements with him to move into the house and was about ready to leave when he said, "I forgot to tell you one thing about the house. It has a swimming pool that is located right behind the trees that are beside the house. Come, I will show it to you." We walked around some trees and there it was. A swimming pool that was about twenty feet wide and thirty feet long came with the house that I had just rented! I could hardly believe it. Tanya was going to get a swimming pool when she came to Africa after all, and I had done nothing to find a place that had one. It was strictly God that had provided this one. It was absolutely amazing to me, but there it was!

I was very happy about finding the house with the pool, but I felt there was no way Tanya was going to get a Pomeranian puppy. As far as I knew, Africa just did not have that breed of dogs. Pat and Tanya were ready to come, and just a few days before they were to arrive, a very well-dressed Swazi man showed up at the machine shop. He came to me and said, "I raise Pomeranian dogs and I have a new litter of Pomeranian puppies. Do you know anyone that would be interested in buying a puppy? I sell them for sixty rand each, and they will be weaned from their mother in about a month."

I told him right away I would buy one for my daughter. He told me that if I purchased one, she could come and see it every day until it was weaned, and then she could have it. I paid him for the puppy and again was amazed at what God had done. This guy had come to the machine shop and talked to me. I don't think he talked to anyone else there about a puppy. It was clear to me again that God had done a wonderful thing in Swaziland for a little girl that had prayed in America for a Pomeranian puppy and a swimming pool when she got to Africa.

Neither Pat nor I had the faith to believe that God would give Tanya a swimming pool and a Pomeranian puppy when she got to Africa. But Tanya prayed for these things, and God was faithful and answered her prayer. True to her prayer, when she arrived in Africa she had a swimming pool and her Pomeranian puppy. Every day her mother would take her to see her puppy before it was weaned, and then came the special day for Tanya when she got to take her puppy home. Tanya and her Pomeranian puppy had many fun hours of playing together. She used her pool a lot and I fondly remembered, as I watched her play in the pool, how God had furnished it without me even saying a word or looking for a home with a pool.

Ch. 25

A Voice from Heaven

Nearly every day Jim took his Toyota pickup truck out on the rough dirt roads to minister in the villages. There were many widows and other poor people in the villages, and he faithfully took cornmeal and other food items to them when he went. Every Sunday morning Jim would start driving early in the morning, making trip after trip to the different villages, picking up people and taking them to church. He usually had about twenty people in the back of his pickup truck. Many times the little truck was so fully loaded that it looked as if it could not go, but it always did. After church, he would make trip after trip taking the people back to their villages.

One Sunday a woman, who was about thirty-five years old, went to church in Jim's truck along with a load of other people. She had her three-week-old baby with her, so Jim had her and the baby sit in the front so she and the baby would be more comfortable. After church, Jim returned this woman along with the rest of the people back to their own area. The woman had a bad case of malaria and died that night. Jim was told about this right after it happened, and it really shook him up because he had no idea if she had accepted Christ as her Savior.

In deep grief he told me how sad and concerned he was about this. He felt that he should have done more that day to make sure she was a Christian. Jim's grief was so intense that I could see it in his face and eyes as he told me about it. I was very concerned for him, because I could see that he might always be concerned, that he did not personally talk to this woman about her soul, and that she might be in hell for eternity.

The night after the woman died, God gave me a vision that I saw with my eyes. It was a scene against a wall in the little house on the mission station that Jim and I stayed in. The vision had a message in it for Jim that said he could rest easy because the woman was right with the Lord when she died. I don't know why God gave the vision to me rather than Jim, but He did. I told Jim about the vision, and he was very relieved, knowing that she was saved and that she would be in heaven for eternity.

I worked at my job as a foreman in the machine shop during the week, but on the weekends Pat, Tanya, and I would make the two-hour drive to Jim's mission station. I would go into the villages with him teaching and preaching the Word of God. We were ministering in many different villages in the area but we had purposely stayed out of a terrorist training area due to the dangers involved for us if we went in there. Many of the people we preached to did not even know who Jesus Christ was. We asked one man if he knew who Jesus Christ was and he got a very serious look on his face as if he was thinking intently. He then pointed in a certain direction and said, "I am not sure, but maybe he lives down the road this way."

Hundreds of people made decisions to accept Christ as their Savior as we taught the Word. Most of the people knew little about the Creation story and man's fall due to the sin of Adam, or that Jesus Christ died for our sins. Often we had to start at the beginning and tell the story about God's plan and what Jesus Christ did for us. The people were very open to listen and respond to the Word.

The terrorist area that we had purposely stayed out of consisted of about two hundred and fifty square miles. After we had ministered in the different villages around the terrorist training area for many months, Jim told me that he felt God wanted us to go into that area and preach the blood of Jesus Christ and repentance in every village. We talked about doing this, but I wasn't sure of us going into this area.

The terrorists were not only teaching the Africans to kill white people but also to kill any African that was friendly to the whites. They tried to make examples out of the Africans that showed any friendship to the whites by killing them and their families. Many white farmers in South Africa had already been killed, so we knew the seriousness of going into the area.

A few days before we started talking about going into that area, Jim and I preached the Word of God in a village that was located near the terrorist area. A few days after we were there, a group of terrorists came running through the village with their guns blazing. They shot every person they could: men, women, and children. Some of the residents of the village were able to run and escape, but sadly, many were not able to get away in time and were shot. Many were wounded and eleven died on the spot from the gunshot wounds. I don't know how many died later. I feel there is a good possibly that the terrorists killed all of those people because they were friendly to Jim and me.

As I prayed and thought about us going into that area, it came to my mind that for two white guys to go into that area would be like two Jews going into a Nazi training area and preaching. They probably would be killed. It was not safe for us to go in there, and we probably would be killed unless God protected us. I also had another problem. By this time I had changed jobs and was working in a plastic molding shop for a man that had escaped out of East Germany. He was a wonderful Christian and we often talked about spiritual matters. He and I became very close friends. He was hungry for the Word of God and questioned me on many different aspects of the Bible. He respected me and I respected him. He grew up in a Communist country and I in the United States, yet we had an excellent friendship in Jesus Christ.

God also used him to teach me plastic molding. I had served an apprenticeship as a tool and die maker and had also been a senior tool engineer for General Motors. My German friend was an expert in plastic molding. I knew little about plastic molding and he knew little about sheet metal tools and dies. He wanted to learn all he could about building sheet metal tools and dies so that he could expand his business into those areas. He told me he would teach me how to build plastic molds if I would teach him how to build sheet metal tools and dies, and every day we gave each other equal time of teaching, hour for hour.

By the time we finished our teaching and learning time together, he had became almost an expert in my tool and die skill and I in his plastic molding skill. He started to quote sheet metal tool and die work from a local industry that used a lot of sheet metal parts. It opened his shop up to thousands of dollars worth of new business. At the time, I only did this teaching to be friendly, but little did I know that God was teaching me an engineering skill from this German that would be of extreme value to me in the years to come.

I was allowed to stay in the country as long as I worked at my job, and Jim was in the country as a director of a mission station. The government only gave me a work permit to stay in the country, and if I stopped working at my job, I was supposed to be out of the country within one week. They wanted to know my whereabouts at all times. Every weekend I would make the two-hour drive to Jim's mission station and minister with him in the villages. This was not a problem as long as I was back on my job on Monday morning.

The law in this country was very strict, and many people were in prison for many years because of some very small infractions. If Jim and I went into the terrorist area full-time, I would have to quit my job, and if I did not leave the country in one week, I would be in violation of their immigration laws. If the police caught me, I would surely go to prison for a long time. On top of that, if the terrorists caught us, we probably would be killed. This was not a good situation, and I was desperately praying about what to do.

Early one morning I was praying about us going into the training area. Suddenly I heard Jim's voice, calling for me. It was so clear! Jim was calling for me with a tone of desperation in his voice that meant come quickly, I need your help. It was Jim's voice, and it sounded as if he was right outside our house. I wondered why he had made the two-hour trip from his mission station to our home in the city so early in the morning. Something was wrong, and he needed my help immediately.

Pat was still in bed; I woke her quickly and said, "Pat, Jim is outside." I ran outside, expecting to see his pickup truck in the driveway, but it was not there. Surprised by this, I knew he had to be someplace outside and he needed me immediately. I ran around the house, expecting to see him in the yard, but he was nowhere to be found. Suddenly, I stopped looking and realized that the Lord had spoken to me using Jim's voice. This time it was not a still, small voice of the Holy Spirit that I was hearing but an audible voice from heaven!

Since it was mainly Jim's feeling that we should go into that area, I knew that God was confirming it to me by using Jim's voice calling in this desperate tone, meaning come and help me now. I had just heard an audible voice from heaven! I don't know if it was the Lord or an angel, but I do know I heard a voice from heaven confirming to me that Jim and I should go into the terrorist area and preach the blood of Jesus and repentance in every village.

I knew then that I was to resign from my job and that we were to go back into the terrorist training area, no matter how dangerous it was. Jim was right in his convictions that God wanted us to do this. In an audible voice, God gave me the confirmation that I had been praying about. I needed this confirmation because of what I was facing if I quit my job and went in this area, and God knew it.

I had just finished building a plastic mold in the tool and die shop and was ready for my next job when God spoke this confirmation to me. The timing was right as far as my job was concerned, because I could leave without putting my friend's work in jeopardy. My friend was also low on work at the time, so the timing was perfect to resign.

I told my friend what God was directing me to do. He immediately realized the seriousness of leaving my job and told me that he would have to report me to the authorities within a week or they would put him in prison. I understood this and called him by his name, saying, "I totally understand that you have to report me. I don't want you to get into trouble. You must do what you have to and I must do what I have to."

Shortly after that I left my job. I knew that I could never go back to it and probably would never see my friend again here on this earth. I have never seen him since that day, but I know I will in heaven. Right after this, Jim and I went back into the terrorist area and started preaching the simple message that God had given us.

Pat and Tanya stayed in our home in the city and worked quickly at getting rid of our belongings except for a few necessities that we would need. She also notified the landlord that we were leaving so he would not be upset. The work took Pat about a week, and Tanya was a big help to her mother in getting the house ready to move from.

That week Pat and Tanya had quite a scare, however. One day a man came to the back door, broke the lock, and came into the house. Pat and Tanya ran toward the bedroom. There was a door in the hallway that had a lock on it (which was on the bedroom side of the door). As Pat and Tanya were running for the bedroom, Pat slammed the hallway door and managed to get it locked before the man rammed the door from the other side. The man continued to ram against the hallway door, but was unable to break the lock or the door. Pat started to pray and rebuke Satan because she had a strong feeling that he, Satan, was leading this man to do this as an attack against us for what we were doing to obey God. The man gave up after a time, and then stole a few things out of the house and left.

After closing up the house, Pat and Tanya came to the mission station and stayed there, waiting for Jim and me to finish ministering in the terrorist training area. Pat knew the dangers we were facing and daily prayed for us.

There were many small villages in the terrorist area, and we knew that the Lord was leading us to preach in every one. The task was great, but we felt the Holy Spirit was telling us to do this job quickly. We also knew that sooner or later the terrorists could catch us or the government would catch me. We felt we should divide up—I would go into some villages and Jim would go into others.

This way we could cover many more villages in the same length of time. We were traveling in Jim's pickup truck to the different villages.

We would usually park it in a location between two villages, and I would walk to one and Jim to the other. When the villagers saw a white guy walking into their village, they would always come out to see us and hear what we had to say. This gave us a wonderful opportunity to give them the Word of God. When the people heard the simple message of the blood of Jesus Christ and repentance, many made a decision to become Christians.

We did not know exactly where the terrorist camp was, but we did know it was in the area where we were preaching. No doubt we ran into some of the terrorists in the villages, but we did not know who they were, as they would have looked like any other person that lived there.

One day as I was walking down a path that led into a village, I saw two African policemen in the village. By their uniforms, I could tell that they were from a nearby city. They were in this very remote area looking for something or someone, and I felt that it might be me. I knew if they saw me in this remote area, they would question me, and I did not want that. I was near a mud hut located right at the edge of the village when I saw them. No one had noticed me walking into the village yet, so I quickly stepped behind the mud hut and stayed there until the police left. After they left, I stepped out and walked into the center of the village. The Africans greeted me very favorably and listened closely as I taught the Word of God.

Every day as we went out, I knew that we could be shot that day. Since the terrorist goal was to kill whites, Jim and I qualified, and we could easily be targets. Most of the terrorist killing was done by hiding in the bushes and shooting their victim from a distance. Many of the white farmers that were shot never saw the person that shot them, and we could be victims in this exact way. I knew God had called us there, but I also knew many people in the Bible and missionaries of our day had been killed in God's service. In spite of this knowledge, we continued to preach day after day. Jim and I were willing to die in God's service, but we were not willing to disobey our wonderful Lord because of fear.

Two months passed and finally there were only two villages left that we had not preached in. One was about a mile's walk up a tall hill from the road we were driving on. The other village was about a mile's walk down into the valley from the road. We decided that I would take the village on the hill and Jim would take the one in the valley. We parked the truck beside the road, and each of us walked to our village to preach.

When I walked into the village, all of the people came to see me. It was strange for them to see a white man walk into their village, but they all listened as I preached the simple message to them. I well remember a blind girl listening so intently to me as I explained the Word of God. When I was finished with my teaching, she said that she wanted to accept Christ. I led her in the sinner's prayer and she accepted Jesus as her Savior. Then I told her that an African Christian pastor from the mission church would come to visit her. I also told the village people where the African pastor lived and where the church was, and asked them to please come to that church. We did this with each group of converts.

I said good-by to the villagers and started my walk back down the hill. The sun had gone down by this time and it was starting to get dark, but I could see well enough to walk. About halfway down the hill, the Spirit of the Lord came upon me and spoke to me in a still, small voice saying, "Get out quickly because they are looking for you." I knew that I had to get out of the country as quickly as possible because I was a wanted man and would be in serious trouble if I delayed leaving.

Jim had also finished preaching in his village and we met at the truck at about the same time. We discussed our day as Jim made the long drive on the dirt roads toward the mission station. Both of us had a very good feeling in our hearts that we had obeyed the Lord in spite of the dangers, and we felt good that we were both still alive. No doubt, many of the men that heard us preach were terrorists, but God had protected us.

In time, the terrorists left the area. Later Jim went back in there, and he and the African Christians built several churches. Today there are hundreds of Christians living there. Many of the ones that we led to Jesus are leaders in those churches, and the blind girl is still going on with the Lord. God used Jim and me to make a difference in that whole area.

As we were driving back to the mission, I told Jim what the Holy Spirit had spoken to me as I walked down the hill. Jim and I agreed that Pat, Tanya, and I had to get out of the country as quickly as possible. I still had another problem that concerned me. To get my exit permit out of the country, I had to go to five different government agencies and have my papers stamped for approval. There was no way around this. They would each check their records to see if I had violated any law, etc., while in the country before they would stamp my exit papers as approved. If any of the offices saw that I did not leave the country within a week after leaving my job, I was in big trouble and could still go to prison.

As I thought about this, I thought about a friend of mine in a neighboring country that was in prison for a year and a half for putting some posters up about a Christian young people's meeting. I knew that these things could be very serious. I was again somewhat anxious for what I still had to do.

With some anxiety, I went back into the city and to the first government agency. It had been two months since my friend had to turn me into the immigration office for violating my work permit. I felt the paperwork showing my violation would surely have reached that office within those two months. With dread, I walked up to the large desk, handed the officer my papers, and asked him for an exit permit. He looked at my papers, got up and went over to a large record book, and took a long time looking at it. All kinds of thoughts were going through my mind as I stood there watching him look into the record book. What would I say if he asked me where I had been for two months? I could not lie to him, and he certainly would be angry if I said that I had been back in the terrorist area for the time. This would certainly open me up to all kinds of questions and problems.

After he finished looking in the record book, he came back toward me. His demeanor was not happy, but I could not tell what he was thinking. You cannot believe my relief when he picked up a large rubber stamp and brought it down on my papers. He signed and dated them, saying nothing as he handed them back to me. He had approved them; my violation had evidently not reached this office yet. I was relieved, but I still had to go through four more offices like this one before we could exit the country.

As I went to each of the other four agencies, I anxiously waited as they went through their records to see if I had done anything wrong while I was in their country. They all ended up stamping my papers, signing and dating them, stating that I was not wanted for anything and that we could leave the country. When the last official stamped my papers and signed them, it was like a heavy weight was off my mind, and I knew we could go home. What had happened?

Was their system so slow that my work-permit violation had not been recorded in any of these agencies? Maybe God had blinded their eyes to it? I don't know what it was, but I do know that God had again delivered me from a problem situation.

Now that we had our exit permits, we were able to get our tickets, and were very relieved to be free from the pressure we had faced. We said good-by to Jim and Mary and a few other Christians and were soon on the plane heading to the United States of America. When we arrived in New York, I had a strange feeling. I even asked myself what it was. I thought for a little bit and realized that for the first time in over two months, I did not have that little fear in my heart of being killed or sent to prison. I felt free because I was no longer a fugitive and was not facing prison. We were back home!

Although I never returned to Swaziland, my brother and his wife ministered there for a total of twenty-two years. Besides their own three children, they were able to raise five African children as well. They managed to come home for a few months every few years, and it was a joy to see them.

I am so thankful God gave us the opportunity to preach His Gospel in this particular terrorist training area. Many people were saved and will be rejoicing in heaven with us for all of eternity due to God's amazing grace.

As I stated previously, Jim went back into the terrorist training area later and built several churches, and today that area is a thriving place for Christianity. Jim would go to each village and teach the Word in the open air or under a tree. When he had about 250 converts in a village, he would build a church. He mentored many African young Swazis, who then became pastors. He also built a total of fourteen churches and homes for the pastors. In addition to this, he also built many water reservoirs in the area so that the Africans could have clean water in the dry season, and he gave food to hundreds of starving Africans through the years. His converts would number in the thousands.

Although Jim and Mary are in America now, they are still involved with their Swazi converts; raising funds to support pastors and helping to feed hundreds of orphan children.

About thirty years have passed since I saw a vision with my eyes and heard God speak to me in a voice that I heard with my ears. Jim and I were just two farm boys from Indiana that ended up preaching the blood of Jesus and repentance in the terrorist training area. We knew the chances of being killed were very high, but we also knew that God had spoken to us through His still, small voice and confirmed it with His audible voice. We were sometimes fearful for our lives, but our desire to obey God more than overcame our fears. May His Name be praised!

Ch. 26

Two Good Women

When we returned back to America, we felt God leading us to become Midwestern representatives for WEC mission, which we did. We quickly got involved in speaking at churches and Bible colleges about missions. Pat became involved in a teaching and speaking ministry in our area and was asked on different occasions to mentor or counsel individuals. As a result, she was very busy in the Lord's work.

One day a very dignified and attractive woman asked Pat if she would counsel her. This woman claimed to be a dedicated Christian. She was very active in her church, and many people looked up to her as a good example of what a Christian woman should be. Everyone believed she had a solid Christian marriage. The woman said she was having some emotional problems and felt Pat could help her. Pat did not know the woman, and she was extremely busy at that time, but she agreed to counsel her.

When they met for the first time, the woman started telling Pat how she was having emotional problems that were tormenting her and that she did not know what to do to stop them. As the woman was talking, Pat suddenly stopped her and said, "You have been having a sexual relationship with your pastor." The Holy Spirit spoke this to Pat in a still, small voice, and she knew beyond any doubt that this woman was in sexual sin with her pastor and that this was her problem. The woman had mentioned nothing about this nor had she even hinted about this sin between her and her pastor, but God knew it, and the Holy Spirit told Pat.

After Pat confronted the woman, she started to cry uncontrollably and repented of her sin. Without the Holy Spirit giving this knowledge to Pat, the counseling sessions might have gone on for months taking up Pat's valuable time, and the counseling session would have been for nothing. The truth of this woman's problem probably would never have come out, and she would not have been helped at all.

God used Pat in a mighty way, but she began to have serious physical problems. Every time she had pain or a general rundown feeling, the doctor would treat her for a kidney infection. We prayed for her to be healed many times, but she continued to be ill.

I got a job as a foreman at Hewitt Tool and Die to support our family. Tony was working for them when they hired me, and he was ready to start as an apprentice as a mold maker when I became the shop foreman. As a result, I ended up being his foreman through his entire apprenticeship and it was a joy for me to be able to teach and work with him.

After five and a half years of working at Hewitt Tool and Die and speaking at many churches, Bible schools, and colleges representing WEC, the Lord spoke to me in His still, small voice, telling me to send a résumé for an engineering job at Delco Electronics where I had previously worked as an engineer. Before I did this, I talked to Ed Hewitt, the owner of Hewitt Tool and Die, and told him what I was going to do. Ed was a very close friend, and I wanted him to know up front what I was planning. He was a dedicated Christian brother, and I did not want to offend him in any way. I had learned a lot about plastic molding working under him through the years and had a very high respect for him as a Christian and also as a friend. He was very gracious when I told him that I was going to apply for a job at Delco Electronics.

I made out my résumé applying for a job as an engineer in plastic molding and sent it in to Delco. The day before they received it, the engineering supervisor had decided to hire another plastic molding engineer. When he received my résumé, he immediately talked to one of the older engineers about me. That engineer knew me well from my position at Hewitt Tool and Die, and he told the supervisor that I was very well qualified and that he had better hire me before someone else did. The engineering supervisor called me in for an interview, which went very well, and then he told the personnel department that he wanted to hire me and turned it over to them.

About two days after my interview, I received a phone call at Hewitt Tool and Die from a man at the Delco personnel department, saying they wanted to hire me and wanted to know what it would take to get me. The Lord had already spoken to me in His still, small voice and given me a figure to give them when they asked. The figure was quite high and I gave it to him.

When the man heard the amount I was asking, he got extremely upset and offered me about half as much as I had quoted him. I told him I would not take the job for that amount of money, and he ended the conversation, saying that they could not pay that much to get me.

The next day I received another call from the same man, offering me about five thousand dollars more per year for the job, but again I refused and told him that it would take the exact amount that I told him in the first place. Once again he ended the conversation, saying they would not hire me for the figure I quoted. The third day he called again and offered me a little more money, but I told him the same thing and refused his offer. We ended our conversation the same way again. He kept calling me for another week and a half, each time offering me more money, but each time it was below what I had originally told him. I kept telling him that I would not lower my price.

Finally he called and made me an offer within two thousand dollars of the original yearly figure that I had given him. Again I refused his offer. He really got upset this time, but I still refused to come down. The next day he called me again and offered me the exact amount that I had originally quoted him, and I accepted the offer and the job.

I gave my friend Ed a three week notice to blend me out of the job. Ed's oldest son was about twenty-five years old and was very qualified to be shop foreman. I had been his foreman through most of his apprenticeship and knew his qualifications well. I knew he would make a very good foreman, and it worked out exactly that way. Ed made him foreman when I left, and he still is to this day. After the three weeks were finished, I went to Delco and started my job as an engineer in plastic molding.

Pat continued to have physical problems and had been to the doctor many times in an effort to get help. Then one evening as we were getting ready to go out for the evening, she noticed a very hard lump in her neck as she was putting on lotion. She asked me to feel it. It was very hard and felt about the size of a golf ball. I became very alarmed, and my immediate thoughts were that it might be cancer. I almost broke out in cold chills, but tried to remain calm. Pat realized the seriousness of it also. Early the next morning we called the doctor, who immediately sent her to a specialist in Indianapolis, Indiana. That day they gave Pat a series of tests which confirmed that it was cancer that had started in her colon and spread throughout her body. The specialist then referred her to an oncologist in Kokomo, only about a half-hour drive from us.

Pat appeared not to worry about her condition; she was handling it much better than I was at the time. My concerns were very deep and profound. From that day on, Pat had different treatments, including an operation and chemotherapy. About three days after the oncologist in Kokomo started to treat Pat, I called him on the phone from work and asked him some questions about her. That was a big mistake on my part because I was at my desk surrounded by other engineers. The oncologist answered my questions, and in the process, he said that Pat had about two months to live, but with chemotherapy she might live four months. He was very sympathetic but was also being honest with me.

When the doctor told me that Pat had only two to four months to live, I started to cry on the inside, and after we ended our conversation, I started to cry openly right in front of the other engineers. All of them were so involved in their work that I don't think they noticed. I knew I could not stay there any longer because I was definitely on the verge of a complete breakdown. I ran to the coat rack, grabbed my coat, and ran for my car. By the time I got there, I was crying so badly that my chest felt like it was caving in. I finally calmed down, drove to a church, went in and knelt at the altar, and did my best to turn it over to the Lord, praying earnestly for my wife's healing. Finally, after a few hours, I was able to get myself together so I could return to work.

Pat continued to be in very good spirits through the rest of her months. The chemotherapy that she took in the beginning made her very ill. Early in her bout with cancer, she spent a lot of time in prayer. She finally decided that if the doctor felt she could only live two extra months by taking the chemotherapy, she would not take it. She decided from this point on she would trust the Lord with the time He would choose to give her. I said that I would honor her decision, and she didn't have any more chemotherapy treatments after that.

After she was diagnosed with cancer, Pat actually lived eight months. Six of those months were fairly good. During this time she taught a class on "The Tabernacle" in our church on Wednesday nights. Her teaching went on for six weeks and her last class was right before she was going to teach on entering into the Holy of Holies. She believed that entering into the Holy of Holies for the Christian represented going to heaven. That week I had to take her to the hospital because she was having trouble breathing. The pastor finished the last lesson of Pat's class as Pat lay dying in the hospital.

This was an extremely hard time for me and also for our children, but there was nothing we could do for Pat except to pray for her and to be with her as much as we could during those last days. During one of Pat's last days, she looked at me and said, "Bob McCauley, you are a good man." Her statement meant very much to me, especially since she said it not long before she passed away.

Early one morning as I was praying for Pat, the Lord spoke to me in His still, small voice and said, "Today Pat will be healed." I was very excited about this because I felt I was going to see the Lord heal Pat that very day. As I was sitting beside Pat's bed that afternoon, I saw her suddenly open her eyes very wide and look up at about a forty-five-degree angle from her bed. From the expression on her face, she looked as if she was seeing something wonderful.

I turned my head and looked that way, but I only saw the walls and ceiling. Finally she lifted a very weak and frail arm toward the direction she was looking and said very clearly, "Come." Shortly after that she closed her eyes and it looked like she went into a deep sleep. Her breathing became very shallow, and later, with all her family present, she went on to be with the Lord. Later the Lord spoke to me again in that still, small voice and said, "I gave Pat the perfect healing." Pat was healed, but not in the way I thought she would be.

Earlier that summer Pat sang "Fill My Cup, Lord" as a solo in our church, and they had taped it. For her funeral, I had the song played, and she sang her own funeral song. After her funeral, I was almost beside myself with grief when the Lord gave me an inner vision as I was praying. It was a vision of Pat in heaven. I was startled when I saw it because she looked exactly like she did when she was seventeen years old, the age she was when we were married. The vision of Pat was very vivid, and she was extremely excited as she stood in the front row of a very large choir, singing. The vision only lasted a few seconds, but I saw it and it made a big difference in me. I still grieved about losing her, but had a peace in seeing how happy she was in heaven.

The days, weeks, and months passed as I lived in grief. Tanya was fifteen years old at the time, and she and I lived together trying to make our home as normal as we could after my wife and Tanya's mother had passed away. Six months later I was still in grief, and one evening as I was praying, the Spirit of the Lord came upon me and said in His still, small voice, "Give Pat to Me." I knew immediately what the Lord wanted from me: He wanted me to turn Pat over to Him and for me to get over my grieving.

God already had Pat, but I was holding on to her also, and He wanted me to let her go. Even though I knew what He meant, it was hard for me to do this. Finally after a long delay I said, "Okay, Lord, take Pat." Then the Lord spoke back to me again in His still, small voice and said, "Now I want you to pray for a wife." I was shocked at this request (and maybe a little angry about it also) and quickly replied, "Lord, I don't want a wife!"

As I continued kneeling there, I felt that the Lord was displeased with my harsh reply, and I did not want that. Finally after a few minutes, I said, "Lord, you know I don't want a wife, but since you asked me to pray for a wife, I will obey. Lord, give me a wife." Then the Lord spoke to me again saying, "Don't date anyone and don't lead anyone on so they might think you are interested in them, but wait upon Me to tell you who the woman is that you are to marry." In my heart I said, "This is going to be easy because I don't want to date anyway." To the Lord, however, I just answered, "Okay, Lord."

A few days later Tanya told me that Michael, Tony, and she wanted to talk to me and told me when they would all meet with me in my home. That day came and Mike and Tony came over; Tanya was already there. We all went into our living room and sat down, and I waited for them to speak. I could see that they were all very uneasy about our meeting and each of them was looking at the other waiting for one of them to speak. Finally Tanya said, "Dad, we have been talking, and we think that it is time for you to meet a good woman and get married."

Before the meeting, I had no idea what my children wanted, and I never would have guessed that it would have been this. I really appreciated their thoughtfulness. Now if God did bring someone into my life, I would be free before my children to pursue a relationship. I was impressed with the mature attitude and thoughtfulness of the children in this matter.

About a month after this meeting was Mother's Day. That Sunday evening I received a phone call from Esther Werdal. I had not seen or talked to Esther for years, and she only said that her son Kevin wanted to talk to Tanya. I called for Tanya, gave her the phone, and walked to my bedroom. As I walked through the doorway to my bedroom, the Spirit of the Lord came upon me so strongly that I fell on my knees at the edge of my bed. I prayed, "What is it, Lord?"

The Lord answered in His still, small voice that I knew so well, saying, "Esther is your wife." The statement was in the present tense, and to say the least, I was surprised. I had not seen Esther in years and could not even remember what she looked like. The only thing I could remember was that she was short. The last I knew, she was a married woman. I was very confused about what the Lord was saying. It just did not add up.

After Tanya finished talking to Kevin, she told me that Kevin was thinking about her not having a mother on Mother's Day and this really bothered him, so he wanted to tell her how sorry he was that she had lost her mother. Esther had only made the phone call for him. I said nothing to Tanya about what the Lord had said to me.

I thought about this word from the Lord a lot that night and through the next day at work. On Monday evening I decided to call Esther and see if I could get any information about her marriage, etc., but I would not say anything to her about what the Lord had told me. I knew if she was to be my wife she could not be married. Since I had not heard anything about her for years, I needed to be sure. I knew she used to live about twenty-five miles north of WEC headquarters, which was located on the north side of Philadelphia, Pennsylvania. Fortunately she still lived there, and I was able to find her phone number from this small amount of knowledge.

That Monday evening I called her, and during our conversation she told me that her husband had left her and her children about five years before this. He had several affairs with other women throughout the years of their marriage and even had a baby from one of them. When he left, she didn't always know where he was, and he paid very little support. A few months prior to this date, her husband had filed for a divorce from a state out west that had a no contest divorce law. This law meant that if one person filed for a divorce, there was nothing the other person could do to stop it.

Esther did not believe in divorce but felt that she needed to talk with a lawyer, who was also a friend, for the sake of her children. She wanted to be assured that she would not lose custody of them. After going through the paperwork and on the advice of her Christian lawyer, Esther signed the divorce papers. Soon after that she was divorced and was able to keep the custody of her children, Kevin and Miriam.

Esther also told me that her husband left her with a large amount of money owed on credit cards and unpaid bills in the community. She said she was not aware of some of the bills until after he left, but her name was on the credit cards and the bills. She felt that he had been using money to have fun with other women and had not used the money to pay their bills. Esther also told me that she had a very difficult time through the years supporting herself and the children plus paying the bills, which included paying off his debts. She told me that at one time they were so poor that she did not have money for milk for their cereal, so they ate it with water.

Esther did many jobs to support her family. She drove a school bus, sold Tupperware, and baked wedding and birthday cakes, all at the same time. Later she got a job as a technical writer for a Turkish company, where she worked for two years. When a better-paying job came up, working in human resources for Richardson Vicks, she took it, and that was where she was working when Kevin phoned Tanya. She also had about a half-acre garden to support her family. On top of that, for a long time she and her children cleaned offices for money.

Kevin worked as much as possible mowing yards and doing other jobs to earn money. They were making it, but it had taken sacrifices on the part of all three. Their church family was also a great help to Esther and the children during this hard time, both financially and emotionally.

I said nothing to Esther about my word from the Lord during the conversation. After we had talked for almost an hour, once again the Spirit of the Lord spoke to me in that still, small voice and said, "I want you to call Esther back and propose to her for marriage, and let me support Esther and her children through you. You are not to go see her first but to just call and propose to her." This really shook me up! It was like God wanted our marriage to be a business deal where He would use me to support Esther. I knew the seriousness of calling Esther and proposing to her and that if I did, it was forever. How could I do this without seeing her first? I just could not bring myself to obey God on this one.

For the next four days I felt like I was arguing with God about proposing to Esther without checking her out first. I did call her back on the phone a couple more times that week, getting more information from her, but I still could not bring myself to propose to her. As the days passed, the Lord was really convicting me for disobeying Him. During this time I said, "Lord, I don't know this Esther, she might weigh three hundred pounds and be meaner than a snake!" After a few minutes of feeling the displeasure from the Lord for this rash statement, I had to repent and ask God to forgive me.

There was another issue that I was very concerned about. If I did marry Esther, I would be marrying a divorced woman. During all of my conversations with the Lord that week, I asked Him to teach me about divorce and remarriage. He very graciously spoke to me and took me through the scriptures on this, especially on what MATTHEW 5:32 had to say about divorce.

> *But I say unto you, That whosoever shall put away his wife, saving for the cause of fornication, causeth her to commit adultery: and whosoever shall marry her that is divorced committeth adultery.* (MATTHEW 5:32)

The Lord made it clear to me that marriage is so sacred that if one person breaks the marriage vow and commits fornication or adultery, then in God's eyes the sin against that person's partner is so great that the innocent party can get a divorce and remarry, and it is not a sin. In addition, no person should put rules or laws upon the innocent party that God Himself has not put on that person. The Lord made it very clear to me that Esther was completely free before the Lord to remarry since her husband had committed adultery, and I was free before God to marry her.

By Friday of that week I knew I had to just do what the Lord wanted me to do. It was time to stop arguing with Him about it. Finally I prayed a very sincere prayer, saying, "Lord, I don't know this Esther, but I do know You, and You have always been faithful to me, so I will call Esther and propose to her." Shortly after that prayer, I picked up the phone and dialed Esther's number. She answered the phone and I said, "This is Bob McCauley. Esther, are you sitting down?" She answered and said, "Yes, but should I be?" I said, "Yes, for what I am going to tell you should be sitting down." Then I continued to speak and said, "Esther, I believe the Lord wants you and me to have a future together as husband and wife."

After I finished saying this I stopped talking and waited for Esther's response. She did not say anything for a while and I just waited. Then she spoke, "What about love? I don't love you." I answered and said, "If God is in this, He will give us love for each other."

After my proposal by phone to Esther, I felt that I had obeyed God, but I could tell that Esther was not convinced that He had spoken to me in that way. We ended our conversation with no commitment on Esther's part to pursue a relationship. After that call, I still felt that I was to marry her just as the Lord had told me. I continued to phone her occasionally through the following days. On one of those calls, I told her I wanted to drive out to Pennsylvania to see her. She lived twenty-five miles north of Philadelphia, making the trip 725 miles from my home to hers. Esther replied to my suggestion that I drive out to see her by saying, "No, I don't want you coming here, but if we are going to see each other, I am coming to see you."

I did not know it at the time, but Esther had thought things out and her thoughts were, "If we do get married, I will have to live in Indiana since Bob's job is there, and I want to see how he is living." Esther went on to say, "I have a long weekend from my job in a week and can come out then. I don't have money for the flight ticket, so you will have to get my ticket."

I agreed to do this, but there was one little problem. The Indianapolis 500-Mile Race was on that weekend. I figured getting a ticket to Indianapolis on that weekend could prove to be impossible. However, I got on the phone right away and was able to find a round-trip ticket at a pretty hefty price of five hundred dollars. I really felt I needed to get the ticket even at the high cost, so I did. I got it in the mail right away so it would get to Esther in time for her to fly to Indiana on the scheduled weekend.

My next step was to inform the kids that Esther was flying out to visit me. They all agreed that this was a good thing and were excited for her visit. Tony said, "Dad, under no circumstances are you and Esther to stay in the same house overnight when she comes out." I totally agreed with this, and said that I would let Esther stay in our house with Tanya, and I would stay with Tony and Marcia.

That Saturday morning as I drove to the Indianapolis airport to get Esther, the thought kept coming to my mind, "You are going to see your wife." Keep in mind the only thing I remembered about the way she looked was that she was short. When I got to the terminal, I went to the gate where the plane was coming in. The small commuter plane that she was coming in on would park in front of the gate, and she, along with the other passengers, would first walk down a ladder and then onto the tarmac, and finally through the doors and up to the gate area. As I stood there watching, I was anxiously hoping that I would recognize Esther when she walked off that plane.

As she stepped off the steps onto the tarmac, I saw her and suddenly remembered what she looked like. At the time she looked very thin and tired, but she was very neatly dressed and to me she looked beautiful. She was my wife even though we were not married at the time. When she walked into the area where I was standing, I said, "Hello, Esther." She greeted me back, and then

I hugged her and we walked to my car. By then I could clearly see that Esther looked like she weighed only about one hundred pounds and was very tired with rings around her eyes as if she had been working long hours with not enough sleep.

I could see the evidence of how hard it had been for her to work making a large house payment, feeding her family, and taking care of all of the cost to raise them with very little support from her ex-husband. I think I started to love her right then as I saw how she was willing to put out the effort to pay her bills and support her family.

Over the long weekend, Esther and I spent time together talking about our possible future. Even though we talked about marriage, she made it clear to me that she did not love me. She spent the weekend getting to meet my children and viewing the area where we lived. On Monday she flew back to her home in Pennsylvania. Even after spending time together on this weekend visit, Esther still was not convinced that we should get married.

I drove out to see Esther nearly every weekend throughout the next two months. I would get off work at 5:00 p.m. Friday evening, drive all night, and be at Esther's home for breakfast on Saturday morning. We would visit during our mornings and occasionally I would get an hour of sleep. Then I usually did some needed maintenance on her two hundred-year-old colonial-style house. She was making very large payments on her house which left little money for maintenance, so I tried to help out by doing the work myself. On Saturday evenings we would go out for a meal and visit some of Esther's friends.

By Saturday evening, I was starting to get very tired as I had worked all day on my job at Delco Electronics, driven 725 miles which took all night, and worked most of the day Saturday on Esther's house or doing other things. Then after we went out on our Saturday evenings, I was very tired and needed some good sleep by Saturday night. Some of Esther's friends had an extra bedroom that they let me use, so I had a place to get some needed sleep at no cost to me.

Then on Sundays we would go to church in the morning, and right after church I would head back for Indiana. The drive normally took about thirteen to fourteen hours, so a large part of the drive would be through the night. In order to stay awake, I drank a lot of coffee. If I did get sleepy, I would pull into a rest stop and sleep for about twenty minutes and then get back on the road.

When I first met Kevin, Esther's son, he and I hit it off right from the start. He had learned to be a good mechanic by the time he was sixteen. He had an old car that took a lot of work to keep going, but he was able to do the work himself. His mechanical abilities helped out the family financially a lot. At one point he told his mother, "If Uncle Bob asks you to marry him, you should do it." Since we had been in WEC mission together years before this, Kevin still remembered that the children called the other missionaries either "Uncle" or "Aunt," and that is why he called me Uncle Bob.

I could see that Kevin was a good worker and was not afraid to get his hands dirty. I certainly admired his abilities and eagerness to work. Miriam, Esther's daughter, was on a missionary trip to France through the summer, so I did not get to meet her during those months.

One Friday night at about 1:00 a.m. the presence of the Lord came upon me in the car as I was driving out to see Esther. The Lord spoke to me in that still, small voice and said something that was so precious. He said, "When Pat went to heaven and saw Jesus, the first thing she did was to ask Him to give Bob a wife that would take her place and be a mother and a grandmother to her children." Then He continued to speak and said, "Esther is that person." Right after that, the presence of the Lord seemed to leave even though I knew He was still with me. For most of the rest of the trip, I thought about what the Lord had spoken to me. Pat was mature enough to know that her children needed a mother, and since she could never again be there in person to help them, she wanted someone else to come into the picture to do what she could not do. God, in His wisdom, chose Esther to be that person.

By the end of July, Esther had decided it was God's will to marry me even though she said she did not love me. She would do it because she felt it was God's will, and not out of love. She also said that since school would be starting in August, we should get married right away so that Kevin and Miriam could start school in Indiana. I agreed to this and we set a date for August 17. Esther told her friends about our decision and they took care of all of the details. A couple that was very close friends of Esther's had a beautiful yard. It was like a well-kept park with lovely flowers, shrubs, beautiful trees, and a very well-kept lawn. Esther wanted an outside wedding, and they offered us the use of their beautiful yard for it.

My children all came out for the wedding. My grandson, Andy, was the ring bearer and my granddaughter, Katrina, was the flower girl. Mike, Tony, Tanya,

Kevin, and Miriam all stood up with Esther and I. Glen Rosenberger, who was a friend of Esther's, and Dwayne Olson, a very close missionary friend of ours, performed the service.

About one hour before the wedding, Esther told me that she still did not love me but that she was going to marry me anyway. That did not deter me one bit because I knew beyond any doubt that it was God's will for us to be married. With about seventy-five people attending, sitting under the trees, surrounded by lovely flowers and plants and our family standing beside us, Dwayne Olson led us in our wedding vows and then pronounced us as husband and wife.

Esther and her children, Kevin and Miriam, moved out to Indiana and into the house that Tanya and I lived in (later we sold Esther's house at a very good profit). Our children have now grown up: all of them have children of their own and we are blessed with eleven grandchildren and six great-grandchildren. And to add to that blessing, we are also blessed that they all live close by. We love every one of them dearly, and pray for them daily.

Over time, Esther and I became extremely involved in ministries to Russia. I have written about some of the events in this book. Wonderful things have transpired through our ministry as we have continued to be led by the still, small voice of the Holy Spirit. At the time of this writing, we have been married for twenty-five years. During this time we have seen many people come to Jesus Christ while ministering in Russia. We have been involved in helping start the first evangelical seminary in Moscow. We were also involved in sending about $1.75 million dollars worth of supplies of food, medicine, and clothing to the Christians in Moscow and a nearby city. We are still very involved in a ministry that we helped pioneer to street children and children living in crisis in St. Petersburg, Russia.

Neither Esther nor I could have launched these projects on our own. God called us together for a multifaceted purpose that He knew about all along. And together we are making a difference to our families and to our ministry.

Esther's biological children are my children and my biological children are her children. They are all our children and grandchildren and great-grandchildren. We continue to be involved with the ministry in Russia and with our family. And, yes, somewhere along the line Esther started to love me, and today she and I love each other very much.

Today I say, "God put two good women in my life, Patricia and Esther."

Ch. 27

DIRECTED BY STORMS

I have faced some very harsh storms in my life. As difficult as some of these were, I learned that God uses us in our storms and sometimes directs us with them. He also teaches us lessons as we pass through these hard times in life. I learned some good lessons about this during my years of being a jungle pilot.

Flying in the jungle is not the normal flying that I was used to before I became a missionary pilot. Those flights in Indiana and the Midwest seemed very mild compared to a day of flying over the jungle in Africa. I don't believe my days of flying in the jungle were any more unusual than those of the other jungle pilots; we all faced very hazardous flying conditions and each had to make adjustments and decisions based on the flying conditions. This happened daily. When you are flying in some of the worst weather conditions on the planet, you have to adjust and not get shook up about it. A pilot needs to flow with the conditions or else he will become so irritated by having to make adjustments that he could become a danger to himself and others.

I often had many redirections caused by jungle storms. At times I planned to go to a certain village and minister the Word of God, and then a storm would be in that area, and I would have to change my plans and go to another place for the night. Almost without fail, some wonderful thing happened as a result of me being at that location for the night. This caused me to consider that the Lord occasionally used storms in my life to direct me.

I have written about a village called Gaguya Town, where I tore up the mission plane. An African evangelist that I did not know well was ministering there and wanted me to come and minister with him, asking that I bring in a medical person with me to treat the sick. I agreed to do this. On the appointed day, the weather was very nice at the mission station, so a nurse and I loaded the plane with the needed medical supplies and took off. The weather was clear until we got to Gagaya Town, and strangely we saw that a storm had surrounded their entire village. It was too heavy to fly into, so we had no choice but to return to the mission station. A few hours later, we headed out again, but were stopped by the same storm. The next day we found the same scenario, and again the third day. We found this extremely unusual, as a storm usually passes through an area in a short amount of time.

This was so unusual that I felt God was stopping me from going into Gaguya Town for some reason. Shortly after this, I heard a rumor that a young girl in the town had accused the evangelist of trying to rape her. I felt something had caused God to stop me from going there, so I decided to check on this rumor. As I was looking into this, I learned the girl in question was actually at our mission station at the current time. I wanted to have a meeting with her along with other missionaries and church leaders. After we all gathered, she told us a story about working on her farm one day when this evangelist sneaked up on her from the bushes, he had been hiding in, and tried to rape her. Thankfully, she was young and quick and managed to get away from him.

Her story was quite believable, which led us to do some more investigating into the past life of the evangelist in question. The investigation revealed that the evangelist was having affairs with other women in the Gagaya Town area. He had become a stench to them with his terrible reputation.

We began to pray and seek the Lord for direction in dealing with this man. It was clear that he had tried to use me in an effort to give him creditability in the village. If we would have arrived as scheduled, I would have stood and ministered beside him, giving the villagers reason to believe that I approved of his lifestyle. I am extremely thankful that God stopped this from happening. The Lord also spoke to me in His still, small voice that we were to deal with this evangelist exactly according to 1 Corinthians 5:4-5.

> In the name of our Lord Jesus Christ, when ye are gathered together, and my spirit, with the power of our Lord Jesus Christ,
> To deliver such an one unto Satan for the destruction of the flesh, that the spirit may be saved in the day of the Lord Jesus.
> (1 Corinthians 5:4-5)

We were to put him out of the church until he repented of what he was doing, and the church was not to allow him to preach the Word of God until he was restored.

We had a meeting with him and talked to him very straight about his conduct. He admitted to trying to rape the girl and also to having affairs with the other women. Rather than being sorry about it or repenting of his sin, he kept feeling sorry for himself and saying over and over, "What is going to happen to me? This is more that I can endure." He seemed to have little remorse over the sins he had committed. The church put him out and after a long period of time restored him to fellowship again, but I don't think he ever preached again.

God used the storm to stop me from doing something that He did not want. This reminded me of another time when God used a storm to direct Jonah when he was running from God. Even the storms have purposes in God's great plan.

One day I was attempting to fly three teenagers of a missionary family back to their mission station after they had spent a week attending a yearly mission conference. They were the Hodgson children named Gordon, Jeanette, and Carol. The three were very musical and sang together. Gordon played a large bass fiddle, Carol played a guitar, and Jeanette played an accordion when they sang. The plane was not overweight, but it was crowded with the three young people, their musical instruments, and their luggage. When we got within about fifty miles of their mission station, we were faced with a black storm front, which was between our location and the mission station we were headed to. It was one of those fronts that I did not want to fly through, so I changed my plan and flew them back to my mission station at Bahn. They were happy about that because they liked visiting our station and hardly ever had the chance to go there. Since it was getting late, the youth also needed to spend the night with us.

Since the Hodgson young people were such good singers, I felt that I should have them sing in a special service in our village that evening. I had an electric generator and some electric lights, so I took the generator to a central location in the village and set it up along with many lights. That evening the young people, along with the Christians, had a special service. It got totally dark by six thirty in the evening and that is about the time we started the service. Many people in the village of about ten-thousand were curious about the bright lights, and many of them came to the meeting.

The Hodgson young people sang many Christian songs and the people really enjoyed them. A pastor for our church had a very good message that night, resulting in hundreds hearing the Word of God for the first time. Most of these people had never attended a church service before. The service went on for about three hours, but the people stayed and enjoyed the whole service.

The service was probably the best one that I ever attended while I was in Liberia. A jungle storm had caused a change in my plans; the Lord had a new and better plan in mind, and He used the storm to get us were He wanted us.

It is not possible to live as a human on this earth without facing storms. When the storm comes, we need to evaluate if perhaps God could be directing us or testing us. Ask God for wisdom in navigating the storm. In the end it matters what we do when facing the storm. Do we give up or do we make up our mind that regardless of the storms we will serve God and let Him use us as He wants? Many times the storms are a testing time in our lives. How we handle those tests can determine how God will use us in the future.

When Pat, my first wife, passed away, I faced a storm. It was the most difficult storm that I had ever faced. The person that I loved with all my heart was dying. I faced the storm for months as she suffered through her bout with cancer. When I was flying the plane and faced a storm, most of the time I could simply turn the plane around and avoid it. There was no way that I could avoid the storm I was facing with Pat. I prayed every day for her healing, but it just did not happen as I wanted it to. When I watched Pat take her last breath, it was heartbreaking for me. I physically cried until I could not cry any more, and I hurt ten times more than I ever thought I could.

The storm could have caused me to stop being a servant of God, but I would not let it. God led me through it and it certainly was a test of my faith. When I finally recovered from it, God led me to marry Esther. Pat and I had had a wonderful ministry, both in America and in Africa. We also raised three beautiful children. Our marriage was like a beautiful flight in the Lord.

I am now on another beautiful flight with Esther. Esther and I have started and still are working with a ministry to children living in crisis conditions in Russia. I often think about this. If Pat were still living, neither Esther nor I could have started the ministry in Russia. Did God use that storm to get me involved in helping to start a ministry in Russia? I don't know the answer, and I probably won't until I get to heaven. I do not believe it was God's will at all for Esther's first husband to leave her. He created a storm for Esther, and it was not of her doing, but she still suffered. I do not believe every storm is of God, but He can still, in His wonderful way, use us after we face a storm created by someone else. In other words, it seems to me that God can take our lives and use them for His work even when someone else creates a storm for us.

The lesson I have learned out of the storms I have faced is to trust God through them all even when the situation looks very dark, as it does inside a jungle storm. Another lesson I have learned is not to fly into a storm if you can find a way around it. I chose to redirect my plans when I was flying the Hodgsons back to their mission. I did not have to go through the storm. There are times, however, when you are caught in a storm that you did not create and that you cannot go around. Sometimes the storms box you in, and you are caught in the center of them, as I have been many times, as I flew in the jungle. Being caught in the center of a storm is not fun. In fact, it can be very difficult, but it can also be a place where God can use you for His glory.

Ch. 28

An Engineering Error and the Still Small Voice

When Esther and I got married I had a job as a manufacturing engineer for a very large company, which made me responsible for getting plastic molds designed, built, debugged, and qualified for production. I led the tool designers and the plastic mold shops that built the molds. After the molds were running well, I trained the production people that were to run the molds on how to process them to make good parts.

My responsibility also included estimating the cost to build the molds and to manufacture the parts. Our company only received the amount of money that I estimated. If my estimate was too high, we might not get the job, and if it was too low, we would lose money. I was constantly under a lot of pressure to make sure each stage of my responsibility was done properly and within cost. I also had a major responsibility of making sure we met the qualification and production dates. If we failed to meet these dates, it could cost my company and our customers millions of dollars. We absolutely could not shut down a production plant because we did not have qualified parts.

My company considered me an expert in plastic molding, and my expertise in this line reflected that. As the years passed, I developed a good reputation of being able to closely meet my estimated cost and deliver qualified and dependable molds on time. There had never been a time when I failed to meet my cost, qualification, and production dates. This was good for my company and also for me. I knew my line of expertise quite well and was comfortable in my job, even though it did take a tremendous amount of effort and dedication to make it all happen on schedule.

I was assigned to a product that had a very special plastic part in it that had to be made to extremely tight tolerances, otherwise it would not function. The production quota of this part was in the millions per year, so we had to have very dependable molds that could run on a very fast cycle to meet this.

During the early stages of this product's development, a young product engineer was assigned to lead the development stage. After designing the product, he had temporary molds built to make a few plastic parts for his development. The process took several months, and the young engineer seemed to be getting along well. He got his parts from the tool shop and assembled them, and they seemed to work well.

He then moved from the development stage to the production stage. This required that high production molds be built to produce the parts. I was then assigned to be the manufacturing engineer for the high production molds of this product.

There were written guidelines for developing a part, and these guidelines required a testing stage. I was not aware at the time, but the young engineer had not tested the product properly during his development stage. The development stage included testing the assembled parts in an atmospherically controlled chamber. During this testing, the assembly would be put through many different temperature and moisture changes to see if it would function in these different conditions.

This testing was not my responsibility, and I had no idea that this stage of the development had not been accomplished. I was assigned to the product after this stage should have been completed. The young engineer's omission of testing the product in the development stage would cause a tremendous problem for me about a year later. The problem would be so great that I would have many sleepless nights and would seek God in a way that I had very few times in my life.

After I was assigned to this product, I found that we were under a very tight time schedule to get the molds designed, built, and qualified in order to meet the production dates. When production started, we needed to make ten thousand of these parts a day, so I was under great pressure to make sure our mold performed well, or we would not be able to make enough to keep all of our customer's plants supplied. If we could not, some of their plants would have to shut down, costing millions of dollars. The pressure was high, but I was not overly worried about it.

With a lot of effort the mold was finished, and we made parts for the production testing stage. After several weeks of testing the production parts in different atmospheric conditions, we received word back that our special parts were failing and that our whole product, which contained many parts, was failing.

By this time the young product engineer had been assigned to another product, and an older product engineer was assigned to the product which contained the special part. The older product engineer started to evaluate what was causing the failures. This took several days, and our production date was coming toward us at an alarming rate.

The older product engineer wondered why the parts had passed the development stage testing and had failed the production stage test. He checked the records and found that the younger product engineer had not run the product assembly through the development stage testing process. He also discovered that the young engineer had designed the part out of plastic material that grew in length when it got in hot, damp conditions. The extra length caused the failure.

Suddenly we found ourselves in big trouble. If we could not get this problem fixed in time for production, every one of our customer's plants that used this product would not be able to operate. We were looking at millions of dollars loss for our customers and for us. This was a major problem! The older engineer and I were faced with a horrible challenge. Neither one of us had caused the problem, but we were the ones that had to figure a way out of it. We did not know how to correct this error in the short amount of time we had left before production started.

We quickly realized that we could not use the plastic material that the molds were designed to run. All plastics shrink, and the mold cavities have to be made larger than the final part size so the part will be the right size after it shrinks. The plastic that the young engineer chose had a very large shrink factor, and our molds were made accordingly. If we ran any other plastic in the molds, the parts would not shrink as much, and they would be too long to function in the assembly.

The young engineer chose the plastic material because it withstands grease and oil. Most other plastics will fail if they come in contact with grease or oil. We had to come up with a plastic that had all of the qualifications of the plastic that the young engineer had chosen and yet did not grow as much in length when it was heated or put in high moisture conditions. We could have used some other plastics that would have qualified, but these all had much less of a shrink factor, and the parts would end up being too long after they were molded.

The older engineer and I spent hours trying to come up with a plastic material that would be acceptable for production. We finally came up with a plastic material that was suitable for what we needed in production, but our mold was not designed to run that type of plastic. There were major differences in how the two different plastics performed during the molding process.

After deciding to use the different plastic material, the senior product engineer looked to me to make it work in our mold. His supervisor and my supervisor were also looking to me to get our whole plant out of trouble. I knew if I did not get the different material to run in our mold, many people would be in serious trouble and I probably would be one of them. I also knew many people could be laid off from their jobs if we did not get this to work in time. I felt extreme pressure from all of this.

Our mold was designed and built with a hot runner system built specifically for the original plastic material. The new material would not run through the system consistently, and when we did make some parts, they were degraded and too brittle to use. This was totally unacceptable! Another expert process engineer and I tried every process we could in an effort to successfully run the new material in our mold, but nothing worked. I talked to many experts in molding, but no one had an idea how to make our system work. I even had an expert from Chicago come to our plant to see if he could make our system run the new material, and he could not do it.

I knew how to build a new mold to run the new material, but I needed at least four months to do it and I only had a few days to get good parts for production. Since there was not enough time to build a new mold, I had to make our mold work, but I just did not know how to do it!

The problem was hitting me very hard, and I had not been able to sleep for days. My stomach was hurting badly, and I was taking antacid pills much too often in an effort to stop the pain. I was almost beside myself wondering what to do. No one could give me any ideas on how to fix the problem within the time element that we were facing. It was up to me!

I went to prayer travailing before God for an answer. I consider God the best engineer ever and knew He was the only one that could help me. As I was praying, the still, small voice of the Holy Spirit told me how to change the mold to make good parts. It was like a combination of the still, small voice speaking to me, and an inner vision showing me a new way to flow the plastic into the cavities. This vision on how to do it was a way that was far different than anything we had ever done in molding before. I had never seen any plastic mold with this type of system on it. It was so far out that I felt some engineers or tool makers would probably laugh at me if I said we were going to change the mold to this system.

The next day I was in a meeting with about twenty-five other people. Fortunately, I was able to sit near the back of the room. I was there physically, but my mind was totally focused on my molding problem. I had a notebook with me that had eight and one-half by eleven sheets of graph paper in it. As the meeting was going on, I drew the system that the Lord showed me on the graph paper. By the time the meeting was over, I had it completed.

After the meeting, I went to the plastic molding department and had the mold taken out of the molding machine and sent to the tool room. I talked to the tool room foreman about how I wanted to change the mold, showing him the drawing I had made. Normally the foreman would have required a completed tool design change, but this time he was willing to do the work from my drawing. He assigned two very capable toolmakers to my project and started on the mold right away.

There were only two weeks left to get the mold changed before we needed to be running thousands of good parts daily. I had a lot of questions going around in my mind at that time, with no sure answers. Could the toolmakers get the mold changed in two weeks? Had I heard God correctly on this? Nobody had ever tried this before, so would it work? I had no backup plan and no time to rebuild the mold, so what would I do if the system did not work?

Due to many sleepless nights, I was so tired that I could hardly keep going and my stomach felt like I had a blowtorch in it. Even though people surrounded me during the day and my wife at night, I still felt so very alone. The only thing that kept me going was the fact that I had heard the still, small voice of the Lord many times before, and His words to me had always been right. I was comforted in knowing I had recognized His voice again in this matter.

The days passed and I was busy on many other molding projects besides this crucial one, but I still checked on the mold's progress several times each day. I was encouraged that although the toolmakers did not have a regular tool design to go by, they were still doing a great job with only my sketch.

The toolmakers finished changing the mold the day before we needed to be making thousands of parts. We had to have parts that day or our customers could not start their production. We were all in big trouble if this did not work! We took the mold to the molding department and mounted it in a molding machine. I was extremely tired and uptight as I waited to get the mold mounted in the molding machine and brought up to heat.

Finally we closed the mold in the machine and injected the molten plastic material into the eight mold cavities. I could hardly stand up as I waited about twenty-four seconds for the molding cycle to be completed. I knew that I was about finished if good parts did not come out of the mold. Then the mold opened and eight perfect parts were ejected from it!

I quickly picked up the parts and checked them. They looked perfect! They were not brittle at all, and when I measured them they were well within the needed print dimensions. I looked them over very carefully and all of the thin walls were very well-filled with plastic. All eight parts looked perfect. I said, "Thank you, God." We continued to run the mold on a fully automatic cycle and eight perfect parts continued to fall out of the mold.

We were molding eight good parts every twenty-four seconds and this was fantastic. Later we reduced this cycle to about sixteen seconds to mold eight good parts. This meant that we could mold forty-three thousand parts in a twenty-four-hour day. In the early production we needed ten thousand parts a day, so we could mold these parts and still have time for maintenance on the mold. Later the volume increased to about sixty thousand parts a day, but by that time we had built two more molds to make the parts for the increased volume. We designed the new molds and built them using exactly the same system that God showed me.

The reliability of these parts through the years was extremely high. As complicated as the product assembly was, there were almost no rejected parts through the years. Ten years later, the older engineer that I had worked with on the project told me that the rejected parts per million were so few that it was as if there were no rejected parts at all. The reliability on the special part was one of the highest of any part that my company had ever molded. We went from not being able to make any good parts to making the most reliable part we had ever molded. How I thank God for this and give Him the credit and the glory. I still thank God for this yet to this day!

Through the years I have heard God speak to me in many different ways, mostly through His precious, still, small voice. Each time, as I have stepped out and obeyed His still, small voice, I have been so pleased with the results, and so glad I did obey. Many times it has been extremely difficult, and at times seemed unreasonable or even strange that He would give me a certain word through His still, small voice. In every single incident, however, when I have obeyed Him, in the end I have been very happy as I looked back and saw the wisdom and the end results of what He told me to do.

Ch. 29

A Snowsuit and Rush to Russia

I was sitting at my desk concentrating on my work as an engineer for Delco Electronics when the phone rang. My wife Esther was on the other end of the line, and she asked me if I had access to our local newspaper. She asked me to read the article about a young Russian man who was an exchange employee for Delco Electronics, and then to call her back.

I went to the cafeteria, where I found the paper and read the article. It was quite interesting, because Russia had just had a major coup and things were very unsettled in the country. The Russian young man shared how few commodities there were in Russia and how expensive everything was. It took one month's wages to buy a snowsuit for his two year old son, and one day's wages to buy an aspirin. When I called Esther back, she said that she was really burdened about the article, and wondered if she could send a box of clothes to the Russian young man's wife and child. As I silently prayed, the Lord spoke in His still, small voice to tell her to go ahead. Little did I know at the time that this would be a major change in our lives, not only for now, but for eternity.

Immediately after our conversation, Esther called Delco and they gave her the Russian man's phone number. When she called him a few minutes later, he told her that another couple, named Ed and Barbara Brown, were also interested, and he suggested that we get together and send a box to his family. Although this seemed like a good idea, Esther was a bit concerned because she wanted to send a Bible and some Russian tracts along with the clothes, and she didn't know where the other family stood spiritually, or even if they were believers. We wanted to send the box of clothing as a testimony for Jesus Christ. God's Word also says that we are not to be unequally joined together, so how could we work with them if they were unbelievers or involved in some false religion? This was a major concern, and we wanted to proceed with caution. After praying about it, we felt we should go ahead and make the contact.

Esther phoned the Browns and Barbara answered the phone. When Esther introduced herself, Barbara immediately said, "I think I know who you are.

Don't you have a Bible study?" Esther replied that she did, and Barbara said that she had heard about Esther and her Bible study and had wanted to meet her. She said that she was also a Christian and that her husband, Ed, had just became a Christian a week ago. Esther was very happy to hear this good news. Barbara added that her husband was the vice president of a large company in Kokomo. Later, this would be a big help!

Esther told Barbara that she felt burdened to send a box of clothes to Russia, and Barbara said that she had the same burden. She suggested that Esther and I come to their house for a meal; she would invite the Russian young man and we would discuss how to go about this. It was a special joy for us to meet him as well as the Browns. After having a lovely meal, we discussed whether we should send one big box or a couple smaller ones. We also decided to purchase a few clothes and then decide how to mail them.

A couple days later when Esther had her Bible study, she shared her plans of putting together a few boxes of clothes for the Russian man's wife and son. After Esther told the women at her Bible study about sending a few things to Russia, all of the women became very excited and wanted to help. They suggested that they look through their children's clothes for things they no longer needed and then go around to garage sales, asking people for donations. When they asked Esther when she wanted to send the boxes she said, "As soon as possible; before the cold weather comes."

It was already the beginning of September, so someone in the group came up with a name "Rush to Russia" for the project and this stuck. From that day on the project was called Rush to Russia. The ladies made posters, RUSH TO RUSSIA, giving details of what we needed to send, and placed them all over the city and county. God was moving and things were getting ready to explode in our effort to just send a box of baby clothes to Russia. Our plan was good, but it was way too small according to God's plan, and we were about to find this out.

The women of the Bible study told other people, and almost within hours we had boxes and boxes of very nice clothes to send to Russia. Our garage filled up with clothes so quickly that we could hardly believe it. Ed and Barbara Brown were having the same results. People were giving very nice things, and within a few days we had to have a larger place to put the clothes. Ed suggested that possibly his company would let us use a large room they had next to their office to store the things in. He talked to the company about this and they agreed, so we moved all the clothes to that room. Then the local *Kokomo Tribune* that had written the original news article about the Russian young man, heard about the project and came to interview us, take pictures, and put it in the paper.

Within weeks our project was like a snowball rolling down a hill, getting bigger and bigger as it rolled. We had so many clothes that the large room we were using could not hold them all. A local builder in our city had a very large warehouse with a lot of room in it that he was not using, and when he heard about our need for space, he offered us the warehouse. We took his offer and moved all the clothes to the warehouse.

Many of the clothes that had come in were for babies, but by now many of them were for children, youth, and adults. We decided that it would be good to send some very warm coats for children and adults as well as the baby clothes. Esther went to Bob Cox, the director of the Kokomo Rescue Mission, and asked him if they had extra coats that we could send to Russia. Bob said they had more coats than they had room for, and we could have them. This contact was the beginning of a long-term relationship between Esther and our Kokomo Rescue Mission.

Some of the coats were like new, but had a missing button or bad zipper or needed some other repairs to make them usable. The coats were very nice and would be a blessing to some person in Russia, but we would not send them unless they were in very good condition. They had to be repaired or rejected. The repairs would take a lot of work, and we needed help to do this.

Through a series of events, Esther met a woman named Marty Miller who would become a lifetime friend. Her husband, Lee, was the pastor of a large Mennonite church in our area. Marty volunteered the Mennonite women of her church to help make the repairs, and she organized the women to come to the warehouse with their sewing machines. Each piece of clothing was examined very carefully, and if anything was wrong with it, the Mennonite women would make the needed repairs. Often many of them took clothes home and washed them so they would be clean and fresh.

We had one rule for all of the clothes that were to be sent to Russia. They had to be clothes that we would wear ourselves here in America, or we would not send them. When the Mennonite women finished with their repairs, the clothes were like new. Some of the coats were very nice but had some stain or dirt on them. A local dry cleaner offered to dry-clean any clothes that we wanted them to at no cost, and the clothes looked like new when they finished.

Next we decided that we would also send food and over-the-counter drugs in the shipment. We heard how people in Russia were having a hard time buying needed food items. We also heard that over-the-counter drugs were very hard to find and extremely expensive for the Russians. This included everything from children's vitamins to aspirins. We prayed about this and it seemed like a miracle how nonperishable food products came in as well as drugs and vitamins. We found a place where we could purchase these items for ten cents on the dollar if they were going to be sent overseas. Money was given for this purpose, so we purchased thousands of dollars worth of food and drugs, etc.

Channel 13 TV Station out of Indianapolis heard about what we were doing and came in, took pictures, and interviewed Esther and a few others. The pictures and interviews were shown on their local news, causing thousands to hear about our project Rush to Russia. We were totally taken by surprise with this television publicity. We had not asked for any publicity at all, but the Lord sure used it to help bring in more donations of clothes, food, and medical supplies.

Our effort which started out to be one box or at most a few boxes of baby clothes to one family had expanded, and now many children and adults would benefit. It was like the project had us rather than us having it. We were amazed at what we saw happening before our eyes. It seemed like our every move was blessed and multiplied many times more than we could have imagined. It was taking a tremendous amount of effort to keep up with the progress, but God was doing it and we were just moving with Him. Barbara and Esther were spending every day working and directing the project, and Ed and I worked with them and others until the late hours every evening.

We had certain guidelines that we had to follow as we packed the boxes. Each box had to be numbered and the contents specified. This information was for the shipping manifest. Our government could check us out by spot-checking a box and comparing the contents with our shipping manifest. If the contents in the box did not match the shipping manifest, they could refuse to let the shipment leave the United States. When the Russian government received the shipment, they did the same procedure, and they could reject the shipment if the contents of the boxes did not match the shipping manifest list. Keeping track of the contents of each box was a big job, but we were able to do it.

At times I would look at the things we had to send and was amazed at how much money it was all worth. The value of what we had sitting before us to send to Russia was worth thousands and thousands of dollars. We were not sending shoddy clothes; every piece of clothing was first class. The medical supplies were also excellent, not to mention all the personal hygiene items such as soap, shampoos, lotions, toothbrushes, toothpaste, and other things that families could use. And we made sure to include vitamins, aspirins, and cold medicines. Esther went to a Christian publishing house in Indiana and got hundreds of Russian Bibles and tracts for free, which were put in the pockets of clothes.

Before long, Ed and I realized that we were going to have to ship a forty-foot-long container because of the vast volume of supplies we had. We knew that a container that large would cost us thousands of dollars, and although quite a lot of money had come in for supplies, none had come for shipping.

One evening Ed, Barbara, Esther, and I discussed this problem. We all realized that we personally did not have the money to send the shipment. It would take a real miracle from God to supply the many thousands we would need to send a container. As we were talking about this, I was reminded by the still, small voice of the Holy Spirit how many times God had supplied our needs in Africa, and I heard His voice tell me that He was going to do it again. I boldly spoke up and said, "Don't worry about it; God is going to provide for the shipping. We don't need the money yet, and He will provide it when we need it!" This statement calmed us all down, and we continued on with our project just as if we had the funds in hand.

I don't think anyone except the Browns and the McCauleys knew that we did not have the money or a way to ship the vast amount of supplies to Russia. Although we knew we needed a miracle, we also knew that we had to take some initiatives to pay for the shipping. Ed and Esther started making phone calls to government agencies asking for help. Of course, although most agencies were encouraging, nobody really said they could help.

Three or four days later, Ed and I put all the boxes in a ten-foot-wide by ten-foot-tall and forty-foot-long row and found that we had exactly enough to fit into a forty-foot container. Except for a few things that we felt we could not ship, we were also out of supplies—God knew when to stop the flow! We all agreed that we were ready to ship, and now it was time to trust the Lord to get the shipping for us. That evening the Browns and Esther and I went home with this on our minds.

That very evening Ed received a phone call from a woman named Linda Green who lived in Toledo, Ohio. She told Ed that she and her husband were the managers of a Christian organization that received foreign aid money to ship humanitarian aid to other countries from America. They wanted to send a container to Russia but had no supplies to send. She went on to tell Ed that they heard from a senator from Indiana that we had a shipment for Russia. She said that if we could get the shipment to Toledo, their organization would send the container to Moscow for us at no expense to us, but they would like to have one-third of the container go to a local Pentecostal church in Moscow. They also would like to send it as soon as possible.

Ed phoned us minutes after he received the call and asked us to contact the organization. Esther called them immediately and got more information about shipping the container. When we called the Browns a few minutes later, we were all amazed at how this phone call came on exactly the same day that we completely finished putting the shipment together.

The timing of this phone call from Linda Green was so amazing that we knew beyond any doubt that it was God that had provided a way to ship the supplies right when we needed it! There was no way this could have happened exactly at the time we needed, if God had not brought this about! God was blessing us and this project for Russia. It was as if we were standing and moving in the presence of God! His power, provisions, and knowledge of what we were doing made us see that God cared very much about the Russian Christians that had suffered so much for years under Communism. God cared for them, and He was using us to make a difference in their lives.

Now we had a way to ship the Rush to Russia project to Russia, but we still had to get the shipment from Kokomo, Indiana, to Toledo, Ohio. We contacted a molding company named Syndicate Sales in Kokomo who had a large fleet of trucks, and asked if they would take our shipment to Toledo for us. The cost to ship would be five hundred dollars, and Ed and Barbara and Esther and I decided to pay the amount ourselves.

Within a few days a nice, bright green semi truck and trailer drove to the warehouse. Many people came to help load the trailer, and lots of people just came to watch; it was an exciting time for so many who had put many hours into the project. The *Kokomo Tribune* photographer was there taking pictures of the truck as it got loaded. Within two hours, we had the truck loaded and ready to go.

Just before the truck took off, Esther walked up to the driver with the five hundred-dollar-check in her hand. As she started to hand it to him, the driver said, "No, we do not want you to pay us. This is our donation to the project. The company is donating the truck and fuel, and I am donating my time." This was another miracle! We had seen God's provision through many different miracles, and once again we were seeing God's faithfulness to us. What a way to send off our project, Rush to Russia, to the people of Russia!

After the truck pulled out of Kokomo with the supplies for Russia, Esther and I drove to Toledo, Ohio, to be there when it arrived. Upon our arrival, we met Stan and Linda Green, who were going to ship the container for us. They were lovely people, and Esther and I were so happy to meet them. They had a very large building that they used for their office and shipping operation.

Early the next morning, the truck from Syndicate Sales pulled into Stan and Linda Green's shipping yard. All our boxes were shrink-wrapped and sitting on skids, so it was easy for Stan and I to unload them from the truck to the container that would go on the ship. Within an hour we had everything done. We spent several hours filling out forms, etc., for our government as well as for the Russian government, and a few days later the container was put on a ship and on the way to Russia. The value of the contents came to one hundred seventy-five thousand dollars. God had provided the entire cost of shipping this container to Russia.

That evening Esther and I spent the night with Stan and Linda Green and had a great time of Christian fellowship. The next day was Sunday, so we went to their church with them. It was a very lively charismatic fellowship, and we really enjoyed the worship and the message.

After the service, Esther and I headed back to Kokomo, glad that this long episode in our lives was finally over. We were tired but at the same time very encouraged. We had been under quite a bit of pressure getting this whole project put together. However, now the pressure was over, and we were both rejoicing that many Russians would be greatly blessed as a result of the huge shipment, and many would read the tracts and have an opportunity to come to know the Lord.

We spent the hours driving home reminiscing about all the events of the past three months. We saw God work through it all! It was exciting to discuss the way God's hand took us step by step in this huge undertaking. As we stepped out to obey Him in an effort to make a difference in the life of one Russian family, He led us to make a difference in the lives of hundreds of Russians. To think of how each step came together almost overwhelmed us. We had experienced the hand of God through it all. God made a way where there seemed to be no way.

We were glad, though, that we could get back home and begin living "normal" lives again. However, little did we know what God's plans would be for our future. We had only finished the first small step in what God was going to do with us concerning Russia. We had no idea what lay ahead of us and would have had a hard time believing what was to come, even if someone would have told us.

Esther and I had planned on putting together one forty-pound box of clothes to send to Moscow and that was it. Little did we know at the time that our lives would be totally changed by Esther's desire to send the snowsuit to the little boy in Russia. If someone had told us we would eventually send $1.75 million worth of food, clothing, and medical equipment to the Christians in Moscow, we would never have been able to believe it. Or that we would be involved in helping to start the first evangelical biblical seminary in Moscow. Or that we would pioneer a ministry to street children and children in prison. It would have seemed even stranger if we would have been told that we would be living in Russia, working with street children and spending time in Russian prisons.

We did not know that this simple action would bring about events that would eventually put our very lives in extreme danger. Or that Esther would have a head-on confrontation with the Russian Mafia. Or that I would be summoned to stand before a high government official and be questioned on our activities. What if we would have been told that we would be ministering in hard conditions in Russian prisons, or that we would be so cold we could barely stand it? This was to be our future as a result of getting involved in sending one box of baby clothes to Moscow. We also didn't know that we would be making close friendships with many wonderful Russian people as well.

This action of putting together this box of baby clothes would end up being the beginning of one of the most blessed ministries that either of us had ever been involved in.

Ch. 30

THE REST OF THE STORY

In 1970 I was in a prayer meeting with some older missionaries from WEC mission. These missionaries were praying for an open door into Russia to minister the Word of God. Their prayer went something like this, "Lord, one more time, please give us an open door into Russia to preach your Word and we will not fail you this time. We will go in and minister your Word to the Russian people." As I heard them praying, I thought, "Don't they know that it is impossible to go into Russia because of Communism?" For a time, my doubts overcame my faith in a God that can open and shut doors according to His will, but very quickly the Holy Spirit rebuked me and I knew that these people were praying for God to change things so we could go in. After that I started to pray as they did, believing God to change the situation so that the Word of God could be preached in Russia.

Not long after that prayer meeting for Russia, I met a missionary from a Christian organization that was asking people to pray for pastors in Russia who were in prison. He had names of many of the pastors and also names of many of their family members. I was very touched by the fact that many pastors were suffering in prison for preaching the Word of God, and I felt so burdened for the wives and children of these pastors. It had to be extremely hard for them, and I knew they were suffering even at the time we were praying. It seemed strange to me that we were serving the same Christ, and yet they were suffering while I was not.

I felt very close to these people even though I had never met them. They were my brothers and sisters in Christ, and I agonized in prayer for them and their families. I didn't think I would ever meet them this side of heaven, but I would pray for them anyway. I prayed for them nearly every time I went to prayer. I just could not get over the feeling of hurt and pain that these people were suffering. Little did I know at the time that I would personally meet some of these people; we would become very close friends and would be living and ministering with them in Russia.

Our Rush to Russia project was on a ship heading for people in that far off country that had been our cold war enemy for many years. Linda Green told Esther that she was going to travel to Moscow to see the need in that country, and she invited Esther to go too. As a result, Esther and Bob Cox from the Kokomo Rescue Mission, along with Linda Green and a small party of her friends, arrived in Moscow at about the time the shipment arrived. Some of the small group stayed with a Pentecostal-lay pastor and his wife named Sasha and Galina Zdor and their five children, while the rest of the group stayed with a Baptist-lay pastor named Nickolai Kornilov and his wife Marina. They also had five children.

Both pastors and their families were friends with each other and they lived in the same high-rise apartment building. Esther stayed with Sasha and Galina Zdor, but she got to know Nickolai and Marina as well. This contact brought about a lifetime friendship between these two pastors and their families and Esther and I. Later they would be in our home in Indiana many times and we would have a vital part in their lives from that day forward. Two weeks later, Linda and her party returned to the States, while Esther and Bob Cox stayed on in Russia for another four weeks.

The Russian government asked Esther and Bob Cox to come to the Kremlin to talk to them about the possibility of sending more shipments of supplies to Russia. When they went there on the appointed day, Esther took eleven Russian Bibles with her into the Kremlin. The Bible was rejected under Communism because they supposedly did not believe in God. Within minutes, however, of Esther going into the Kremlin, she gave away all of the Russian Bibles. They told her that she was the first person to ever give away Bibles inside the Kremlin.

The officials hoped that Esther and Bob would send them more shipments of supplies and also told them that they had very few supplies in their hospitals. In an effort to convince Esther and Bob of this, they took them to one of the hospitals, and while they were showing them the rooms, etc., they showed Esther and Bob one operating room and bragged that they had performed eighty thousand abortions in that room. They were so proud, but Esther and Bob were shocked to be in a room where so much sin and destruction of life had taken place.

The Russian officials assigned a Russian woman named Tatiana to be the interpreter for Esther and Bob; however, Tatiana had other obligations, so she asked her friend Olga (who also interpreted for the Kremlin on occasion) to interpret for her. Olga was a very gracious woman of about forty-five years of age. She treated Esther and Bob with great respect.

As they were traveling through the city in a van, a conversation started up between Esther and an official named Alexander. Olga was interpreting during this conversation. Alexander said he was a Communist and an atheist but wanted to ask some questions about the Bible, even though he did not believe it. Esther answered his questions and began explaining the plan of salvation, when the group arrived at a certain place and everyone dispersed.

Alexander seemed to have lost interest in the conversation about the time the group was dispersing but Olga, who had been interpreting, and of course hearing the conversation, was more interested than ever. As she was preparing to leave, she was concerned that she did not know the "end of the story." She came to Esther and said, "I want to hear the rest of the story, but I know that you can't stay to tell me, and I have another obligation to go to, but please keep in touch with me. I want to hear the rest of the story about Jesus Christ." Then she gave Esther her phone number and said, "If you need an interpreter at any time, please call me and I will interpret for you."

"I want to hear the rest of the story" is a very unusual statement when we think about Olga's background. Olga had worked for the Communist Party in the Kremlin, and her husband, Slava, was in security for the whole Soviet Union back in the fifties when Russia put up the first satellite, named Sputnik. Slava (means "praise" in Russian) had a very high position in the Communist government at that time. Now his wife was asking to hear the rest of the story.

The next day, Esther and Bob were planning on traveling to a city named Molyarslovits, which was about a four-hour drive south of Moscow. That evening they received a phone call from the interpreter that was planning to go with them saying she could not go; immediately Esther called Olga, and she said that she would be happy to go. Olga met Bob and Esther at the appointed place, and they all made the four-hour drive to Molyarslovits in the Pentecostal church van. The van had no heat in it, and it was well below freezing outside. In addition, the seats were so worn that there was almost no padding on them, which made for a very tiring four-hour drive.

Esther and Bob were going there to talk to two Russian Pentecostal pastors about sending them shipments of supplies. The older pastor, Stefan, had spent eighteen years in prison for preaching the Word of God. Many years before, when he was pastor of a local Pentecostal church, he was arrested and spent six years in prison; when he was released he began preaching again and once again was imprisoned. This happened three times, causing him to be in prison for a total of eighteen years.

The third time that this happened, Vladimir, a member of Stefan's church, took over preaching, and he too was arrested and sentenced to six years in prison. Both pastors were in the same prison and were put into the worst part of it because they were classified as political prisoners. While they were in prison, nearly everyone that was in their cell became Christians. Even some of the guards were converted to Christianity.

Vladimir told us that the prison officials did not like this, so to stop it they put him into solitary confinement in one of the worst cells in the prison to keep him from spreading Christianity. He nearly starved to death through the process, but another inmate found a way to get food to him and this saved his life. While Vladimir was in prison, his wife, Olga, was questioned many times in an effort to get her to tell names of other Christians in their church. but she would not divulge names to the Communist officials.

When the van arrived at Stefan's home, Esther got out and walked into the house slightly in front of Olga. As Olga entered the room, she suddenly stopped and spoke in a fearful and amazed voice, "Oh, what is this? I have never felt anything like it. What is in this house?" Olga had a confused look on her face as she was standing there slightly inside the doorway. She was looking around and seeing nothing except the contents of the room, but feeling this strange presence around her that she had never felt before. Esther spoke back and said, "Olga, it is the Holy Spirit you are experiencing. The Holy Spirit is in this place."

Olga had never experienced anything like this. Now she was in the home of a man and woman that had suffered greatly for their faith, and the anointing of the Holy Spirit was upon them. It was not only upon them, but it filled their home, and Olga was feeling and experiencing this for the first time in her life. During the day, discussion took place about shipments of supplies, and there was Christian fellowship between the Russian and American Christians. Olga was interpreting and also witnessing all of this for the first time in her life.

Late that evening, the guests left Stefan's home and started on the four-hour drive back to Moscow. Esther was very tired and cold and wanted to get some sleep on the drive back to Moscow, but the Holy Spirit spoke to her in His still, small voice, saying, "Tell Olga the rest of the story." Esther was so tired that she said, "Lord, I will talk to her later. I just want to sleep now." The Holy Spirit spoke back in that same still, small voice and said. "Talk to Olga now!"

Esther tapped Olga on the shoulder and said, "Olga, do you want to hear the rest of the story now?" Olga replied, "Oh, yes, please tell me the rest of the story." With that reply, Esther explained the entire plan of salvation to Olga. With tears streaming down her face, Olga accepted Jesus Christ as her Savior and Lord. There in that old van she was born again. Today Olga says that Esther is her spiritual mother because Esther birthed her to Jesus Christ.

From that day until now, Olga has had a wonderful ministry in Moscow and in other places in Russia. She has worked with Billy Graham, Co-Missions, and is now working full-time with a Christian doctor named Doctor Bill. Olga is the director of Doctor Bill's Medical Clinic and Pharmacy. She has been involved in helping to bring the Word of God and medical help to thousands of people living inside Russia.

Esther McCauley and Bob Cox returned to Molyarslovits once more before they returned to the States. It was a very cold February day in Russia; the ground was covered with about a foot of snow and the local river was frozen over with about four inches of ice. The political situation in Russia had changed, and the Christians were, for the first time in many years, allowed to baptize people freely. They wanted to do this at that time and in that weather, because they were fearful that things might change quickly and they would not be allowed to baptize people freely.

The Christians went out into the river and broke the ice in an area about fifty feet along the river's edge and about thirty feet back from the bank toward the center of the river. The water was icy cold with a very swift current flowing under the ice. The Christians brought musical instruments to the river's edge and played and sang many Christian songs. Then about four church leaders waded out into the freezing water, and about forty Christians, all dressed in white, waded out with them to be baptized.

Those that were baptized struggled out of the freezing water after they were baptized, slipping and sometimes falling as they walked up the snow-covered bank in their bare feet. At the top of the bank, Christians waiting there for them quickly wrapped them in blankets. The sight of these Christians suffering this cold in order that they might be baptized was very touching.

When Esther returned home from Russia, she shared with me the events that took place while she was there. My heart was very touched as I listened to her give the details of how God led and blessed. I was especially blessed to hear about Olga accepting Jesus Christ as her Savior. To hear about her reaction when she felt the presence of the Holy Spirit upon entering the home of Stefan was such a blessing and encouragement to me. When I heard about the Christians being baptized in the freezing river, it nearly caused me to weep.

Then Esther told me that she and Bob Cox had promised the Russian officials and the Christians that we would send a total of fourteen shipments of humanitarian aid to Russia. We had already sent one shipment, so that meant we had to send thirteen more shipments. I was shocked and said, "Esther, you didn't promise fourteen shipments, did you?" She said, "Yes, we did." I was quickly counting the cost to do this and I said, "Esther do you realize the shipping alone for this is about one hundred and fifty thousand dollars, and the cost overall is more than a million dollars."

Esther also told me that Russian officials said, "We have learned one thing about Americans; when they say they will do something, they do it." I knew they believed that when Esther and Bob said we would send a total of fourteen shipments, they would receive thirteen more shipments. I was very concerned about this promise and did not even know if it was of God. I just wasn't sure I had enough faith for Esther's promise—one million dollars? I also knew that since Esther and Bob said we would send a total of fourteen shipments to Russia, we had to do it.

Since I was very concerned about Esther and Bob's promise to send the fourteen shipments, she explained to me how this came about. She told me that when the Russians in the Kremlin and the Christians asked them to send more shipments of food, clothing, and medicine, she felt that God told her in His still, small voice to tell them that we would send fourteen shipments in all. She emphasized that God gave her this number of fourteen. As a result of this, she gave them that number.

After hearing this, I believed that she had heard the still, small voice of the Holy Spirit, and I agreed with her that we should send the fourteen shipments. I also felt that God would provide the cost to do this. I knew that it would take a tremendous amount of work to put this together. I also knew Bob Cox would do all he could to make this happen. I felt sorry for Esther because I knew much of the labor would fall upon her to pack the boxes etc. I was, however, completely at ease with it after hearing Esther testify that God gave her the number. Within days after returning home, Esther started making plans to put together the second shipment.

Ch. 31

"God Just Told Me"

I believe many people desire to hear the still, small voice of the Lord, and I think they hear it many times, but fail to obey. I think this happens many times when people feel they should give a certain amount of money to the Lord's work but they refuse to do it. Many times people are tested as they hear that inner voice telling them to help with a certain thing, or give financially to a need. If we aren't faithful in the small things that God asks us to do, then we limit how much the Lord will speak to us for greater things. Can He trust us in all cases to obey Him at any cost? If not, then He will probably not use us as He would have, because He cannot trust us to obey.

Shortly after Esther and Bob Cox returned back home, they were asked to speak in different churches about their trip. On one such speaking engagement, both Bob Cox and Esther were to speak at the Lutheran Church in Kokomo. Our neighbors, Ralph and Lois Grotrian, were members of that church and they invited Esther and me to ride to church with them that morning. Ralph, a bank manager in our local city, was about sixty-five years old at the time. He was a respected member of the community and very successful in his business. He always dressed very properly, and presented himself in a very dignified and formal way. He just had the looks of being a successful bank manager. Lois was also very proper in her manners and her Christian life. She was a woman that a person could not help but love and respect.

When Bob Cox spoke that morning, he told about Nickolai and Marina Kornilov and their ministry in Moscow. In his speech, he told about his desire to have a rescue mission in Russia, and that he felt it would be good for Nickolai and Marina to come to America to visit the Kokomo Rescue Mission. As he spoke, I felt that it would be good for them to come here to meet American Christians and for people here to meet some Russian Christians. Bob and Esther both did a good job speaking that morning about Russia, and the Lutheran pastor and people treated us very well.

As we drove back home after the service, Ralph and Lois were seated in the front seats of their car and Esther and I in the back. Ralph was very proper in his driving, with both hands placed directly on the steering wheel as he drove. Lois was sitting very properly in her bucket seat beside Ralph. We were all talking about how the service went and about Nickolai and Marina coming to America.

All of a sudden I heard Ralph speak. I was very surprised at what he said. Still properly holding the steering wheel and not even raising or adding any special expression to his voice, he said, "Lois, God just told me that you and I are to bring Nickolai and Marina to America." Without even a moment's delay and also with no change or special expression in her voice, Lois quietly said, "Well, that is fine, dear. Let's do it." It was as if it was very common for God to speak to them in this manner.

As I heard this, I thought, "This expressionless event that I just witnessed cost them about two thousand five hundred dollars." I was very touched and impressed by the simplicity of it. Ralph was very sensitive to the still, small voice of God. He did not suggest to Lois that they seek God about it or to even put out a fleece about it. He also did not say, "I think God just told me—. It simply was, "God just told me," and Lois answering, "Yes, dear, let's do it."

A two thousand five hundred-dollar-decision to obey God was made before Esther and me with no fanfare or even any additional expression in either one of their voices. The way Ralph broke into the conversation was as if God had just spoken to him and he and his wife immediately obeyed. It all took place within less than one minute, and I knew that God had spoken to Ralph to do this. To say the least, I was amazed at the simplicity of the event and the quick obedience of Ralph and Lois.

Ralph and Lois did fund a trip for Nickolai and Marina Kornilov to come to Kokomo shortly after that, and the Kornilovs stayed with Esther and me for the three weeks they were here. They met many American Christians from the Kokomo area, and the people loved them. They were such a humble and gracious Christian couple, and by the time they left, were well known by many people in our area. Later this would prove to be very vital for what God was going to do in their and our lives.

Nickolai and Marina spent a lot of time at the Kokomo Rescue Mission, but as they prayed about it, Nickolai did not feel God was leading him to start a rescue mission in Moscow. God had a totally different plan for the Kornilovs. He was using their visit to America for something far greater than what we thought was His original plan.

God was going to use Nickolai to help start the first evangelical seminary in Moscow, which would have students that would preach all over Russia. Nickolai would be a professor in that seminary and would also be used to start a radio program in Moscow that would reach hundreds of thousands of people with the message of Jesus Christ. Nickolai's contacts, in and around Kokomo, Indiana, would be vital in helping to establish all of this.

Ch. 32

RENEWED STRENGTH AND A JUNGLE RUN

When we started packing the second shipment for Russia, both Esther and I were extremely tired. Esther had put in many fourteen-hour days packing boxes or driving to some city to get food and medicine for the first shipment. At times I had worked eight hours or more a day on my job and about six hours on packing or getting the supplies for the first shipment. Many other people had worked hard at packing the first shipment, but most of them could not help us on the second shipment due to other responsibilities. Regardless of being tired, we started on the project of packing the second shipment, knowing we had a few more years of intensive work to put together the rest of the fourteen shipments we had promised to send to Russia.

A few years before this, the Holy Spirit taught me a very important lesson that I have never forgotten. One day when I was so tired that I could hardly walk, He told me in His still, small voice to run. What happened after that is amazing. The lesson I learned is this: If God gives you something to do, then regardless of how tired you are, you start doing it as hard as you can, and God will renew your strength as you go. You start first in faith and then let God give you what you need to continue. The following scripture best explains this.

> But they that wait upon the LORD shall renew their strength; they shall mount up with wings as eagles; they shall run, and not be weary; and they shall walk, and not faint. (ISAIAH 40:31)

Esther and I had been waiting upon the Lord. This does not mean that we were doing nothing, but we were in motion, moving with the leading of His Holy Spirit and also waiting for His leading as to what we were to do. Before we got involved with a ministry to Russia, we were prayed up and letting God lead us in everything we did. We knew that He had spoken to us in His still, small voice to send the first shipment, so we never questioned that after we began. We just did not realize how big the project was going to be. Waiting upon God to direct us and then doing it with all our heart was a way of life for us.

250

After we started packing the second shipment, our strength was renewed and once again we were excited about putting together the shipment. I want to emphasize that this renewed strength came after we started the work and not before. I will give an example of doing this when I was in Africa.

Early one morning when I was in Liberia, Africa, I walked at a very fast pace for about fifteen miles to get to a village called Sea-ap-lee. The villagers were making a bush airstrip in the jungle to enable me to fly to their village with our medical evangelism team to treat their sick and to bring the Word of God to them. On this particular day, I walked to the village to make sure they were making the airstrip correctly so I could land the plane there.

I needed at least a five hundred-foot-long strip of fairly level ground to land on (though I was hoping they could find a way to make a six hundred-foot airstrip, which was much safer), and I also needed the trees cut back from one end of the airstrip for an approach as I came in for a landing. This was very important. It was hard to find five hundred feet of fairly level ground in the jungle, and I did not want them to waste their time making the strip in a place where I could not land, so my visit with them was very important.

On this particular day, as I was helping work on the strip, time got away from me and I ended up staying in Sea-ap-lee longer than I had intended. About three o'clock in the afternoon, I realized that I needed to leave and walk back to my mission station. An old African man said that it was too late in the day for me to get there before dark. He tried hard to convince me not to go, but I insisted on going.

When I started walking back, I found that I was very tired. The fifteen-mile walk at a very fast pace that morning and the work during the day had put its toll on my body. I knew that it got pitch dark at six thirty in the evening, so I had about three and half hours of daylight to walk the fifteen miles. I was tired but still felt I could make it, but I had not counted on one fact that the old man knew. I was soon to find out what he meant when he said I could not make it before dark.

After I had walked very fast for about three or four miles, I saw that the narrow path through the jungle was quickly getting dark. I was walking at a good pace, but because I was tired, I was not walking as fast as I needed to. I was putting out as much effort as I had on my walk to Sea-ap-lee that morning, but I was not covering as much ground as I had earlier. On top of this, the sun was getting lower in the sky and the extremely tall trees were filtering out its light; the smaller trees overhung the small path, and it was like I was walking in a tunnel through the jungle. The sunlight was just not getting down to where I was walking. I soon realized that I did not have three and a half hours to make the fifteen miles, because it was going to be dark in the deep jungle much sooner than I thought.

I still had about ten or eleven miles to go, and I estimated that I only had about one or maybe one and a half hours of light left before it was totally dark. If I tried to return to Sea-ap-lee, I was so tired that I might not make it before dark there either. I also knew that my wife and the other missionaries at the mission station were expecting me to be home that evening. If I did not get home, they would think something had happened to me in the jungle and would be very worried. I did not want this. I also knew that it was very dangerous to spend a night alone in the jungle with all the poisonous snakes and wild animals. Then there were the mosquitoes that would make a night in the jungle very difficult.

I knew I was in trouble and had to trust God for my help. I asked Him to help me and He spoke to me in His still, small voice saying, "Run home at a very fast pace." During my high school years, I was a sprinter. I won a lot of races and received a lot of ribbons. Most of my running had been as a short-distance runner, but now I was more than fifteen years older and had to run a long, hard run. I knew I could not endure running ten or eleven miles back to the mission, but the Holy Spirit was telling me in His still, small voice to take off running. I knew I did not have the strength within me to do it, but I prayed, "God, give me strength." After saying this prayer, I started to run almost as fast as I did during my days of running the dashes in school.

I knew I could not continue the pace very long, but then I realized I was not getting tired. It was amazing! I was able to hold the pace for a much longer time than I had the strength within me to do it. I was shocked at my endurance! I should have started to feel exhausted, but I was not feeling it. I had set up a fast pace and was holding it! It felt so good. Even in my best days at running when I was younger, I was never able to keep up a fast long distance pace like I was doing right then. It took effort on my part, but as I put out the effort, God was giving me the strength that I needed.

The shadows along the jungle path were getting darker as I ran. I had to watch my step very closely on the uneven path and still keep up my pace. The terrain was difficult with lots of steep hills as well as gullies and an occasional jungle stream that I had to jump over or cross on a fallen tree. I ran right through some streams. There were many jungle obstacles along the way such as exposed tree roots, huge rocks, fallen trees, and vines that I could easily get tangled up in, but I did not fall or even stumble on any of them, although some of them did slow me down.

As always when I was in the jungle, I was watching out for deadly snakes laying on or near the path or hanging from a tree or vine ready to bite any victim that passed by. On top of that, I was constantly watching for huge constrictor snakes that might drop on me from a tree. Some of these snakes are very large and can kill a man by wrapping tightly around him until he cannot breathe. With all of these obstacles, I was still able to keep up the pace, and I did not faint.

Mile after mile passed, and shortly before dark I could see the outlaying huts of our local village of Bahn. I did not slow down but ran on a path around the village toward my mission station, which was at the top of a very steep hill. By the time I arrived at the base of the mission hill, it was dark. I could just barely see well enough to follow the path but not well enough to see what was on the ground. There were a lot of flat rocks on the path that led up to our mission station, and poisonous snakes liked to lie on them to warm themselves. During the daytime a person could see these snakes, but it was so dark by the time I got there that I could not see well enough to avoid them, so I just kept going. I knew that if I stepped on one of them, they could kill me within minutes after the strike.

I personally knew of five people that died in one year from bites from these snakes, but I kept running and trusting God to deliver me from being bitten. I knew God had given me strength to run, but I still was on edge as I took every step, knowing that I could come into contact with one of those deadly vipers. It was very dark by the time I got to the top of the hill, but within minutes I was home. My wife and daughter were there waiting for me with our supper ready when I arrived. They had no idea what I had just gone through and greeted me as though it had been a perfectly normal day. It was good to be home, and I thanked God for His strength.

My strength to run came after I started and continued to be with me as I ran. God was my Provider. He helped me to mount up with wings as an eagle and to run, and not be weary; and to walk, and not faint. That day I saw ISAIAH 40:31 literally come true in my life.

As Esther and I started working on that second shipment, we saw God renew our strength. Again I will say, "The strength came after we started." It did not come before this. We were tired when we started, just as I was very tired when I started to run on the jungle path in Africa. We were, in a way, mounted on the wings of an eagle as the scripture says, and running and not growing weary. We were running to get this shipment put together and sent to God's people in a land where the followers of Jesus Christ had suffered so much. He had called us to do it. We were obeying, and He was blessing as we did.

It was a privilege for us to let Him use us to make a difference for these people. It took great effort and hundreds of hours of our time, and help from others, but the shipment was put together and sent to the Christians in Russia just as the other shipment had been. The wonderful thing was, this renewed strength for Esther and I stayed with us mile after mile as it had for me on my jungle run. Actually it stayed with us for shipment after shipment or for the full fourteen shipments.

As we were putting this second shipment together, we had the Kokomo Rescue Mission warehouse building to work in. The mission director, Bob Cox, was a big supporter of sending supplies to the Christians in Russia, and the board of directors was also united with us in this ministry.

Bob Cox found an organization that shipped all the rest of our containers of humanitarian aid to Russia for free. All we had to do was to put the shipments together, and when we had a shipment ready to go, Bob would call them and set up a date, and they would send us a semi truck with an overseas container on it. The trucking company gave us two hours to load the container after it arrived. We had many volunteers from different walks of life come and help us load, and we always had the semi loaded in two hours!

This worked out great, and the second shipment left Kokomo, Indiana, in the early months of 1993. Once again, we were excited as we watched the semi-truck pull out of the rescue mission parking lot, knowing that soon all of these supplies would be in the hands of many Russian Christians, and that they would make a difference in the lives of hundreds of people living there.

As tired as we were when we started this shipment, God helped us to mount up on wings as eagles, and to run and not grow weary. We were so thankful for the strength that He gave us as we spent the next four years packing and sending containers to Russia. It is so important that we know what God wants us to do and then do it with all of our might, trusting Him to give us strength and provisions along the way.

Ch. 33

First Evangelical Seminary in Moscow

As we are walking with the Lord, we may encounter obstacles. Our reaction when this happens can mean the difference between succeeding or failing in our call to obey God. Many times when we stepped out to obey God, obstacles got in our way to hinder or even stop us. When these times come, we need to do all we can even when the job seems impossible for us to accomplish, such as happened in this next story.

The second shipment of supplies to the Christians in Moscow was worth about one hundred and eighty thousand dollars, so we needed to do all we could to make sure it went to the right location. The shipment arrived at Moscow in late March 1993 and Esther was there to make sure it went to the Christians as we intended. Every detail went great and it was put into the hands of the very needy Christians. They were thrilled to have the huge container of food, medicine, and clothing, and they felt the love of the Christians in America. They distributed the supplies to their needy as they saw fit. Esther again had a very blessed ministry speaking in churches and making friends with our Russian brothers and sisters in Christ.

Esther went to Moscow several times, making sure that the shipments arrived safely and were distributed as we intended. On her return home, after going to Russia in April 1993, she promptly told me that the Mennonites and Baptists in Moscow had approached her and asked if we would be the United States sponsors to bring Nickolai and Marina Kornilov and their five children to Indiana so that Nickolai could study at the Mennonite seminary in Elkhart, Indiana. This request included us helping with the funds to get them to America and for all their expenses while they were here.

The Baptists and Mennonites wanted to start the first evangelical Christian seminary in Moscow and wanted Nickolai to teach church history in that seminary. Nickolai had been a school teacher in a Russian government school teaching Russian history, but after he became a Christian he refused to teach history starting with evolution. As a result, he left the school and was no longer teaching. Nickolai was a very good historian and was extremely well respected in Christian circles all over Moscow. He was also a leader in his own local church. The Christians felt that Nickolai would be an ideal person to teach church history in their new seminary, but he needed a degree in church history. Esther went on to tell me that they wanted Nickolai and his family to be at the seminary by the first of September to start his schooling in the fall. Esther accepted their request, and told them that we would be the United States sponsors for the Kornilov family.

My mind went back to Esther's first trip to Russia, when she promised we would send a total of fourteen shipments of aid. I was shocked then, when I heard what she promised. Now I was shocked again when I heard, that she had made this promise to the Baptists and Mennonites. How could we take care of all of the details to do this in such a short time? We were already well into April. I also became quite concerned about the finances, when Esther told me that the Russian Christians wanted us to help with all the expenses of getting Nickolai and Marina, and their five children to American and also for them while they were here.

Then when I thought I heard her say that they were to come here in about four months, I became very concerned. I said, "Esther, you mean a year from this coming September, don't you?" Esther replied, "No, this coming September." My heart nearly sank when I heard that. There seemed no way that we could get this done, unless God was in it, and worked out all of the details for us, including finances.

Seeing God supply funds to do the things He had called us to do was not uncommon to me. I had seen Him provide thousands of dollars in the past. I had also seen him supply thousands of dollars to fund flying the mission plane for evangelism. I knew God could provide funds, but in the back of my mind, I still did not have the faith for this one because I was not sure it was of God. My faith at that time just seemed to drop out from under me and I replied, "Esther, how can we ever get all the money and support before September?"

Esther didn't have an answer for my question except to say that we would trust God for it. I settled down and said, "Where do we start?" Even as I said this, I knew the answer. From years of doing the Lord's work, I knew that we had to start with prayer. I also needed to hear the still, small voice of the Holy Spirit speak to me that this was of God. If bringing the Kornilov family to America was of God and I knew it, I would go at it with all my heart, and I knew Esther would do the same. I settled down, and Esther and I had a very serious prayer about this situation. As we prayed, we also waited on God to speak to us as He had many times in the past. Soon that still, small voice of the Holy Spirit that I had heard so many times gave me a confirmation that this was of the Lord and that He would provide.

I now knew this was of God and would never doubt it again. From then on that question was answered. It was as solid in my mind as if it were engraved on stone. Now, if we had hard times, I would not have to go back and wonder if we did the right thing by starting this work. From years of being in God's work and going through many very difficult times, I knew that we probably would face difficult times in getting the Kornilov family to America. When those difficulties came, as they were bound to, I would know with all my heart that we were doing the right thing. When the difficulties came, we would need to step back and ask God for direction on where to go from where we were.

Not only had God confirmed to me as we prayed that this was of Him, but in addition to this, the Lord gave Esther a word of wisdom. It was an answer to my question, "Where do we start?" I have learned that God has given Esther the spiritual gift of wisdom many times when we have needed it. She said, "I believe we should invite to our home Bob Cox from the Kokomo Rescue Mission and some of our friends and pastors who might be interested in helping start this seminary."

These were all people that had gotten to know Nickolai and Marina when they came to Indiana in 1993. Esther went on to say, "I feel we should tell them about this request from the Mennonites and Baptists. Then I think we should form a board of directors from these people for the project." This seemed to be a good place to start, and I asked Esther to take care of the details, which she did. From that day on, I was fully dedicated to getting the Kornilov family to Elkhart, Indiana, by September of that year.

Esther made several phone calls and arranged a meeting in our home for about a week later. In the meantime, I had to be at my job, and Esther continued packing things for the third shipment of supplies for Russia. When the time for the meeting came, Esther had our house looking very nice with finger foods, coffee, and soft drinks for our guests. When our guests arrived, Esther led the meeting and gave them the details about the request of the Mennonites and Baptists in Moscow.

I could denote a bit of excitement in the room as our guests heard how they could be a part of starting the first evangelical seminary in Moscow. This was a major step forward for all of us. We all knew that we could be a part of starting this seminary in the country that was formerly our cold war enemy, and which we had feared for many years. The possibility of our involvement in this seemed like a very good idea to all of us. Much to our delight, every person there agreed to be a part of this ministry and to be on the board of directors that would help direct this new ministry. As our guests left that evening, there seemed to be an excitement in all of them. A bond between all of us had been formed, and today we all are very close friends.

We knew difficulties could come in our effort to get the Kornilovs to Indiana, but we did not expect what would be our very first one. I thought it would be getting enough funds together to bring them here and then funds for their living expenses. Although difficulties and roadblocks come, they do not mean we are out of God's will. In MATTHEW 14:22-33, we see the story about Jesus telling His disciples to go to the other side of the sea in a boat. As they started rowing toward the other shore, the disciples encountered some very bad weather.

They were doing exactly what Jesus told them to do, but still the sea roared and the waves and wind came against them so hard that they made almost no headway. They kept rowing as hard as they could, but the wind was blowing at them from the direction of the other shore, and with the wind came the waves from the same direction. Were they out of God's will by trying to row their boat to the other side of the sea? No, they were not, but they still had the wind and waves coming straight at them as they rowed.

I know from past experience that we can have problems when we are doing exactly what God wants us to do. This does not mean that we are to stop rowing our boat, but rather we need to see Jesus coming to our aid, walking above our problems. As the disciples were being hindered in their efforts to obey the Lord, they saw Him walking toward them into the wind and on top of the roaring sea. He had the same strong wind and waves coming against Him as they had, but the wind and waves gave Him no problem at all. When Jesus arrived, He took care of the disciples' problem. When we face problems, we need to see Jesus walking above our problems and delivering us from them. We needed to see this very quickly after our first meeting to bring the Kornilov family to America.

A few days after the meeting, we received an e-mail from Nickolai in which he gave details about his meeting with the American Embassy people in Moscow. The embassy flatly turned down his request to come to America with his family. They said they would allow him to come by himself, but they would not allow his family to come with him because they would all stay in America and not return to Russia. If he came by himself, he would return to Russia because his family was there. Nickolai told us that he could not leave his family for two years. He did not feel this would be right or fair to Marina or to his children, and he would not even consider coming to America without his family. Nickolai said, "I do not know what to do to change the minds of people in the American Embassy in Moscow."

This seemed like a very large roadblock, and Esther and I shared it with our new board. None of them had an answer. After much prayer about this, Esther and I felt we should go to Moscow and personally talk to our embassy personnel; however, a major roadblock that I had was leaving my job for three weeks. This was not an easy thing for me to do at the time, because I was right in the middle of a very heavy workload.

I was responsible for getting millions of dollars worth of plastic molds designed, built, and qualified for production that was to start in August of that year. It was a very difficult time for me to leave my job, but I felt I had to do it for God's work. I did my best to work out things on my job so that I could be gone for about three weeks. I also kept my supervisor well-informed on every detail of what I was doing. He seemed satisfied that I had every detail covered on my job, and he permitted me to leave.

We purchased our airline tickets and flew to Moscow. I was looking forward to seeing Nickolai and Marina again and meeting their children. They were my brothers and sisters in Christ from Russia. During the years that I prayed for the Christians in Russia, I never thought it would be possible for me to see any of them except when we all got to heaven. Now I was going to meet many of them. I was excited about that and was planning on doing all in my power to help them start their new seminary. I was in constant prayer about this. I knew my God could move mountains, and we needed a mountain moved to get the Kornilovs to Elkhart, Indiana. The mountain was the American Embassy.

When we arrived at the airport, Nickolai and Marina were waiting for us. It was so good to see them. Nickolai had a small car to take us and our bags to their flat. From the time our plane circled the city to land and as we drove, I could not help but notice the general condition of the city and the buildings. The buildings and streets were in need of major repairs and had been that way for years. Many streets were full of large potholes, and unfinished building projects were standing in many places. It looked like a city living in great poverty. I had been involved in enough construction in my life to see that the buildings had been in need of major repairs for at least a generation or forty years.

The condition of the city was not my concern, however. It was in obeying and doing what we knew God wanted us to do. We were with a very dedicated Christian couple whom I had great respect for. I also knew God had His hand upon them for a great ministry, and I was to do my part in making it possible for them to come to America.

The drive to the Kornilov's flat took us about an hour. Nickolai and Marina could both speak English fairly well, and we had a very good visit as we made our way through the streets of Moscow to their flat which was on the outskirts of Moscow. The Kornilovs lived on the fifth floor of their building. As we entered their flat, we immediately took off our shoes in their small entryway. It is strictly against Russian culture to enter a home with your shoes on. This was easy for me to adjust to because it is also an insult to enter a Canadian's home with your shoes on. Since Esther is a Canadian, I am very used to taking my shoes off at the entryway. We do this in our own home even though we live in Indiana.

We met all five of the Kornilov children that evening. Esther already knew them from her trips to Moscow, but it was my first time. The children were all very gracious to us and seemed very excited to have us in their home. Marina had a lovely Russian supper for us shortly after we arrived, and we had very good fellowship with all of the Kornilov family that evening.

About two days after we arrived in Moscow, we got up at four o'clock in the morning and headed for the American Embassy. The trip across the city took us about an hour, and we arrived at the embassy at about 6:00 a.m. Nickolai knew from past experience that we needed to be there at 6:00 a.m. and stand in line for two hours in order to get in to talk to the authorities. When we arrived, there was already a line of about thirty people. We walked up to the end of the line and started our long wait. Many people came after we arrived, and the line became very long. The people's behavior in the line was quite different from what I had experienced standing in line in America. It seemed to me that the longer the line got, the more pushing and shoving there was. Some latecomers were pushing and getting in front of people that had stood there for a long time.

We were getting farther and farther back in the line, and I started to wonder if we would be able to see the embassy personnel that day. The press against our bodies was more than I had ever experienced. One young man behind me was pushing on me so hard that I turned around and said in English, "Why are you pushing me so hard?" He answered in very good English, "You are in Russia, and in Russia everyone pushes." Well, I sure had a lesson to learn about this part of their culture. Later in our life we would live in Russia and would find out how true his statement was.

By the time the doors opened at 8:00 a.m., we were well back in the line. We kept standing and trying to maintain our place, but we were getting pushed farther and farther back. After about five or six hours, I thought that we would not be able to see the embassy personnel that day. We had arrived at six o'clock in the morning and now we were very far back in line because of the mass of people shoving and pushing to get to the front.

It seemed to me that hundreds of people wanted to get out of Russia to America and were doing everything they could to accomplish this. To even have a chance of getting to America, they had to get to the front of the line, and they were willing to do all they could to do it.

I thought, "We are Americans and cannot even get in to talk to our own American Embassy personnel." By about two o'clock in the afternoon we were very tired and were far from the front of the line. There were probably two hundred people in front of us, and the doors closed at 4:00 p.m. I had been praying throughout the day and kept feeling that the Lord was telling me that He would get us in to see the embassy personnel. Logically speaking, it was impossible unless God did a miracle.

The pushing and shoving seemed to intensify as the time for the doors to close drew nearer. The press was so bad that to even leave the building through the door we came in would be nearly impossible. By the time the situation became impossible for us to make it in that day, an American man came out of a door on an elevated platform above where we were standing and said in English, "Are there any Americans here?" Esther and I yelled out and raised our hands that we were Americans.

We were the only Americans there, and he told us to come forward. He stood there above the crowd making sure that the people let us through, which they did. When we got to the front of the line, we told him that Nickolai and Marina were with us, and he let them come to the front also. He permitted our request and took us into the room where they were interviewing the people that wanted to come to America. We gave him the name of the embassy official that had interviewed and rejected Nickolai and his family's request to come to America.

As soon as that official was available, we were taken to him. He was about forty years old, slightly balding, well-dressed, and had the appearance of a person that was well-educated, very strong-willed, and highly qualified for his job. Nickolai and Marina were with us, but the official did not want to talk to Nickolai again and told Nickolai and Marina to stand off to the side as Esther and I talked to him.

The embassy official had Nickolai's file before him and told us quickly why he had rejected Nickolai. He said that if he let the Kornilov family go to America, just as soon as they got off of the plane, they could apply for welfare from our government, and our government would have to support them fully. Then, since all of the family was there, they would refuse to return to Russia, and our government would be stuck with supporting them for years through welfare.

I spoke back and said, "They are Christians and will return to Russia just as they said they would." The interviewer barked back at me, "Christians are the worst of the lot." I thought, "That sure did not go over well at all." I replied strongly, "I know they will return to Russia." He looked at me squarely in the eyes and said, "You prove to me that they will return to Russia and I will let them go." I then asked the question, "How can I prove to you that they will return?" Still looking straight at me, he replied, "That is not my problem, it is yours." With that I knew our interview was over. I thanked him for his time, and we all walked out the back door where there was no press.

If God had not spoken to me in His still, small voice back home in our living room when Esther and I were praying and given me the word that this was of Him, I think I would have given up on this venture. My thoughts would have been, "This obstacle in front of us is just too great. I know no way to go around

263

it, over it, or through it." This would have been my normal way of thinking, but I knew something far beyond what this man knew. I knew it was God's will for Nickolai and his entire family to come to America.

As we walked out of the building, I could see that Nickolai and Marina were very discouraged. Esther was upbeat and she tried to encourage them, but even with her effort, they still seemed very down. I could see that the obstacle that we had just encountered looked impassable to them. What we needed was another word of wisdom and guidance from God on where to go from here! God had given this to us many times before, and we needed it desperately again.

Confused about what to do and very tired, we started our long trip back across Moscow to Nickolai and Marina's flat. We had not eaten since about four fifteen in the morning and had not even had a bathroom break since then. From all of the pushing and shoving, and just plain standing and waiting, we were all very tired. The harsh interview, with what seemed like no results, made it even worse.

We were four people that had grown up and lived in very different conditions. Nickolai and Marina had lived under Communism in their early years. They were both about thirty-five years old at the time, but seemed much older than that. Esther had grown up in a logging camp in western Canada and had a much different background than the Kornilovs or I. My life, as a farm boy and living in the flatlands and Bible belt of America, was much different than all of theirs.

Here we were, brought together by God for a purpose, and we were tired and not knowing where to go from here to do what we believed God wanted us to do. We just wanted to get back to the apartment, get something to eat and drink, and then get some rest. We hardly knew what to say as Nickolai drove his little car across Moscow that evening.

Because of the time of the day, it took us much longer to get back to Marina and Nickolai's apartment than it had taken us to get to the embassy in the early morning, and by the time we arrived, it was well into the evening. I had no idea of what we needed to do to get the Kornilovs to America. There just seemed to be a wall in front of us with no way around or through it. In the back of my mind I knew there was a door in that wall, but I sure could not see it.

I did not know where to go from here. Esther and I felt we should come to Moscow to personally talk to the American Embassy personnel, and we had done that. The only results that I could see from doing this was in knowing that we had to convince a man of something that he seemed determined that he was not going to be convinced of. Back at the Kornilov flat, we ate and had prayer together, each one realizing that all we could do at this point was to pray and ask God for His wisdom.

After that prayer, I was still very tired, but things started to clear up in my mind, and God spoke to me in His still, small voice, giving me a plan and the directions that we needed to take. After a good night's sleep, I told Esther, Nickolai, and Marina that I wanted to have a meeting with the elders of the Mennonite church, the elders of the Baptist church, the president of the new seminary, and the leader of the Russian Ministries that Nickolai worked for. I asked Nickolai to set up these meetings as quickly as possible. He wasted no time and had the meetings all arranged within a couple of days.

The first group of elders we met with was the Mennonites. Nickolai, Esther, and I traveled about halfway across the city to a very clean but small apartment where one of the American Mennonite missionaries and his wife lived. They took us into their little living room, where we sat down on their clean but worn couch and were served tea and some Russian sweets. About ten minutes after our arrival, several other Mennonites arrived. We were impressed by their love and concern for the Russian Christians. There was some small talk in Russian between Nickolai and the elders. Nickolai was very respectful of Esther and me and interpreted each word that was spoken. Then it was my time to talk since I had called the meeting.

I started out by greeting them. Nickolai had introduced me, but I needed to tell them a bit about Esther and I. Then I asked them one question, "Why do you want Nickolai Kornilov to go to America?" I think my question surprised them, but they each took a turn to answer. They all said the same thing. They wanted Nickolai to go to America so that he could get the qualifications to teach Russian history in the new seminary.

Then I asked them another question, "Do you believe Nickolai Kornilov will return to Moscow after he finishes his training in America?" They all answered, "Yes." Then I had one more question, "Would you be willing to put your answers that you just gave me in writing on a paper with your letterhead?" Almost in unison, they said, "Dah." I knew enough Russian to know that they said, "Yes," after which I asked if they would do it as soon as possible and get it to Nickolai. Our meeting was over very quickly, and I was completely pleased with the outcome.

Nickolai worked for an organization called Russian Ministries, and we went there next. Russian Ministries works with many evangelical churches in Russia, helping them with literature and other Christian supplies and in business-related matters. Their headquarters is located in Chicago, Illinois, but they also have a headquarters in Moscow and are a well-respected ministry in all of Russia. Nickolai did office work for them and received a salary for his work. The director of Russian Ministries was a man from Chicago. He was a very big man that looked like he lifted weights. He looked very Russian with a full head of dark hair and a beard. He dressed in a Russian manner and could pass as a native Russian.

After our introduction, I asked him the same question I had asked the Mennonites, "Why do you want Nickolai Kornilov to go to America?" I was surprised at his answer. He quickly and almost gruffly said, "I don't want him to go." This took me by surprise, but then he said, "I don't want him to go because he is a very good man here and I don't want to lose him, but I feel he should go to America in order that he might teach in the new seminary. He will be of more use to Christianity there." I asked him if he believed Nickolai would return after he finished his training, and he said he would. Then I asked if he would put his answers on a Russian Ministries letterhead, and he agreed to do so.

We also went to the Baptist church located near the center of Moscow and met with the president of the new seminary. I asked him the same questions and he answered exactly like the Mennonites had. He also agreed to put his answers on a letterhead for the new seminary.

Last we met with the Baptist elders in Nickolai's apartment. There were about ten of them, and they reminded me a lot of the Mennonites except they were probably about ten years younger. When I asked them why they wanted Nickolai to go to America some of them started to cry openly. This was really a surprise to me. It took them a while to get their composure back enough to answer my question. All of them said that Nickolai was such a good leader in their church that they would miss him very much if he went to America, but they wanted him to go there in order that he might become qualified to teach in their new seminary. They all believed Nickolai would return to Moscow to teach, and they too agreed to put their answers on a letterhead.

Within a few days I received signed statements from the four groups just as I had requested. I felt I had completed what God had told me to do while we were in Russia. Shortly after that, Esther and I flew back to our home in Indiana. When we returned home, we had another meeting with our board. Esther and I made a report to them about what we had happened while we were in Moscow. We then asked each pastor and individual if they would write a letter telling why they wanted Nickolai in Indiana and why they believed he would return to Russia.

When we spoke to our board, we shared with them that the American Embassy stated that we had to have twenty-five thousand dollars-a-year support for the Kornilov family if they came to America. This amounted to over two thousand dollars a month. All of our board gave us amounts of how much their church, organization, or individuals would give toward their monthly support. Bob Cox said the Kokomo Rescue Mission would give a certain amount of food and clothing a month, which would come to several dollars a month. Within a few days we had the twenty-five thousand dollars pledged to support the Kornilovs while they were in Indiana. The Seminary had a five-bedroom house right across the street from the seminary that we could rent for a very low amount. This was a great blessing because neither Nickolai nor Marina had a driver's license or a car, and Nickolai was able to walk to all his classes.

Esther and I wrote a letter for ourselves to the American Embassy in Moscow in which we gave our personal word that we would take responsibility for the Kornilov family while they were in Indiana and that we personally would see to it that they returned to Russia after Nickolai's schooling. We also filled out a form from the American Embassy in which all of the support for the Kornilovs was detailed out.

All of the papers from the Christian groups in Moscow and the papers from the individuals, churches, and Kokomo Rescue Mission in our area were neatly put in a large envelope and sent to Nickolai to hand carry to the American Embassy in Moscow. After the American Embassy went through these papers, they gave Nickolai Kornilov and his family permission to all come to America.

After we received the e-mail from Nickolai telling us the good news that the American Embassy had given the whole Kornilov family permission to come to America, we quickly got busy furnishing a home for a family of seven. We needed everything from furniture to food to make the home complete. The

Kornilovs would bring their personal clothes and a few other small things from Russia, but nothing as far as setting up a home.

Esther, along with several other friends, was extremely busy for the month of August finding all the necessary things for the home. It was a two-hour drive one way from our home to Elkhart where Nickolai would be attending seminary, so she spent hours on the road in addition to hours of working. I could not help her a lot because of my job, but I did what I could. A few days before the end of August 1993, Esther and I and Bob Cox drove our vans to the airport in Chicago and picked up the seven Kornilovs, taking them to the seminary and to their new home where they would be for the next two years. They were there exactly on time for Nickolai to begin school in early September.

By the time the Kornilovs arrived, the home was beautifully decorated and everything was in place to make it a very lovely place to live. The refrigerator and freezer were full of good food items; towels and washcloths were hanging in place, all the beds were made with nice sheets and quilts, etc. The place looked lovely when Marina and Nikolai and their family walked into their American home. Esther even had toys for the children. They all were excited about what they saw and seemed to appreciate it very much.

Nickolai started his classes right on time in September, at the Mennonite seminary in Elkhart, Indiana. Four of the five children, John, Demetri, Peter, and Ksenia, also started their classes in the Elkhart, Indiana school system in September. The fifth child, Alex, was too young for school so he stayed at home. The children could not speak English well at that time. The Elkhart school system did a wonderful job of helping them learn their new language and adjust to their new school and subjects.

Esther could speak some Russian, so she made the two hour drive, from our home to Elkhart many times, helping Marina and the children understand what the teachers were saying. She also made countless trips taking food and clothing to the family. Bob Cox gave the Kornilovs a car, and Marina worked hard to get a driver's license, so they had transportation while they were there and they also would come and spend at least one weekend a month with us.

Nickolai did very well in his classes and graduated after two years. He and Marina, along with their family, then returned to Moscow and he started teaching church history in the new seminary in Moscow. Today, fifteen years later, Nickolai is still teaching in the seminary, plus holding biblical seminars in many cities in Russia. Nickolai is having a very successful ministry in Russia and Esther and I thank God that He let us be a part in it.

There seemed to be no way that our embassy would allow Nickolai and his family to come to America. We did not know what to do to make it happen, but God did. We just had to know what He was saying, and do it. It was then that I heard the Holy Spirit speak to us in His still, small voice; we stepped out on what He told us to do, and the Lord did the rest of it. It was very important that we heard His still, small voice and then obeyed it. When we did, God brought about what He wanted.

Ch. 34

SLAVA, HERE IS YOUR SON!

God is multifaceted in the fact that He can do different things with us at the same time. Both Esther and I thought our ministry to Russia was only in sending supplies to the Christians in Moscow. It did start out that way, but God was going to use us in a multifaceted way, the results of which we could never have imagined in our wildest dreams.

As I said above, when Esther went to Russia in 1992, she had the wonderful privilege of leading her interpreter, Olga, to the Lord. This developed into a wonderful friendship between Esther and Olga as well as between us and her husband, Slava. While we were in the process of putting together another container of supplies for the Christians in Moscow, we both started to feel that we should invite Olga and her husband, Slava, to come to the United States to visit us.

They accepted our invitation and we paid for their tickets to fly to Chicago from Moscow. When the day came for them to arrive in Chicago, Esther and I made the four-hour drive to the airport and picked them up. On our way back to our home in Indiana, we drove them through the center of Chicago, stopped, and let them walk around so they could see some of the city. They both enjoyed their short time seeing the sights of Chicago.

Slava had been married to another woman before his marriage to Olga. He had a son from that marriage that he had not seen in a long time, and he was very worried about him. His son had come to America about two years before on a visitor's visa. He took a tour bus to see America, and while he was on the tour he ran away, and no one knew where he was. Slava had received the information that he had left the tour, but had heard nothing from his son since then. From Moscow, Slava had tried different ways to find his son, but nothing worked out, and he hoped that when he was in America he could find him.

For about two and a half weeks after he arrived here, Slava made many phone calls to different agencies in an effort to locate where his son was, but nothing worked out. About three days before he and Olga were to return to Russia, Slava became very depressed because he was not able to find his son.

Slava, Olga, Esther, and I were all visiting in our kitchen as Esther was preparing a meal. I could see that Slava was very depressed. He told me that they were going back to Moscow in just a few days, and he had been unable to find his son. I could hear the pain in his voice as he spoke. The Lord spoke to me in His still, small voice to pray that Slava would find his son before he returned to Moscow. I told Slava that God knew where his son was, and that I wanted to pray that God would make it known to him before he returned to Moscow. Slava agreed with my request, and Olga interpreted for him as I prayed. I tried my best to let the Holy Spirit lead me as I prayed, and my prayer was very positive that Slava would find his son before he returned to Moscow. Since Olga was interpreting my prayer, it took longer than normal.

Just as I was finishing my prayer, the phone rang. God had been hearing my prayer and was answering even as I prayed. Esther answered the phone as I was saying my closing "Amen." Very quickly she called Slava and said, "Slava, here is your son!" I looked at Slava and his face went white. He got up from his chair, and it looked like his legs would hardly hold him as he walked to the phone. Esther handed it to him, and Slava started speaking in Russian to the person on the other end. It was his son. God had answered our prayer while I was praying! This was an absolute miracle. There was no way this could have happened on its own.

Slava's son was in prison in southern Florida where he had been for quite a long time. After he jumped the tour, he started selling drugs and was caught, arrested, tried, and given a prison sentence. Before the police arrested him, he threw his Russian passport away so that he would not have it on him if he was caught. He told his father he would be released from prison if the Russian government would let him back in the country. Since he did not have a Russian passport they refused to allow him to return. He added that he knew of no way of getting a Russian passport while in prison. He also informed his father that the Cubans that were in prison were treating him very badly. Slava's son had a major problem, and there seemed to be no way out.

When Slava stopped talking to his son, he was as shook up as he was before the phone call. His son had received permission to call his mother in Russia, and she gave him our phone number, knowing that Slava and Olga were with us. The son immediately called our number. This all took place as we were talking and praying with Slava. God heard our prayer and He was working as we prayed. Slava's desire to find his son was fulfilled. However, Slava was not happy about what he heard from his son, and he was still very sad and depressed. Then I said, "Slava, I want to pray again for your son. I will pray that your son will get out of prison and back to Moscow quickly." This time Slava quickly agreed and bowed his head as I prayed.

Three days later Esther and I drove Olga and Slava back to the airport in Chicago. They flew back to Moscow, and to their surprise, their son, who had been in prison in Florida, was waiting at the airport for them. I still don't know all the details of how he got there so quickly, but I do know that God answered our prayer and made it happen. Slava and his son both have become Christians. The son then went to work full-time in the same ministry that Olga works for. Also, I had the privilege of baptizing Olga while they were in America.

Many times in prayer God has given me faith that I would not have had on my own. I believe this was one of those cases when I had faith to boldly tell Slava that God knew where his son was, and that we should pray and ask God to show him where he was. The reason I had such faith was because I had heard the still, small voice of the Holy Spirit tell me to do this. This act not only helped Slava to believe, but it also blessed Olga, strengthening her faith and also the faith of Esther and me.

God saw us sitting at our kitchen table near Greentown, Indiana, and He could also see Slava's son sitting in prison in southern Florida at the same time. The amazing thing was how quickly the phone call came, just as I was finishing the prayer. God did answer prayer that day, but it was like a miracle to me that He answered it immediately as I was praying. This was just one multifaceted thing that happened to us in our Russian ministry, and there were many more to come that we did not know about but would see as the days, weeks, months, and years passed.

Ch. 35

THE LITTLE GIRL FROM THE LOGGING CAMP

Esther continued the huge task of sending shipments of supplies to Moscow. She worked long hours nearly every day filling boxes and doing all the paperwork required to ship them. Trip after trip was made to different locations, getting supplies to fill the containers. About every four months, a shipment left Kokomo headed for the Christians in Moscow. Esther followed up on most shipments by going to Moscow when they arrived to make sure things went well there. She was tired much of the time, but hundreds of thousands of dollars of supplies were sent to Russia as the result of her and her helpers' efforts.

In addition to this, the Kornilov family came to our home at least one weekend a month, for the two years they were here. We got to know and love the family very much; however, it did require extra work for us and especially for Esther. We also made many trips to Elkhart to help the Kornilovs in various ways, plus we made trips there just to visit them. Then God gave Esther an additional workload. She was at the Kokomo Rescue Mission so much that the board of directors and the mission staff got to know her very well. Esther and one of the mission staff named Bebe Jo Dorris became very close friends during that time (and still are to this day). Shortly after Esther started packing the supplies for Russia at the rescue mission, the mission board of directors asked her to be on the board of directors.

Esther and I knew this was going to be an additional workload for her, so we wondered if she should accept the position. As was our usual way of doing things, we prayed about it, expecting an answer from the Lord in His still, small voice. The Lord spoke and made it clear to us that this was of Him. As a result, Esther accepted the position. Nothing, however, slowed down in packing things for Russia or taking care of our responsibility to the Kornilovs. Esther just found additional time to be a member of the board of directors.

We also had five married children and several grandchildren that we wanted to spend time with whenever possible. We love them very much and they are a major part of our lives. Esther made time to have large family dinners and enjoy our children and grandchildren. We also had many overnight guests in our home during this time. This was additional work for Esther but God helped her to use her time wisely. We watched very little television, and I helped Esther every hour I could. It was amazing how much more we got accomplished compared too many people that we knew who spent hours every evening watching the tube.

Our lifestyle was centered on living and making a difference in our world for Jesus Christ. In doing this, it seemed as if God was blessing our very strength and health. Even though we worked long hours nearly every day and well into most evenings, we still had plenty of strength for the next day. Yes, we did get tired, and I might even say that we got very tired at times, but God continued to renew our strength. He had placed before us an open door to minister in Russia, and we were doing all we could to take advantage of what He had given us.

In REVELATION 3:8, the Lord said good things about the church of Philadelphia. He said, *"I know thy works: behold, I have set before thee an open door, and no man can shut it: for thou hast a little strength, and hast kept my word, and hast not denied my name."*

It seems that the Lord was pleased with the church of Philadelphia. They were doing the right things and the Lord gave them an open door to increase what they were doing for the Lord. In MATTHEW 25:15, Jesus told the story of the talents. The men had a responsibility to use the talents that were given to them so that their master could make more money. The two men that used their talents in the right way were rewarded.

They were not rewarded with money for their personal use, but rather were given more responsibility. You could say that their master gave them more responsibility for their faithfulness. This would amount to a greater workload. They could be trusted, so the master put more responsibility upon them. It seems that the Lord did this also for Esther when He put another open door before her of being involved on the rescue mission board, which created more of a workload.

When Esther was young, she learned responsibility. Not only did she learn responsibility, but she took responsibility. One example was when she started her first Sunday school in the logging camp deep in the forest of British Columbia located in western Canada. There were five or six children in the logging camp, and Esther decided they needed a Sunday school class. She knew very little about Sunday school as she had lived most of her life in the deep forest, miles from a church. She was able to get some used Sunday school books, and she used those to teach from. The children loved the class and were faithful in attending.

It may not sound unusual for Esther to take the responsibility for a Sunday school class in a logging camp until you find out that she was only eight years old at the time. She had turned her life over to the Lord and accepted Jesus as her Savior when she was about six. From the time that Esther was twelve years old, she was sent off to a boarding school, which was located about five hundred miles from her home. Esther traveled those five hundred miles by train at different times by herself when she was thirteen years old. It took two days each way for her to make the trip. She was home very little during the rest of her years in school, which included four years of Bible school. During those years she really learned responsibility.

As Esther continued to pack things for the Christians in Moscow, she spoke about Russia in many churches in our area and even in other states. With her speaking and her involvement in sending the shipments to Russia, she became very well-known in the Kokomo area. Soon the rescue mission board of directors asked her if they could put her name up to run for president of the board. If she was elected, this would be an added responsibility on top of what she was already doing. As we prayed about it, the Lord spoke to us in His still, small voice and said that she should accept this nomination. When the election came, she was elected as president of the board of directors of the Kokomo Rescue Mission.

This was a tremendous additional responsibility. Then to add to that responsibility, she was faced with a situation that greatly increased her workload as president of the board. The Kokomo Rescue Mission building was literally splitting in two. The foundation on each end of the old building was settling into the ground, while the center part of the foundation of the building was staying firm. This was causing the building to crack right through the center. Some of the water pipes were pulled apart as a result.

The city of Kokomo condemned the building but gave permission for the mission to continue to use it for three more years, after which the building had to be torn down. The Kokomo Rescue Mission needed to continue to use the condemned building to house and feed the men until a new building was completed. A new building would cost a few million dollars, and there was little money to fund this. This put more responsibility on Esther because she had to lead the board of directors as they decided what to do. Esther's borders of ministry just kept expanding, but we knew God was directing her to be involved in it all.

The board made the decision to build a new building, but there was not a suitable place to build it on the rescue mission's property. Since there was no space to build the building on the mission's property, they had to expand their borders, but there was no property for sale next to their existing property. There seemed to be a wall before them that they could not find a way over.

The board knew that God would provide, but they knew that they had to take steps toward this as well, so they set aside three different times of prayer and fasting for the board members, the staff, and the public. Many people came and prayed that God would provide a place to build the new building, and that He would provide the funds to build it.

Esther and her friend Bebe Jo Dorris and Bob Cox, the director of the mission, started speaking in churches and businesses in the area presenting the need for a new building. Delco Electronics, a division of General Motors, let Bebe and Esther speak to each department in the plant. The company gave their employees time off from their jobs so they could hear about the new building and the need for it. The employees were not forced to come to the meetings, but most did. There were several departments at Delco, and Esther and Bebe spoke in most of them. After the speaking was all finished, each department gave its employees a chance to donate to the new building, and a high percentage of them did. The Delco plant also gave a large gift for the building. This went on in many industries in the area.

Meanwhile the board was continuing to pray about property for the building, and before too long, a law firm that owned a house and parking lot right across the street from the Kokomo Rescue Mission gave the property to the mission to build their new building on. What an answer to prayer this was.

The new building was designed, and the quote to build came to about $2.5 million. Though not all the money came in at that particular time, a big amount was given, and many had pledged to give toward the building. Before long the day came to "turn over a bit of dirt" for the official groundbreaking; Bob Cox,

Esther, and a couple of contractors (who were donating time and materials) used little shovels to do this duty.

It was a great day of rejoicing when the building was finally built and ready to be dedicated to the Lord. The Kokomo Rescue Mission had a special ceremony with speeches from city and government officials as well as one from Esther. Box Cox, Esther, and the vice president took part in cutting the red ribbon for the dedication and opening of the new Kokomo Rescue Mission building. The local newspaper took pictures of the ribbon cutting and had a good article along with it. They showed pictures of the building too. The three-story brick building had a commercial kitchen from which to feed about two hundred people every day, a very large sleeping area for the men, classrooms, a beautiful chapel, and offices to be used to run the ministry. Thousands of people have been ministered to in that building since it was built.

It took a united effort to get the building erected, and it stands there today as a testimony of God using His people to make a difference in the lives of other people. Jesus Christ is being preached and taught as the only way to eternal life. The Word of God is being taught; some of the clients are coming to Christ, and their lives are changed for eternity.

I know God used that little eight-year old girl as she taught the five or six children in their Sunday school class at the logging camp. Then I believe God used her dedication and drive to get things done in many different places and with different ministries. God used her to pioneer the ministry of shipping $1.75 million worth of supplies to the Christians in Moscow. He also used her to help pioneer the first evangelical seminary in Moscow, and God used her to help get the new Kokomo Rescue Mission building funded and built.

Through all of this, many lives were touched and people saved, such as Olga from Moscow, who herself is now in full-time Christian work. Esther is very well known in the Kokomo area now. When she and I were married twenty-five years ago and she moved to Kokomo, Indiana, she was Bob McCauley's wife. Now I am Esther McCauley's husband. She is much better known now in my hometown than I am.

Was God finished with Esther after all of this? No, He would use her to pioneer the largest ministry that she had been involved with.

Ch. 36

The Little Russian Girl with Cancer

In July of 1995, right after Esther returned home from taking a team to Turkey, we received the shocking news that our friends Sasha and Galina Zdor's eight-year-old daughter Lena was diagnosed with cancer. Her father, a Russian Pentecostal pastor, had taken her for medical treatment in Russia, but the doctors said there was nothing they could do for her. They had given her very strong chemotherapy, but the Ewing's Sarcoma, a large mass on her lungs, ribs, and liver, had not responded to it, and the Russian hospitals didn't have resources or medical equipment for surgery.

Sasha and Galina contacted Linda Green, who ran an organization called Christian Medical Services, to see if they could help Lena. Immediately upon hearing from the Zdors, Linda contacted different hospitals, etc., and was able to get medical aid for Lena from Children's Hospital in Columbus, Ohio. Sasha and Galina then brought Lena to America and Linda took care of the details of getting her into Children's Hospital.

Late in July, Lena received a very extensive surgery at Children's Hospital, removing the tumor, part of one lung, a piece of her liver, as well as three of her ribs. They also inserted three artificial ribs made in a special way that could "grow" with Lena, to keep her chest in place.

After the surgery, Lena needed a place to live while she took chemo treatments. Linda Greene had several children from other countries living in her home, and she was not able to keep Lena because of the restrictions that had to be in place as precautionary measures to keep Lena healthy. As soon as we heard of the need, the Lord spoke to us in His still, small voice to offer our home to Lena and her parents.

Esther and I drove to Columbus, a four-hour drive, to talk with the doctor, nurses, etc., to find out how to care for Lena when she came to our home. A Christian doctor spent about two hours talking with us and her parents about

Lena (the hospital even provided a Russian interpreter to communicate with Sasha and Galina). He explained that we needed to wash our whole home and furniture with disinfectant, and we had to be very careful not to have sick people in our home; even a common cold could jeopardize her immune system. He also told us that Lena had a very serious cancer and they were going to be doing some experimental chemotherapy on her; they were unsure of her prognosis at this time, and all of us needed to be aware that Lena might not make it through this. He also reminded us that God was the author of healing and He was the One that could bring her through this cancer.

When we brought Lena home, Sasha and Galina came with us because they were going to be staying in the United States for a few weeks. It was a wonderful time of bonding for all of us; our children and grandchildren all came to meet the Zdors, and we had a delightful time together, even though the Zdors could speak very little English. Our granddaughter Tiffany, who was five at the time, went to Esther and said, "Grandma, how come Lena doesn't know how to talk!" because she could not understand her. We had many fun times while the family was here, but the time soon came when Sasha and Galina had to return to Russia to go on with their responsibilities and take care of their other four children.

Sasha had to give us guardianship of Lena to enable us to make emergency decisions and sign papers, etc., if necessary, and that was very difficult for him. Because of the language barrier, he was unable to understand the meaning of "guardianship," and he was afraid that we would keep Lena and never let her go back to Russia. After several days of discussion, Sasha phoned a former Russian friend who lived in New York to discuss this situation. The friend tried very hard to explain things, but still Sasha could not understand; he had heard so many horror stories of Americans who wanted Russian children!

Finally the friend drove all the way from New York and spent a whole day at our home explaining the necessity of what Sasha had to do and why. Sasha finally agreed to give us guardianship, and within a few hours we went to our family lawyer and got all the papers written up. We assured Sasha that as much as we loved Lena, she was his daughter, and we would make sure that she got back to Russia.

As a result of talking to the medical staff at the children's hospital, Sasha and Galina, as well as Esther and I, knew there was a good possibility that Lena would not survive. We were told that the Ewing's Sarcoma cancer is very aggressive and difficult to cure. There could be cancer cells in other parts of Lena's body, and if the chemo did not destroy them, she would die. If this happened, we would be faced with burying Lena in America.

This knowledge put a terrible strain upon Sasha and Galina. They had four children back in Russia that they needed to be with. One was a three-year-old that was crying every day, wanting her mother, and then they had a very ill child in America that they felt a great responsibility to. On top of that, Sasha was a pastor and had a responsibility to his congregation.

The painful decision to leave Lena was almost more than they could bear, but they knew they had to do it. Esther and I felt a great responsibility also, as we would be responsible for Lena in place of her parents. Our hearts and love went out to Sasha and Galina, and we wanted to do all we could to relieve their worries about their daughter's care.

Sasha and Galina had suffered so much in the past as a result of their Christian faith in a Communist country. Sasha had been forced to leave his city for a long time as the result of his preaching. This meant that Sasha and his beloved Galina had been separated for a long time as a result of Sasha preaching the Word of God. This seemed so tragic at the time and was very difficult for both of them. God, however, is able to take what Satan meant for evil and turn it around so that it will turn into a blessing. In Sasha and Galina's future, God was going to turn Sasha's persecution into a blessing, but they had no idea at the time what He was going to do for them.

Every third week, Esther would take Lena to Indianapolis to a pediatric oncologist, and they would check her and do blood work to see if she was well enough to have chemo. If she "passed" all her tests, the next week Esther and Lena would make the four-hour drive to the Columbus Children's Hospital, where Lena was first hydrated and then would have five sessions of chemo for five days. The day after her last session she would be hydrated again, and then they would return home.

The poor little girl was completely exhausted from the chemo and would sleep most of the way home. On one such trip, Esther stopped at a Cracker Barrel for some dinner. When she asked Lena what she wanted to eat, after much thought Lena said, "Chicken and noodles." The waitress informed Esther and Lena that they didn't have chicken and noodles that day (they only made it on

Monday!) and soon Lena had big tears running down her skinny white cheeks. She didn't have an appetite for anything else and didn't see anything else on the menu that she wanted.

Pretty soon the manager of the restaurant came up to them and said, "Is this the little girl who wants chicken and noodles?" When Lena nodded (she still spoke very little English) the manager said, "We don't have any today, but I will make some just for you." And he added, "I am the manager of all the East Cracker Barrels, and if she ever wants chicken and noodles, you just give them my name and tell them that they MUST make chicken and noodles for her!" And off he went to make a meal for this little bald-headed Russian girl.

Lena was exhausted when she got home. Esther would then lovingly hold Lena on her lap, and rock her until she was asleep. We made a special bed for her in our study so she would be close to our bedroom, but yet would have privacy. Many times when she was asleep in her bed, we would check on her. She looked so pale and still that we thought perhaps she was already with the Lord.

Although Esther spent most of the time taking care of Lena for the eight months she was with us, I was the one who took care of her "medical needs at home." For ten days after Lena's chemo treatments, she had to have shots to help bring her immune system back up, and I was the one who had to give them. We did the shots right after our dinner meal, and I would let her decide where she should get the shot. Her little legs were covered with black and blue marks from all the needles she had to have, as were her arms.

But each time I would ask her where she wanted the shot, she would point to a place and then she would say, "But let's pray first..." in her little Russian accent, so we would pray, and then she would change her mind as to where the shot would be until finally she decided, and I would give it to her. Never once did Lena cry while she had the shots or when she was in the hospital, though Esther said that she did cry when the dentist spent two hours trying to take out cement fillings from her teeth and replace them with proper fillings.

Some of you have heard the old African saying, "It takes a village to raise a child." We experienced the village coming together to share in the care of Lena. Many people helped in various ways, but I hesitate to write names, lest I miss someone. One family made chicken and noodles every week and brought a special homemade lemon and orange drink which Lena loved. Another friend took Lena shopping and out for lunch every couple of weeks. Friends with children Lena's age would take Lena to their home to play with their children; a neighbor took her to a hair dressing shop, bought her a wig, and then took her to Sears and had her picture taken. I could go on and on, but it would take a whole book to write all that was done for Lena during her time with us.

In December we were told that The Wish Foundation had chosen to send Lena and a friend to Disney World! We chose our granddaughter Amanda to go with us, since they were the same age and were also good friends. What a wonderful trip that was for all of us. We flew to Orlando where we were met by members of the foundation waiting for us at the airport. They rented a lovely car for us and put us up in a beautiful duplex on their property.

Many other children and their families were there, and the girls had a great time playing and enjoying all the facilities. And then of course, we had three days in Disney World. Never have I seen a happier child. Lena had her ninth birthday while we were there, and the highlight of the trip was when we got a phone call on her ninth birthday telling us that all Lena's tests came back saying that she was cancer-free at that time. What rejoicing!

Upon our return home from Florida, we began preparing to take Lena back to Russia. Lena had been given many toys, stuffed animals, and clothes, etc., and of course she wanted to take EVERYTHING back home–she would go through all her items and say, "This is for my baby sister, and this is for my older sister, and these are for my brothers." We knew that she could not take everything home, so she and Esther went through everything and decided what to give away and what to take–it was so encouraging to see this little nine-year-old girl choose to take things for members of her family and for friends and not many for herself.

Finally the day came for Lena and Esther to fly to Russia. It was a bittersweet day for me as I had come to love Lena as my own child, I wondered if I would ever see her this side of heaven again, but I knew that she was God's child and He would take care of her. I did see Lena again about four years later when Esther and I went to Russia, and it was a joyous reunion.

In 2007 Sasha and his whole family immigrated to Washington state. When George W. Bush was president, he gave special status to Christians who had been persecuted for their faith and allowed them to come to the United States. When Sasha heard about this, he remembered how he had suffered for preaching God's

Word. He and Galina had been to America when Lena had her operation, and they loved our country. They wondered if it was possible for them to get permission to come to America with their family. They would love to come if they could so they prayed about it, asking for God's will to be done.

Then Sasha went to the American Embassy to apply for immigration. Unbeknown to Sasha and Galina, the American Embassy had a list of Russians that had been persecuted for their faith. Sasha's name was on that list. When he started to tell the authorities his story, they interrupted him and said, "Sasha, we know your story; welcome to the United States," and with that he was given permission for him and his whole family, including his mother, to immigrate to America.

God knew about Sasha's persecution for preaching His Word. Satan meant the persecution for evil, but God turned it into good for Sasha and his family. This included little Lena (who now had grown into a beautiful young lady). As I was thinking about how our government knew nearly all the names of the Christians that suffered persecution under Communism, the Lord spoke to me in His still, small voice and said, "I also know every name and detail of those that suffered for being my servants, and I will greatly reward them."

What a joy it was for us to attend Lena's wedding in September of 2009 in Vancouver, Washington. My thoughts could not help but go back to when Lena was a little baldheaded girl with cancer and how we wondered if she would live. Now she was a beautiful bride with hair down to her shoulders, looking very healthy and so happy. Lena married a young Russian man whose family had also immigrated to America. How thankful we are that we followed the leading of the still, small voice of the Holy Spirit when He spoke to us about taking Lena into our home. She has enriched our lives!

Ch. 37

Project Hope and the Sewer

Early in 1997 Esther received a phone call from Phyllis Kilbourn, the director of Rainbows of Hope, which was a ministry to children living in crisis. It was also an arm of Worldwide Evangelization for Christ. Esther and I were at the time, mid-western representatives for WEC. An American man had been to Russia and found that many children were in prison in St. Petersburg. The man contacted Phyllis and told her about the children in prison. Soon after hearing this, she decided to send a team to check things out.

I got to know Phyllis when I was a pilot in Liberia, West Africa. Phyllis knew that Esther and I had been heavily involved in Russia for a long time, and she also knew that Esther spoke some Russian. As a result she called and asked Esther if she would take a team of college students to St. Petersburg and check out the situation of the children in prison. She wanted Esther to see if there was the possibility of starting a ministry to these children. Esther did not give Phyllis an answer right then, but said we would pray about it and call her back.

Esther and I went to prayer about what to do concerning Phyllis's request. We wanted and expected a word from God on whether or not she should go to St. Petersburg. Again, as we had heard so many times in the past, the still, small voice of the Holy Spirit spoke to us and said she should go. Neither of us had any idea how great an impact this event would have on our lives. We had been going hard for about five years in our humanitarian aid ministry to the Christians in Moscow and also in Esther's work on the Kokomo Rescue Mission board. Of course, I was still working as an engineer for General Motors. We had been very busy for years, but God was still not finished with us.

It was during this time that the Holy Spirit spoke to me in His still, small voice and gave me an invention that saved my company three million dollars the first year and a million each year after that for years to come. I know beyond any doubt that God gave me the knowledge on this invention. I was getting good raises and my salary was increasing as a result. Through all of the very busy times of packing for Russia, I was still prospering on my job, and God was greatly blessing me.

Yes, we had been very busy, but things were slowing down enough that we thought we could get back to a normal life. Nickolai and Marina and their children were getting along fine. Nickolai had extended his schooling to include getting his doctorate, so he was still in school. His children had all settled down to the routine of going to school in America. The new rescue mission building was built, and Esther's workload there had slowed down a lot. We had also finished shipping the fourteen shipments of aid to the Christians in Moscow, so that workload had diminished. Yes, maybe we could get back to a normal lifestyle. This, however, was not in God's plans for us!

Esther called Phyllis back and said that she would go to St. Petersburg, Russia, take and work with the team, and check out the situation of the children in prison and the possibility of starting a ministry to them. Phyllis herself also planned to go to Russia while the team was there.

A few weeks later in May 1997, Esther and her team flew to St. Petersburg, Russia. The city of six million people, was named after Peter the Great. The city's name was changed to Leningrad in the early years of Communism, but after the fall of Communism, the name was changed back to St. Petersburg. Shortly after arriving in St. Petersburg, the team was taken to the International Church building where they were to stay during their time in St. Petersburg. The pastor of the International Church was an American who helped establish the church, and he was the contact person in St. Petersburg for Esther and the team. There were some small rooms in the building that the team used as bedrooms. The living quarters were not fancy at all, but the team was thankful for them.

Esther and her team were settled into their rooms, and after they had a night's sleep, they started the preparations to go into one of the prisons for boys. It was then that they hit a big roadblock. They could not get permission to go into the prisons at that time. They did, however, start the paperwork and process to get permission, but they quickly saw that this was going to take time.

God had other plans, however, which included not only a ministry to children in prison but also to street children. Shortly after the team arrived in Russia, the *St. Petersburg Times*, an English Russian newspaper, came out with a front-page article about street children in that city. The article reported that thirty to eighty thousand children and youth lived in the streets of St. Petersburg. Above the article was a picture that was obviously taken on a very cold, windy, and snowy day in St. Petersburg.

In the center of the picture was a sickly and skinny-looking street boy. His clothes were not fit for the cold Russian winter, and he looked like he was very cold. The boy's eyes had the look of hopelessness, and his general physical condition said that he was cold, hungry, needing shelter, and had no hope of getting any of them. It seemed as if the boy was saying, "I need help and no one cares." The article also told of many children who were living in the sewers for shelter and warmth.

Esther saw the article and her heart was touched. She decided if they could not get into the prisons, they should check out the situation with the street children. The team then spread out over the city checking out the situation of the street children. It was not long before they saw that the article in the *St. Petersburg Times* was probably right. There were thousands of children living in crisis conditions in that large city.

The team divided into groups, and every afternoon each group went to a different metro site (subway entrance) where the children hung out, begging or stealing food. Each team gave them the Gospel as well as food, consisting of boiled eggs, bread, a piece of fruit, and a drink. At other times they gave sausage, bread, and yogurt. For many children, this was the only decent meal that they had each day.

Esther met a woman from Finland while she was there, named Helena. Helena came to St. Petersburg to see about starting a ministry to the street children. Almost from the very beginning of meeting each other, Esther and Helena became very close friends. The two women had very different backgrounds but also had some similarities. Helena grew up in Finland and learned to speak English as a second language. Esther grew up in western Canada and also learned English as her second language (her first language was Ukrainian). Esther was fifty-five years old at the time and Helena was about forty-five, so they were close in age. Both had a desire to make a difference in the street children's lives, and they both were willing to give of themselves to do it.

On a very cool, rainy day Helena, Esther and two other team members went to a metro site to feed the children. It was strange that they could not see any of them, but within a few steps of walking out of the metro entrance, they saw a little girl begging. The girl was about eight years old, wearing a very dirty and badly worn dress and a shaggy coat; she looked haggard, and from her general appearance, she looked underfed. Esther went to her, and after giving her some food, asked her where all the other children were. Usually the street children do not want to disclose where they live because they do not trust people, but the little girl must have been touched by Esther and Helena's compassion for her, and she said, "In the sewer."

Esther was shocked at her answer and asked if she would take them to the sewer, but the little girl declined, saying that she had to continue begging because she had to have a certain amount of money when she went home in the evening, or else her father would beat her and make her sleep outside. But just at that time a young street boy around nine years old came to them and said, "I'll take you to the sewer."

The little boy led the way, as Esther and her group, followed him through back streets to an area of abandoned buildings. Some of the buildings had roofs missing and almost all the windows were broken out. Many had entire sidewalls that had fallen in. There was also a lot of trash spread out among the broken-down buildings. It was unsafe to go into that area, but they continued to follow the little boy through all of this. Finally the little boy walked up to a manhole above a sewer and said, "They are down there."

Esther, Helena, and the two other team members, thanked the little boy for his help and then did something that very few people would do. They climbed down a ladder into the sickening stench of the sewer gas. At the bottom of the hole was a little room about eight feet square. As their eyes adjusted to the darkness, they could see that the floor was covered with a layer of raw sewage. Then they saw an extremely sad sight. About seven children ranging in ages from about six to ten years old were down in that sewer. They were sitting on some cardboard and boards above the sewage. The sight almost broke the hearts of the team. Never in their lives had they seen anything like it.

The sewer gas had to be hard on their little bodies. The children didn't have blankets to keep warm; they only had the heat from the sewage. They were sitting and sleeping on boards and cardboard that had been placed over sewer pipes and on stones in such a way as to make a platform, which was their bed. The platform was just a few inches above the raw sewage.

Helena and Esther could not help but think of the children in their homelands. They had clean beds with lovely blankets, bedspreads, and pillows, as well as stuffed toys. They also had loving parents to care for them and tuck them in at night. Here these children were having a sewer for a bedroom with no parents to care for them at all. The germs in the sewage just below their sleeping area put these children's very lives in danger.

The team had a challenge to keep out of the sewage themselves. Esther and Helena had some bread and boiled eggs with them, and they gave these to the children. The children quickly ate the eggs and bread. Esther and Helena then told them about Jesus Christ and His love for them. One girl, however, seemed very bitter when Esther and Helena mentioned love. The girl spoke back and said that no one had ever loved her and no one ever would. The girl was angry inside. She, no doubt, had been on her own for as long as she could remember, living in harsh conditions and surviving in any way she could. This girl was going to have to see love in action, or she would never believe that any person loved her or that God and Jesus Christ loved her.

After Esther was in the sewer for about twenty minutes, the sewer gas started getting to her, and she developed a very severe headache. She did not know how the children could live and sleep there without having the same thing happen to them. Possibly they had developed some tolerance to the gas so it didn't bother them. Esther knew the reason that they lived there was to get out of the bitter cold during the Russian winters.

Esther's and Helena's lives were permanently changed from the day they entered the sewer. Never again would they be the same after seeing what they saw that day. They had to do something about it, but what could they do? Both women returned back to the sewer or the metro sites many times with a backpack filled with food for the children. They got to know them by name and developed a love for each one of them.

One day as Esther was walking to the sewer, a black Mercedes car came right at her and almost rammed her into a concrete wall. The car stopped just short of smashing her body against the wall. This was no accident; the driver had purposely calculated just how far he could push Esther without killing her. During Esther's trips to Russia, she had grown used to seeing the black Mercedes autos in Moscow, and here one of the same types of cars had nearly killed her in St. Petersburg. From her past experience in Russia, she immediately knew that this was a Mafia car. They were about the only ones that drove the solid black Mercedes autos. The driver of the car told Esther to stay away from the street children. He said, "They are our children, and you stay away from them."

Before Esther went to St. Petersburg, we heard a report that the Mafia had killed one woman that had tried to help the street children. Now Esther was facing them for the same reason. A man in the car asked Esther why she was going to the street children. Esther replied that she was taking food to them. The man then said, "We will feed them." Esther looked inside their car and said, "I don't see any food in your car, and I have food in my backpack for them." The man in the car was very angry when he said, "Don't come back to the street children!"

Just before the car drove away, Esther said, "I won't come this way again." And she didn't; she found another way to get there—a way that they could not see her. After they left, Esther continued on her way to the sewer and ministered to the children. She knew her very life was in danger by continuing to go to the street children, but she also knew that God loved them and wanted to use her to make a difference in their lives.

The Mafia used the street children for their own needs. Many pedophiles came to Russia, and organized crime would furnish them with young boys or girls. The pedophiles would pay a lot of money to get a child to satisfy their perverted sexual desires while they were there. The Mafia would also use the street children in different ways to help them in their crime. As a result of this, they did not want Esther or anyone else interfering with what they were doing or how they were using some of the children.

Esther and her team continued taking food and sharing the Gospel for the remainder of the six weeks she was there. Esther made friends with a boy named Kalill. He was about ten years old and lived on the streets and slept in the sewer when necessary. Kalill came daily for food, and Esther got to know him well. One day when Esther went to the metro site, Kalill was not there, and none of the other children knew where he was. Kalill did not come back all that week.

A few days later as Esther was getting ready to go to the sewer, she kept thinking about a child's hooded sweatshirt that she had brought with her. She just could not get this off of her mind. The Lord was speaking to her in His still, small voice to take the hooded sweatshirt with her, but it did not make any sense to Esther. It was now July and the weather was very warm that day, so she couldn't figure out why she should take the hooded sweatshirt, but she decided to take it anyway. Just as she was about to leave her room, she took the shirt and put it in her backpack. As she was closing the door to her room, a tube of first aid cream and some gauze bandages fell off of a shelf onto the floor. This seemed kind of unusual, so Esther grabbed them and put them in her backpack as well.

As Esther got near the area of the sewer, she saw Kalill sitting on the sidewalk curb all bent over as if he was in pain. As she got close to him, she could hear him crying out in pain and rocking back and forth, holding a rag over his head. Esther went over to him and said, "Kalill, what is the matter?" Then Esther saw his head. All of his hair had been shaved off and he had a long, deep cut across the top of his head. Esther looked at it and saw maggots in the cut. It was very infected.

As Esther talked to Kalill, she found out that the police had arrested him for something. They had taken him to jail and shaved off his hair. This was the customary thing that was done if the police arrested a street child. They did this because nearly all of them had lice. Someone had hit Kalill very hard on the top of his head with a solid object that cut him deeply. Flies had laid eggs in the cut, and now maggots were eating Kalill's infected flesh. The sun was very hot that day, and as it shone down on Kalill's shaved and infected head, the heat made his condition feel even worse.

Esther immediately knew why she had felt led to bring the hooded sweatshirt and why the first aid cream and bandages fell off the shelf. She sat down on the sidewalk beside Kalill and, as carefully as she could, she dug the maggots out of his infected flesh. Esther always carried "Wet Ones" with her, so she got those out and started cleaning Kalill's wound. The Wet Ones had some alcohol in them that helped kill the germs and clean the wound. Then she applied the first aid cream and the bandages to the wound. After that, she had Kalill put on the sweatshirt and pull it over his head. This protected his head from the sun and was also an added protection against flies and dirt getting into the wound.

Kalill was very thankful for Esther's tender love to him. He had probably never had that before in his life. Through the following weeks, Esther did follow-up on her first aid treatment to Kalill and his wound healed nicely. This was the start of a love that Kalill would have for Esther for years to come.

Phyllis Kilbourn came to Russia while Esther was there and held seminars teaching how to start a ministry to street children and children living in crisis conditions. The pastor of the International Church and other people that were interested in starting a ministry to the street children were involved in the meetings. One of these was the man who had originally spoken to Phyllis Kilbourn; he was back in St. Petersburg and was very involved in starting a ministry to the street children.

After much discussion, the group decided to establish a ministry to the street children called "Project Hope." The term Project Hope was decided upon because they wanted the ministry to give hope to the hopeless children living in crisis conditions in St. Petersburg, Russia. A Russian woman named Vera Zhuravleva, who was a member and employee of the International Church, had all of the qualifications to be the director for the new ministry of Project Hope, so they asked Vera to become the director of the ministry. After praying about it, Vera and her husband Sasha felt that this was of the Lord, so the ministry was established, but they had no money and no building. They only had the streets to minister from.

Esther was nearly heartbroken when she returned to America. She felt that they had only put a bandage on a very large sore, and what they did was only temporary. They needed something permanent. Soon after Esther returned home, she shared her concern for the street children in Russia with a close friend named Linda Hewitt. Linda asked Esther what she thought should be done, and how could it be done.

Esther, having worked with the Kokomo Rescue Mission for years, thought about a rescue mission type of ministry. She said they needed a place to feed, clothe, give medical treatment to the children, and teach them the Word of God, but it seemed like an impossible dream because it would take a lot of money. Linda then said, "If you can raise ten thousand dollars, Ed and I will match the ten thousand dollars, and you will have some money to start it." Linda's offer encouraged Esther, but she felt there was no way she could raise the ten thousand dollars. God could raise it, however, so it was up to Him to do it.

Esther shared this with our pastor, and he said he would give her five minutes to speak the next Sunday morning. The following Sunday they would take up a collection for Project Hope. Esther and I worked hard on a five-minute speech; five minutes is not very long, but we were determined to put as much as we could into that allotted time. We prayed about it and felt that God led us. We typed it all out, and Esther went through it so many times that she almost had it memorized. Esther gave her five-minute speech almost exactly as we had written it out. It came from her heart, and people could feel her compassion as she gave it.

The following Sunday morning came, and I went to our church. Esther was in Pennsylvania speaking that morning, but she was wondering how much money would come in from our church for Project Hope. Well, after the service, the money was counted and our pastor told me that eleven thousand dollars had been given for Project Hope. I could hardly believe it. I called Esther and told her that we had eleven thousand dollars and she was very excited about this. Then the mission board decided that they had some extra money, and they added four thousand dollars to make the total fifteen thousand dollars.

I was elated, to say the least. After Esther returned to Indiana, she and Linda met. Linda asked Esther if she had gotten ten thousand dollars yet. Esther replied, "Yes, in fact we have fifteen thousand dollars." Linda said, "Then Ed and I will match the fifteen thousand dollars." Within less than a month after Esther returned home from Russia, we had thirty thousand dollars to start a ministry to the street children in St. Petersburg, Russia.

In the meantime, Helena had continued to minister to the street children in St. Petersburg. She was working long hours in the street with little rest, living very poorly herself. In addition, she was using a lot of her own money to buy and take food to the children when she went out. As time went on, she was ministering to many children in the streets, but had no building or place to take them. Most of the time she just had an open area in a parking lot or on the street in some out-of-the-way area to feed the children and have a Bible study with them.

Helena really wanted a room someplace where she could meet with the children and feed and teach them. She thought about a church that was in the area where she was meeting the street children. The church building was very large and quite beautiful. There were very few like it in all of St. Petersburg. We had heard that the church was built with money that came from churches in America.

Helena went to the pastor of this church and asked him if she could use a Sunday school classroom through the week to minister to the street children. She said they would not use it on Sundays. The pastor told Helena that he did not want street children in his church because they would disgrace it with their presence. He flatly turned down her request. Helena was devastated by his answer and his attitude toward the street children.

After Esther received the thirty thousand dollars, she sent it to WEC Mission, and they wired it to St. Petersburg, Russia. In December of 1997, the Project Hope staff looked for a place that they could rent for their new ministry. They found two adjoining apartments that looked very suitable for what they needed.

They could use the two apartments to have a feeding program, a place where they could minister to the children's physical needs, and also rooms that they could use to teach the children Bible lessons and school lessons. The rent was about four hundred dollars a month, which was reasonable at that time, so they signed a six-month rental contract for the apartments. The place was small but it was a beginning, and Project Hope was officially on its way.

During this time, the pastor from the church that I spoke about previously found out that there was a forty thousand-dollar grant available from Finland to be used for a ministry to street children in Russia. The terms of the grant were that the money had to go to an existing ministry, and it had to be spent by December 31, 1997. The pastor knew that Helena was now involved in an existing ministry to the street children. He contacted her and said, "I can get forty thousand dollars from Finland, but it has to be used for an existing ministry to street children. If you will say that I am involved with you in your ministry, I will get the money and will split it with your ministry."

This meant that he was going to keep twenty thousand dollars for himself. Helena was very upset with the dishonesty of this pastor and told all of us what had happened. We all said that this man was not with us and, even for the whole forty thousand dollars, we would not lie and say he was. Helena, being from Finland, told the people there about our existing ministry, and shortly before the end of 1997, we received the full forty thousand dollars for Project Hope.

This meant that we had a total of seventy thousand dollars at the very beginning of Project Hope to start the ministry. With that money we paid the rent on the building well in advance. We purchased a cooking stove, a refrigerator, a washer and dryer, some computers, and had money to purchase a lot of food for the children. Vera registered the ministry with the Russian government, and Project Hope was well on its way. Project Hope became the very first registered ministry to street children in St. Petersburg, Russia.

Today the Russians say, "Project Hope started when Esther and Helena went into the sewer."

Ch. 38

HARSH TREATMENT BECOMES BLESSING

The Project Hope Center became the center of activity for feeding and ministering to street children. Sandwiches and boiled eggs were made in the center to be carried into the streets to feed the street children. Many very fine and dedicated young people came from Finland, Russia, and other countries to be a part of Project Hope's ministry. Most of the street children were very fearful of coming to the center for food, but they would gladly take it from the teams as they went into the streets.

The street children were, in general, afraid of the police because most of them had been involved in stealing food items from the sidewalk vendors. As a result they did not trust anyone very quickly, including the Project Hope workers. Sometimes it took weeks for the Project Hope workers to gain the trust of the street children before they would come to the center for food, clothing, bathing, and the Bible lessons.

After the Center had been open for about three months, many street children were coming regularly. Most of these children had not had a bath in months and maybe in a few years. Many of them slept in the sewers, and the sewer gas had saturated their clothes so much that their odor was almost nauseating. Usually they had sores on their skin, their hair was full of lice, and their clothes were filthy. Many times these children looked very tough for their age, due to their harsh living conditions. As Christians, it was easy to see that they were hurting children in need of much love and care. Not everyone was Christian, however, and that fact brought about our very first opposition after Project Hope was started.

Some of the people that lived near the Center saw the street children in their area and did not like it. They contacted the police and government officials of the area, including the person who owned the apartments that Project Hope rented. The people demanded that Project Hope be shut down. There was so much outcry against the street children being in their area that the owner of the apartments said Project Hope would have to leave after their six-month contract was finished, which was on the last day of June 1998. The police backed him in his decision.

The staff was devastated by the actions of the owner of the apartments, the police, and the neighbors. None of these people seemed to care about the hurting children. The lack of love and compassion for the children seemed harsh and unfair to the Christian staff. The hard fact was, their attitude in this was a reality. The staff of Project Hope had to be out of the center within about two months, and they had no place to go.

Esther arrived in Russia in May of 1998, which was shortly after the staff was told that they had to be out of their center by the end of June. The staff and Esther had to find a new location for the center, but it had to be located in an area where they would not have opposition from the neighbors. It also had to be a place they could afford. They knew this was going to be very difficult to find, and after praying and committing it into God's hands, they started to look for a new location.

The pastor of the International Church knew the city well and drove Esther and Vera all over the area looking for a suitable building to rent or purchase, but they could find nothing. Most of the buildings that could be purchased were in deplorable condition, and they wanted from half a million to a million dollars for them. Then it would take about a quarter to a half a million dollars to rebuild the buildings. Purchasing a building was totally out of the question. For weeks the staff continued to look, but they just could not find a place.

Satan seemed to have put a tremendous obstacle for getting a suitable place to minister from, and the Project Hope staff knew no way around it. God never has and never will be outsmarted by Satan. If Satan tries to stop God's plans with an obstacle, God has a way around Satan. Many times, things end up even better than they might have originally been when God moves to foil what Satan is trying to do. Our Lord has a way of turning what Satan meant for evil into good. The loss of our two apartments was one of those times when Satan may have tried to stop Project Hope's ministry to the street children, but the end result was going to be better than it was in the beginning.

Even in the midst of our troubles, I still had the knowledge in the back of my mind that God had told us in His still, small voice to start this ministry. It was a deep comfort to both Esther and I. We knew God was in it, and He was going to do whatever He wanted to make the ministry a success.

When we started Project Hope, we did not know it, but God had also led a group of young missionaries from Youth With A Mission (YWAM) to start a ministry to street children as well. They called this ministry "New Life." The leaders of New Life were Ricardo and Rachel Cyrino. Ricardo was from Brazil, South America, and his wife, Rachel, was from England. Both were dedicated Christians that had the anointing of God upon them. Through working with the street children, both Project Hope and New Life got to know each other, and Ricardo and Rachel became friends with Vera and her husband Sasha, and also with Esther and Helena.

Project Hope had to move out of their building on the last day of June 1998. Not one day of ministry to the street children was lost, however, because Ricardo and Rachel asked the Project Hope staff to bring their street children and join them in a month-long summer camp in the forest, starting on the first of July. On that day, New Life and Project Hope gathered up all of their street children, and they traveled about one hundred miles north of the city into the deep Russian forest where they camped for a month. This was not a simple thing though, because the staff had to provide everything for the children-from toothbrushes to sleeping bags! The children had none of their own possessions.

The street children were elated with this trip. They slept in clean tents, had clean clothes, and enjoyed good food for the month. They were able to swim daily in a beautiful lake and live among the very high pine, fir, and spruce trees. They ate food cooked on a homemade stove and from a campfire. They were not breathing the sewer gas, but rather the clean air scented with the smell of evergreen trees. They were loved and mentored by Christians and played games to their hearts' delight. Many of them made a life-changing decision for Jesus Christ during this time.

Through the month, the staff of both missions and also the street children got to know each other well. As a result, there was a kinship formed between Project Hope and New Life personnel. God was forming a bond that would continue after the month of July; He was turning Satan's opposition against Project Hope into something good. God's plan was forming, and it looked beautiful. After the summer camp was finished, Project Hope and New Life joined forces and became one large ministry with a very large staff committed to making a difference in the lives of children living in crisis in St. Petersburg, Russia. Project Hope then moved their ministry to the New Life Center. Since Project Hope was already registered with the government as a Russian ministry to street children, we decided to continue to call the new partnership Project Hope and Vera was to continue to be the Russian director.

Satan brought opposition against Project Hope at their original center. The hatred for the street children, rather than compassion for them, was a fruit of the flesh and of Satan. Satan had his hand in the opposition, and God turned it against him. In the end, Project Hope was much stronger than it was in the beginning. It could meet the physical and spiritual needs of many more children much better as a larger ministry than it could have with two smaller ones. God simply used the opposition, turning the tide against Satan, and brought about a much better ministry to meet His goals for the street children.

Ch. 39

RETIRE AND GO TO RUSSIA

At the same time that God was bringing New Life and Project Hope together in a partnership, He spoke to me as I was praying and said in His still, small voice, "After the project you are working on is finished, retire and go to Russia."

At that time I was a senior project engineer working on the 2000-model year Chevy and GMC radios. My area of responsibility was the plastic molded parts. When the Lord gave me those words, I was in the final stages of getting all of the molds sampled and qualified for production, which would start in August 1998. My part of the project had to be finished by July 1; so after the Lord spoke to me, I knew that I should retire shortly after that.

I planned to work longer so I would lose some money each month by retiring that summer. I had also learned a long time before this to simply obey God when He spoke to me in the still, small voice of the Holy Spirit. I still had three weeks of vacation left, which meant I could leave my job three weeks before my retirement date, so I told my supervisor that I wanted to retire on August 1, and he agreed. This would allow me to leave at the end of the first week in July, which would be right after I finished my 2000-model year project and would be in line with what the Lord told me. Both Esther and I felt good about this, even though I would lose some retirement money each month as a result.

When my retirement date came, my department had a big party for me. I received many nice letters and comments about my job performance, my abilities, and my ethics. My family also had a retirement party for me, and it was wonderful as friends and family came to visit and congratulate me. Throughout the day, many of our friends asked us if we were going to go to Florida and enjoy ourselves, or were we going to just travel and have fun. When this subject came up, we told our friends that we were not retiring to just go out and have fun but rather were headed for Russia to work with street children. Some of our friends may have wondered about us going to

Russia at our age, but we knew God had directed us to go there, and we planned to do all we could to obey Him.

Shortly after I retired, we made a quick trip to western Canada to visit Esther's elderly mother before we left the country. My brother, Jim McCauley, and his wife, Mary, said they would take care of our home while we were gone, so that took a big concern off of our minds. We had to get our visas and tickets and do all the things that needed to be done in order to leave our home for several months. We knew we would miss our five children, their spouses, and our grandchildren very much, but we needed to obey our God and go to work full-time in St. Petersburg, Russia.

We had been to Russia before and knew we would be living in harsh and cold conditions, so we had to pack clothes for very cold weather, and even some food items that we wanted but could not obtain there. We also knew that it was hard to get medical supplies there, so we packed antibiotics and other medicines that we thought we might need for any sickness we might face. Also knowing that we would be around a lot of children with lice, we took some "Lice Kits" with us to treat ourselves if needed. Most of the people that worked with the street children did catch lice from time to time, so we figured we would also. With our bags packed and ready to go, we said good-by to our family, went to the airport, and flew out on our way to Russia.

There are many times in life when we cannot see the end result of a decision or event until years later. God knows the end and the beginning of all events for all time. He knows what will happen in years to come as well as He knows what has happened in the past. It is sort of like this. After I see a movie, I know what happened in it from the beginning to the end. If I see the same movie again, I know what is coming because I have already seen it. It is the same way with God, because He can see the future just as He sees the past. God knew what would happen to me if I stayed on my job and retired at a later date. I felt that I lost a fair amount of money by retiring early, but now I know this was not the case at all.

I worked and retired under General Motors. If I had stayed for a longer period of time, I probably would have retired under a completely different company. General Motors spun off the division I was working for into another division, and they became a separate company. Six years after I retired, that company went bankrupt, and their employees now are very concerned about what is going to happen with their retirement and insurance. There is a good chance that they will lose some of their retirement income and much of their insurance. I could have been one of these employees if I had stayed on my job to get a better retirement. Today I am very happy that I obeyed the still, small voice of the Holy Spirit and retired under General Motors and not under the company that went bankrupt. I thank God for this!

Ch. 40

A Jungle Ride and Impassable Objects

Can lessons that God taught us in one traumatic episode in our life be remembered and used when we face another situation? I believe the answer is yes. When David was going to face the giant, he said, "God delivered me from the paw of the bear and the mouth of the lion, and He can deliver me from this uncircumcised Philistine." He had faced two very traumatic situations where he could have been killed, and he remembered how God delivered him from both of them. This gave him faith to face the giant.

I have faced traumatic events in my life and have learned that God is able to deliver us from situations where there is no way in the natural to overcome them. Can lessons learned on a long jungle ride on motorbike help a person when they face a traumatic situation in St. Petersburg, Russia? Yes, they did for me. They helped me to know that God can deliver us when it is impossible to be delivered.

One day when I was in West Africa, I made a very long trip through the jungle to get back to my mission station. I had not seen my wife or my children, Tony and Tanya, for about a month. I was away from them because I had severely damaged the airplane in a jungle airstrip, and my brother and I were rebuilding it at my brother's mission station. This story is told in the chapter "A Plane Crash and a New Bible School." We had worked on the plane for about a month doing the needed repairs, but one of the struts was badly bent and I needed to replace it. I had an extra strut at my mission station and needed to get back there to get it. Since I had been away from my family for so long, I was really looking forward to seeing my wife and children while I was there.

Weeks before this, I had flown my son Tony and his motorbike to my brother's station so that Tony and his cousin Mark could spend some time together. Mark was about the same age as Tony and also had a motorbike. The two boys had a good time together doing different things in the jungle, especially exploring the different trails on their bikes. I had taken Tony back to our mission station on one of my flights but did not have room to take his motorbike back because I had too much cargo on the plane. As a result, his 125 cc Yamaha motorbike was still at my brother's station. I was going to use that motorbike now to get back to my mission station.

I have found in life that we can run into obstacles that we never planned on or even thought about. This was going to be one of those times. I left my brother's station after breakfast that morning and headed down a combination of a jungle road and a jungle trail. I had flown over this area many times, so I knew that this trail and road wound through the jungle in the general direction of my mission station. I felt confident that I could get back to my home using it, even though I could not see the trail very well when I was flying because it was covered over in many areas by high trees.

I knew my brother's mission station was about one hundred miles from my home in a straight line, but the jungle trail had so many curves that it could be as much as one hundred and fifty miles back home using the trail. I wanted very much to get back home before nightfall because it is very dangerous to be out in the jungle alone during the night.

When I started out that morning, I was riding on a very rough, narrow road and could not make very good time. I went though many villages, and the little children would hear the sound of the motorbike coming, so they would be watching for me as I rode by. They were excited to see me on the motorbike. I would wave at them, and they would smile and wave back at me.

I felt sorry for them because, as is usual in the villages, their little tummies were bloated out severely, which was a sign that they were malnourished and filled with worms, which is very common. In addition, their belly buttons were almost always pushed out to about the size of an orange due to improper care in cutting their umbilical cords when they were born. Even with that, the children were lovable and I enjoyed seeing them as I rode by.

After about ten miles, the jungle road turned into a jungle trail. It was very rough and almost like an obstacle course for a motorbike with all the hills, rocks, and tree roots, etc., to ride over. It was sure giving Tony's little motorbike a workout, but I needed to keep riding as hard as I could in hopes of making it home that night. In one area the trail was fairly smooth, so I speeded up and then came to a hill, which was about fifty feet high. I continued at that speed as I rode up the hill. This was a mistake since I could not see what was on the other side. As I came over the top of the hill, I saw the whole back side of it had either washed away or slid away to my left side. I quickly applied both my front and back brakes, but it was too late. I could not stop in time, and my bike slid out from under me and to my left.

I fell half on the bike and half on the ground, and both my bike and I slid down the steep slope clear to the bottom. I felt no pain when I fell, but shortly after I stopped sliding I saw that I was bleeding badly from the palm of my left hand. The cut was very deep and blood was gushing out profusely; I knew I could bleed to death if I did not get it stopped quickly. I could also get so weak that I could not travel on. I was miles away from any kind of medical help, so I knew God had to help me get it stopped. At first I just did not know how to do this however.

Then the Lord spoke to me in His still, small voice and reminded me of a big red handkerchief in my pocket that would make a good bandage. I pulled it out with my right hand and folded it in such a way as to give it the most length. Then I used my right hand and my teeth and tied it very tightly with the knot in the palm of my hand covering the cut. I held the knot in place with my left hand fingers and thumb. The knot turned red with my blood, but the flow finally stopped as I squeezed the knot as tightly as I could. Then I had to continue to squeeze the knot to keep it stopped. This was very difficult but it did work.

After stopping the blood flow, I checked to make sure I was not hurt anywhere else. I was skinned up some and felt like I had a few bruises, but otherwise I was in pretty good shape. Next, I checked out the bike to see what kind of damage I had done to it. I was pleased to see that it had fared better than I had. It had a few scratches on it, but other than that it was fine. Using my right hand, I lifted the bike back on its wheels and pushed the starter button.

It fired up immediately, and since I was already at the bottom of the hill, I only had to get the bike back on the trail and take off again. This time, however, it was much harder to ride my bike because I could only use my right hand to control it. I could not let up holding the knot with my left hand or the blood would start flowing again, so there was no way I could use it to help me control the bike as I rode on the rough trail. The throttle and clutch were both on my right handlebar and my gearshift was a foot control, so I did not have to use my left hand to ride the bike. If I had hurt my right hand, it would have been nearly impossible to ride the bike because I would not have been able to use the throttle or clutch. I was not happy about hurting my hand, but I was thankful that it was my left and not my right.

Controlling the bike with only one hand on the rough and hilly terrain was very difficult. After about an hour of the one-handed driving, I was very tired and not making much time. Finally I laid my left hand down on top of the left handle bar to help me control the bike. I continued to grip the knot, however, but the small amount of additional control I got from having my left hand lying on the handlebar helped me a lot.

Soon I got back into a routine and started feeling somewhat comfortable at it, and once again I was making fairly good time. Then I came around a curve in the trail and over a little hill and there in front of me, to my surprise, was a raging river. I had no time to stop and without even thinking about it, I laid the bike on its left side, and again the bike and I slid down the slope toward the river. This time, however, sliding with the bike was not as bad because I had purposely laid it down in a controlled manner. I was able to slide with it in such a way that I was not hurt at all. The bike and I stopped within a few feet of plunging into the river.

I got back on my feet and sat the bike on the wheels with the kickstand down. Then I stood there in the deep jungle looking at the obstacle in front of me. Evidently a jungle storm had poured tons of water somewhere upstream from where I was, causing the river to rage.

Since the trail went right into the river, my guess was that a person could cross it on foot when it was at its normal level. Walking through a river is a very common practice in Africa. My bike could go through about twenty inches of water with no problem; however, although the river was only about sixty feet wide, it was flowing at a great speed and was probably over my head in depth. It would be very dangerous to even try to swim across it. About one hundred feet to the right of where I was standing, a very tall tree had fallen down across the river. The roots and base of the tree were on one side of the river and the top on the other.

I looked at this tree for a while trying to see if I could figure out a way that I and my bike could get across the river on that tree. Finally I thought to myself, "No, if I fell off, both the bike and I could be gone. No, I would not take a chance on that." Praying, I said, "God, how can I get across this river?" There was just no way for me to cross this obstacle, but God could see far beyond what I could! I suddenly found myself in a terrible predicament. An impassable obstacle was in front of me. I was in the very high and dense jungle. I had a very serious cut in my hand. On top of that, I could see no way that I could continue on my trip.

As I was looking and praying, suddenly some African men showed up on the other side of the river. They saw me and crossed over to my side on the tree that I was looking at. I had no idea what tribe they were from, but all of them seemed very friendly. They quickly saw my predicament and offered to help me. They could only speak a few words of English, but it was enough that I could understand them. They told me that there was a train bridge that went over the river, and they could take me to it.

This sounded good to me! The men started walking on a very small trail through the jungle. I pushed my bike and walked with them. We walked for about a mile and then came to a very high railroad bridge that was used by an iron ore mine. The embankment up to the bridge was so steep and high that I could not push the motorbike up by myself, so the Africans helped me. They said we could cross the river walking on the railroad ties.

When I saw that the bridge was at least a quarter of a mile long, I became very concerned about the possibility of a train coming along while we were on the bridge. This would especially be true with me pushing a motorbike between the railroad tracks. My question was, "Could a person get out of its way and not get run over?" I looked the bridge over very closely and saw that there was enough room on the outside of the rails to lay a bike down on the ties and to also lay oneself down and not get hit by the train. This gave me some peace of mind, so I decided to cross the bridge with the Africans. They led the way and I followed, walking as fast as I could to keep up with them as I pushed my bike.

As we walked over the river, I had to push my bike between the rails and over the railroad ties. They were so rough that it was hard to push the bike. We finally made it across the river but were still on a high embankment of dirt, which supported the railroad ties. Outside of the ties was about a foot of level ground and then a very steep embankment, which went down about sixty feet to the original ground level.

When we got to the embankment on the other side of the river, I found it was easier to push my bike on the one foot of level ground rather than on the railroad ties. This worked quite well for a little way, but then suddenly the wheels slipped in the loose dirt, and the bike started sliding backward down the embankment. I held on with all of my might, even using my hurt hand, and I was able to stop the bike from sliding farther down the bank. I was almost lying flat on the side of the embankment when I finally got it stopped. I kept holding and pulling on it until I got it back up to the level area.

The Africans were walking so fast ahead of me that I don't think they even saw what happened. After a lot of effort, I got the bike back on its wheels and started pushing it again on the narrow, level area beside the railroad ties. Finally we got to a place where I could push the bike down a gradual slope from the railroad bridge and back to the trail.

I thanked the Africans for helping me and then got on the bike and pushed the starter button. The motor would turn over but would not start. This was unusual because this bike would normally start instantly. Tony had always kept it running perfectly, so starting was no problem. I kept trying until the battery was almost dead, but it would not even fire. I knew the bike well but just could not figure out why it would not start. I was starting to think that I would have to stay all night with these Africans and possibly start walking the rest of the way the next day without the bike. It would probably take me three days to get the rest of the way home if I walked very quickly. I did not like that possibility at all.

When I was at my wits end not knowing what to do to start the motor, God used the most unusual man to help me get the bike started. An old man was with the group that had led me to the railroad bridge. He wore only a loincloth as a covering and looked very wrinkled and feeble. This old man spoke to me and pointed at the back of my bike. I looked where he was pointing and I saw that my exhaust tailpipe was plugged up with dirt.

I immediately knew what had happened. When I nearly lost my bike as it slid down the embankment backward, my tailpipe had scooped up dirt and was filled solid. This kept my engine from starting. I was extremely surprised that this old man, who had probably never in his life worked on a motor, saw the reason that my bike would not start. I believe God spoke to him in His still, small voice and showed him my problem. I don't know why God spoke to him to show me the problem, but He did.

I very sincerely thanked him, found a stick, and dug the dirt out of the exhaust tailpipe. I got on the bike, pushed the starter button, and it fired right up. After thanking them, I rode off, and as I left I kept thinking about the old man in the loincloth and how God had used him, and also how He had used the men to help me get over the raging river. Without them I never would have found a way to cross the river. God can use anyone or anything to get what He wants to bless his children, as He did for me that day.

After crossing the river, I drove on for many more miles through the deep jungle. The farther I went, the better my left hand felt, and I was able to start making good time again because I was able to control the bike more easily, using my left hand as I went around the sharp turns and over the hills, etc. The jungle trail led to a road near my home, and that evening I was back with my wife and children. My ride had been long and hard, but I also saw God deliver me from two things that day, and I praise Him for it. I have never forgotten the lesson I experienced that day as God made a way around an impassable river for me. Remembering how God delivered me from one situation is very precious when facing another obstacle that there seems to be no way around.

Shortly after we started our partnership with New Life and Project Hope, we faced what seemed like two impassable obstacles. The Salvation Army in St. Petersburg let Ricardo and Rachel use their unfinished basement for their New Life Center. Ricardo and Rachel did not have to pay rent for the area but they did have to renovate it into usable space. They, and about ten of their street children, worked hard renovating it for their feeding and teaching center. It was rather dreary in appearance, but it was space out of the Russian cold where street children could come to be fed and taught. For a child who has a sewer for a bedroom, a dreary looking, but clean and warm basement is like a palace. Just finding any place in the center of the city of St. Petersburg to feed street children was very difficult, so we were glad to have this place.

Not long after New Life and Project Hope formed a partnership, we encountered our first obstacle. The Russian Board of Health said that our facility was not fit to feed the children in. Then the police accused us of harboring criminals. The police and the board of health gave us a list of regulations that were so strict that we could see no way we could continue ministering to the children. As I looked at these regulations, I thought, "Thousands of children are living in sewers and abandoned buildings; very few are doing anything about it, and they are saying that we have to have perfect conditions to feed these children." I just could not understand their reasoning.

The police said that some of the children or youth that we were feeding might be criminals. Most of these children that lived in the streets had nothing to eat and did steal items of food from the street vendors, so I guess that made them criminals. The police said that before we could feed any child, we had to have complete background records on them. This meant that we would have to have hundreds of background records and spend countless hours investigating each child before we could feed them.

The board of health also said that we had to have what would be equivalent to a commercial kitchen to feed the children, and it would have to pass their inspection before we could use it. In addition to all this, Vera, our Russian director of Project Hope, was ordered to report to the police, and there was the possibility that she could be arrested. The combination of the requirements from the board of health and the police seemed like an impassible obstacle ahead of us.

On a cold and damp day in November of 1998, the newly formed Project Hope staff was going to meet to discuss what to do concerning the problems facing us. Before Esther and I left our apartment that morning, we had a very sincere prayer asking God for His leading in the meeting that we were going to attend and for His protection on us personally. We were concerned about our own safety from the moment we walked out of the door of our flat each day. Some people did not like Americans, and they could do us harm.

It was also common for the apartments of foreigners to be broken into while the residents were out. Consequently, we were concerned about the few things of value that we had in the apartment, such as a laptop computer and our hidden money. To keep from losing everything in one incident, we carried some of our money with us and left some in the apartment. The most valuable possessions we had were our passports and visas. A thief could get at least a thousand dollars for them. We tried our best to protect these by carrying them on a cord around our necks, which hung down under our clothes.

We walked out of our apartment that morning and down the nine flights of stairs with heavy hearts, thinking about the seriousness of what we were facing. Outside, a freezing rain was coming down, so we were soon damp and cold. That morning we spent about fifteen minutes riding a bus and then about thirty minutes on the metro (subway), and then walked for about a half hour to get to the center. There was a lot of ice and snow on the sidewalks even after some of it had melted in the light rain. This left about an inch or two of slush on the sidewalks, making our walk difficult and our feet wet and cold.

When we arrived at the center, we went down a flight of stairs from the outside of the building to the basement. As we walked into the basement, we could smell food cooking and we saw Rachel cooking at the end of the long hallway. Then when we turned a corner of the hallway, we saw children and youth seated at the forty-foot-long table in the hallway, eating their breakfast. These youth and children were very poor. Their clothes were not much more than rags, and combined with the smell of the food, we could also smell the odor of sewer gas that clung to their bodies. The smell left no doubt that they had stayed all night in the sewers to get out of the cold.

At the end of the hallway, was a ten-foot-square room with a very low ceiling where the Project Hope staff was meeting. Most of them were young Christians that had very little themselves. The majority of them were young Russians, but there were also others from different countries such as Ukraine and Finland.

As I looked around the room, I saw that all of the people looked poor themselves. I knew that all of them were God's people trying to make a difference in the lives of the children out in the hallway, and they desired to make a difference in the lives of many more children living in the streets. By the time the meeting started, there were about twenty people in the tiny room. Most of them were standing because there were very few chairs and no room for chairs even if we had them. One well-dressed woman that I did not know was there. She looked to be about fifty years old and her name was Yelena. She almost seemed out of place.

When Vera started the meeting, I could see that she was bearing a heavy burden. She looked like she was ready to cry as she gave the details about the regulations that the police and the board of health were putting upon the ministry. I looked at Ricardo and Rachel and could see the pain and seriousness in their faces as well. They had worked so hard at getting this place ready to feed the street children, and now its very existence was in jeopardy. After Vera told about her summons to the police department, most of the young people were nearly in tears.

My mind went back to the early Christians, who probably looked like this group in many ways. But, in spite of their conditions and problems, God used them to make a huge difference in their world. I knew that God could also overcome the restrictions that were being put on us in this situation. After Vera gave the details about the police and the board of health, she asked everyone to pray. Within seconds that little room was alive with people praying. Everyone was travailing before God for His answer and for deliverance. This prayer went on for a long time; then it seemed that all at once everyone stopped praying, and Vera very quietly gave a closing prayer.

I had seen God deliver before when there seemed to be no way, but I could not see how it could be done in this case, however, I did have faith to believe God was going to do something. Again, as I had looked at the raging river on my jungle ride in Africa, I was looking at this raging river in front of us now! God was going to give us a way around this impassable object, but I sure could not see how it could be done.

Shortly after the prayer, the well-dressed woman named Yelena started to speak. As she spoke, I realized that I had heard of her before. Esther had told me about this woman who worked for the Russian government. She was a licensed social worker. At one time she had been involved in helping Vera with some social issues concerning the street children. As she was working with Vera, she saw what Project Hope was doing to help the street children. She made the statement to Vera, saying, "You people really love these children. I have worked with the government for twenty-four years and have never seen anyone love them." Yelena was very impressed with Vera and what she was doing.

Yelena told the group who she was, and that she was personally going to try to help Vera concerning her summons to the police. She would also do all she could to work with the police and the board of health concerning the regulations they were imposing on the ministry. Upon hearing her speak, it was obvious that she had some authority with the government. This gave all of us some hope. Esther, in the Bible, made a difference when she spoke to the king about her people, and maybe Yelena could make a difference when she spoke to the authorities on behalf of Vera and Project Hope. It seemed to all of us that Yelena might be God's answer for Project Hope to continue as a ministry to the street children.

Yelena intervened, and Vera had no trouble with the police after that. The board of health backed off and we were able to continue our feeding program in that location. We did, however, have to keep records on every child that came to Project Hope. We did it by feeding them first and working on the report next.

Yelena became a Christian shortly after this incident. She quit her twenty-four-year job with the government and became Project Hope's social worker. Now

Project Hope had a social worker that was licensed and recognized by the Russian government. She set up a very professional program of interviewing and keeping records on every child. From that interview, she would learn about each child, and then the Project Hope staff would minister to that child according to their special needs. Through it all, things became better than they were before all this trouble began.

Vera had a doctorate in teaching teachers to work with children and Yelena had a degree as a social worker. Both of these women were a great blessing to Project Hope. In answer to our prayer, God sent Yelena to help us over our impassable object just as He sent the African men to help me over my impassable object of the raging river and the man in the loincloth to help me see what was wrong with the motor bike.

Ch. 41

A Better Center

Things were going well at the Project Hope Center. The problem caused by the opposition from the police and the board of health had been settled. The ministry was in a daily pattern of serving the street children and youth that were coming to the center for food and Christian teaching. Many of the children and youth were making decisions to accept Jesus Christ as their Savior. Vera was busy directing about twenty people, who were working in the streets or in the center, cooking food and teaching classes. We also had a doctor who was treating the children's physical needs.

Some of the staff was going into two prisons, one for boys and one for girls. They would take in food (which included fruit) and other items that the boys and girls needed such as blankets, shoes, toothbrushes, toothpaste, personal items for the girls, etc. The Word of God was also being taught in these prisons with positive results as some of the inmates were accepting Christ as their Savior. Things were going great in this new ministry.

However, there was a negative side to where our center was located. It was in a basement with no windows and absolutely no room for expansion. We had no playground and no way for outside activities at all. In addition, our office space was located a couple miles away, which was very inconvenient and took a lot of time walking back and forth between the two locations. Our location was okay for a short time, but it was not what we needed for long-term ministry.

About two months after things settled down with the board of health and the police, the Salvation Army wanted to expand their ministry, so they asked us if they could have the space back that we were using. We had to find another place.

Day after day we went from building to building, looking for something that we could use as our center. Most of the buildings we looked at were in terrible disrepair both inside and out. It would take thousands of dollars to make them usable, and we did not have that kind of money. Then one day Ricardo and I and a few others went to a building that we heard was for rent. It had been built by the railroad as apartments for the employees and as a day care center for their children, but they had not used it for years. The building was very large, and next to it was about an acre of playground space with a large stone wall around it. The playground area came with the building.

A Russian realtor had possession of the building, and he wanted to rent about five thousand square feet of it for two thousand dollars a month. We looked the building over inside and out. All the plumbing had been torn out, as well as most of the electrical wiring. The space was located on two floors, with a stairway leading from the first floor to the second. To make this space usable, we would have to put in all new electrical wiring and plumbing, which would include sinks, showers, and toilets. We would have to build a kitchen, dining room, and classrooms, etc. The cost to do all of this would be New Life / Project Hope's responsibility. It would take a lot of work but we could do it. However, the work wasn't the problem; we did not have enough money to cover all the expenses.

Before we said we would rent the building, we prayed about it, asking God to show us His will in this matter. After our prayer, we felt God wanted us to rent the building. We needed some cash immediately to rent it and to make the repairs. One of the single missionary ladies from Finland named Helena Reinikainen had a large sum of her personal money that she donated. Helena's gift was a blessing, as it covered the first three month's rent. She was the woman that went into the sewer with Esther when she came to St. Petersburg the first time. Then Ricardo and Rachel had a good sum of money that they had been saving and they gave it to start the repair work on the building. These generous gifts allowed us to rent the building and to start the repairs.

It took about three months of intense work to get the building ready for us to occupy. In the meantime, the Salvation Army allowed us to continue using their facility until ours was ready.

Three months passed quickly, and we moved our center into our new building. It was a much better building and location than we had been in. The children had a large playground where they could play their favorite game of soccer and other things. We had a large kitchen, dining room, classrooms, pantry, supply room, craft room, wood shop, medical room, and offices, where we could feed, teach, and minister to many children and youth. Most of the rooms also had large windows, so we could see out as well as benefit from the light that came in (something we did not have in the basement). Our new building and play area were such an improvement over what we had previously.

As I look back on what happened that caused us to relocate our center, I know God was using it to get us out of the basement and into a much better place. We had quickly become a bit like the baby eagle sitting in his secure nest, when there is a whole world out there for him to spread his wings and fly. The mother eagle knows this, and there comes a time when she kicks her little eagle out of the nest and forces him to fly to the heights that God intended for him. Yes, we were kicked out of our secure nest, but it was for our good. God wanted to bring us out into the light and give us space to minister from. And as a bonus, He gave us a playground area for the children and youth.

We ministered out of this new location for seven years. The board of health was happy with our kitchen and dining room. The police were happy with our record keeping and ministry programs, and things went very well. With our loving Christian staff, we were able to meet the children's physical, emotional, educational, and most important of all, their spiritual needs. Every child heard the Word of God, and many had a life-changing experience of being born again.

Ch. 42
MAKE IT RUSSIAN

During these years Esther and I had a flat (an apartment) in St. Petersburg that we rented for four hundred dollars a month. We would live there for about four months, return back to our home in Indiana for a short time to spend time with our family, and then return to Russia. We always paid our own expenses. We did not take one penny from funds that were given to the ministry for our own use. Sometimes we were given personal money to travel or live on and we took it, but we never took money that was given for the ministry to the children. While we were there, we helped lead the ministry and also spent about three days a week ministering in one prison for girls and two for boys.

During the years, we had a few close calls due to personal attacks from thieves and people that did not like Americans. One time as I was climbing the nine flights of stairs up to our flat, a thief grabbed me from my back, right in our stairway. I thought he might have a knife, but I was not sure. Esther was a few flights of stairs behind me, as she had stopped to pick up some mail for our flat. When she saw the thief holding me, she started shouting at him as loud as she could in Russian telling him to let me go. Since Esther speaks Russian with a Ukrainian accent, the thief thought we were both from Ukraine. He then disgustedly said, "Ukrainians are poorer than Russians, so he has no money." Then he let me go.

I was grabbed another time from my back in a headlock as we were waiting on a bus. That time I was with a young Russian man who was part of our Project Hope staff. The young man slowly started walking toward the thief, quietly speaking to him in Russian. I don't know what he said, but the thief let me go. Other similar things happened, but I won't get into them now.

About two years after we moved into our new building, the Holy Spirit started to speak to me in His still, small voice saying, "Make it Russian, make it Russian." I knew exactly what He was saying. Esther and I were to do everything we could to put ourselves in the background and to put the Russians fully in charge. I told Esther what the Lord had spoken to me, and she fully understood and agreed that it was the right thing to do. It seemed that Ricardo and Rachel were thinking the same thing as we were. They slowly blended themselves out of any leadership position and started another ministry to adult people living in crisis in Russia.

We started to let the Russians make more of the major decisions. At first they were reluctant to do this, but slowly they saw that they needed to. As time passed, Esther and I backed out more and more, telling the Russian staff that they were the leaders, and that it was their ministry, and their people that they were ministering to. Soon they were making the major decisions and only seeking our advice on some difficult decisions. They also put themselves under the covering of a very good Russian church and used their pastors to help them teach the Bible in their classrooms and at their summer camp. Since they were Russian and knew the culture better than we did, the change worked out wonderfully.

About a year after God spoke to us to make it Russian, we felt it was best to spend less time in Russia. We felt God was saying that it was good to help support the ministry from America and other countries, because the Christians in Russia were so poor. This, however, did not mean we were to run the ministry from America or other countries. This transfer of leadership worked out well, and soon the Russians were fully running Project Hope.

Later we saw how important it was that we made it Russian. The Russian government passed a law that foreigners were only allowed to be in the country three months and then they had to leave and go back to their home country and apply again for a visa before they could return. This caused long delays in getting back into the country, and sometimes their visas were refused. We know some American ministries in which the missionaries did not make their ministry Russian, and when this change came, it greatly hurt their ministry. We were so thankful we heard God's still, small voice about this and obeyed. God knew this was going to happen and we were fully prepared for it. The change in policy did not hurt our ministry at all.

As the years passed, the financial situation in Russia greatly improved and the nation started to prosper. Along with this came fewer and fewer street children. There were, however, many children living in crisis conditions, but most of these were from conditions caused by parents who were alcoholics. Some of the home situations were so bad that the children were living in conditions about as bad as the children living in the streets. As a result of this change, Project Hope's ministry started to change from one that ministered mostly to street children to one that ministered to children living in crisis due to situations caused by child neglect.

Most of the children and youth that came to Project Hope had life-changing experiences through Jesus Christ. Many of them went on to have very good jobs after they grew up, and best of all, several went on to serve the Lord. We know the stories of many children's lives but I want to tell about just two of them. When Esther first went to St. Petersburg and checked out the situation with street children, she met a young boy named Peter (not his real name) and a young girl named Olga (not her real name) who both lived in the streets.

They were in such bad shape physically and emotionally that Esther wondered if we could even help them. Both of the children were very dirty, full of lice, bitter, and hateful. They trusted no one, and yet they needed help, and no one previously had reached out to help them in any way. They had lived on the streets for a long time and had probably stolen food, etc., and did whatever they could to survive. Olga went to school spasmodically but Peter had not, so he could not read or write, and Olga was limited in her literacy.

Peter and Olga were in the first group of street children that Project Hope ministered to. Esther and the loving staff at Project Hope reached out to them and did all they could to meet their physical, emotional, educational, and best of all, their spiritual needs. The staff of Project Hope mentored both of the children and brought them up to the grade level they needed to be in to get into the government school. To get into the government school they had to take a government exam to see if they could pass a test at the grade level they should be in for their age.

Every person in Russia has to have a passport, and if Peter and Olga failed the exam, the officials would stamp "Retarded" on their passport, and that word would be on their papers for the rest of their life. It would then be nearly impossible for them to get a job because they would be classified as retarded. When these children took the exam, it was extremely important that they passed the exam the first time so that they did not get the dreaded classification.

The Project Hope staff spent months working with the children in an attempt to make sure they passed the test the first time. When the day came to take the test, both children passed it very well. Now they were able to get into school at their age level. Olga did so well in school that she made the top grades in her high school. She then received a full, government-paid scholarship to college where she also received the top grades. Olga today is happily married and doing very well. Peter also did so well that he now has a very high-paying job as a supervisor in a St. Petersburg business.

It took a lot of sacrifices and effort from people that gave to support the ministry, plus a lot of work from the Russian staff and missionaries to run Project Hope through the years. I know it was worth it, however, when I see the results that our ministry had on children such as Peter and Olga and hundreds more like them that lived in the streets and prisons.

Ch. 43

PROJECT HOPE MERGES INTO CHILDREN'S ARK

A few years before Esther was asked to go to St. Petersburg to check out the situation with children in prison, God had given a Russian man named Jack Kerbs the vision of building a large building in St. Petersburg, Russia, for orphanages and children living in crisis.

God blessed Jack and his vision for the children and he was able to get the funds, mostly from Germany, and built a very large building that they called Children's Ark. The building was beautifully designed and built with ceramic floors, a commercial kitchen, a large beautiful dining room, lovely bedrooms, and classrooms for many children and youth. This beautiful, well-built building probably cost in the millions of dollars. After the building was finished, the Children's Ark Orphanage was started.

Lydia, the director of Children's Ark, and Vera, the director of Project Hope, became close friends. Lydia knew that Vera had a doctorate in teaching teachers to teach children and also had experience in working with children living in crisis. As a result, Lydia asked Vera to teach the staff of Children's Ark about working with children living in crisis and then to counsel some of the children. Vera agreed to do this, and for about a year and a half she spent several hours each week of her own time working with the staff and children at Children's Ark.

During this time, Project Hope was again forced to leave their building because the owners wanted it back. When this happened, Lydia suggested that they relocate their ministry to the Children's Ark building. She said they had unused space that Project Hope could use. She suggested that Project Hope keep their identity and Children's Ark keep their identity, and the two ministries could work together for a common cause of helping children living in crisis. Before this could happen, however, the board of directors of Children's Ark had to approve of it.

When Esther went to St. Petersburg, Russia, in the fall of 2007, the founder of Children's Ark and some of the board of directors from Germany were in St. Petersburg at the same time. The leaders of Children's Ark had a meeting with the leaders of Project Hope while Esther was there. The first question they asked Esther was, "Does Project Hope have the goal of bringing the children to a life-changing, born-again experience through Jesus Christ?"

Esther was very happy with their question because she knew their goals were the same as ours; we could work with them only if they had the same goals as we did. Esther was pleased to answer their question with a very strong, "Yes, we do." After some discussion, the two organizations were very happy that they all had a common goal for the ministry. The founder of Children's Ark and the board members that were there all agreed that it was of God for the two ministries to work out of the Children's Ark building and help each other in the ministry. The partnership of both ministries working out of the same building was a wonderful combination that God brought about.

After this meeting, the Project Hope ministry and their equipment were relocated to the Children's Ark building, and a wonderful working relationship began. In December 2007, the Russian government of St. Petersburg evaluated all of the ministries to children in the city. As a result of the evaluation, they rated Children's Ark as the best in the city of six million people. For the next two years, the staff of Project Hope and Children's Ark worked together, ministering to children living in crisis.

In the fall of 2009, Esther and I were back in our home in Indiana when the Lord spoke to us in His still, small voice, telling us that we needed to go back to Russia and visit the ministry in St. Petersburg. It was a time of the year when we both were very busy, but we obeyed God's still, small voice, got our visas and tickets, and flew to St. Petersburg, Russia.

When our plane broke through the clouds as it was landing in St. Petersburg, I looked out of my window to get a view of St. Petersburg from the air. I was surprised to see that the snow was coming down so hard that I wondered how the pilot could see well enough to land. Everything was covered with snow, and it looked very cold out there. I should have expected it, however, because we were back in Russia.

Vera and Sasha were at the airport waiting on us and it was so good to see them again. After a few hugs and greetings, we loaded our bags on a cart and headed out to the parking lot and on to their van. The large snowflakes were coming down so heavy that all of the cars, including Sasha's van, were covered in white. It was beautiful Russian snowfall. As we drove out of the snow-covered parking lot, we started asking Vera and Sasha questions to get caught up on how things were going with them.

One of the first things they told us about was the situation with them in their small flat. We were aware that Vera's father had passed away in the past spring but didn't realize that her mother had to move in with them. Her parents had lived about one hundred miles outside the city in a very small cabin (called a "dacha"). Vera's seventy-six-year-old mother was a complete invalid, unable to walk or feed herself. Her husband had taken care of her for years, but when he died, Vera and Sasha had to bring her to their six hundred-square-foot apartment and care for her there. Sasha's eighty-four-year-old mother also lived with them.

When Vera and Sasha were at the Children's Ark orphanage, Sasha's mother had to care for Vera's mother. Since she could not feed herself or walk, this made the situation very difficult for Sasha's mother. Russia has very few nursing homes, and those that are there are only available to the very rich, and it is not possible to find someone to care for an invalid. It must be done by the family.

Vera felt that her responsibilities as director of Project Hope meant she should be at the orphanage nearly every day, and she and Sasha did not get back home until late in the evening, so this was making an almost impossible situation at their home. As they were talking to us, Vera said, "I am just so tired. I am burnt out!"

Vera told us that she was also feeling God was leading her to start holding more seminars on ministering to children living in crisis. She is probably one of the best Christian teachers in all of Russia on this subject. Through her years as director of Project Hope, she has held seminars in different cities in Russia, some as far away as Siberia. Several ministries to children living in crisis began as a result of her seminars. Sasha said that if Vera did hold seminars, he would stay at home and care for their parents while Vera was away. They told us that three different places had already asked her to hold seminars for them. One of them was in Ukraine.

As Esther and I heard about the problems that Vera and Sasha were having, our hearts were very touched. We could feel the pain in their voices as they told us how difficult their situation was. We love Sasha and Vera very much and did not want them to hurt like this. We feel God always has an answer to problems, and we need to trust Him to speak to us in His still, small voice letting us know what to do.

As Sasha made the ninety-minute drive from the airport on the south side of St. Petersburg to the apartment Esther and I would be staying in on the very northeast side of the city, the snow kept falling at a constant rate. Our conversation continued throughout the whole trip, and we assured them that we would be praying for God to give wisdom to all four of us.

We were going to be staying in Lyuba's apartment while she was in America visiting her son and daughter in the United States. Lyuba had been the director of our prison ministry for ten years. We had worked with her and had stayed in her flat before, so we were glad to be someplace that we were familiar with.

Later that evening after Vera and Sasha returned back to their apartment, the Lord started to speak to me in His still, small voice about His plan for them. It was very clear what He wanted us to do. At the same time He was also showing Esther the same thing. God was telling us both that we were to totally merge Project Hope into Children's Ark, and that Project Hope was to cease to exist. This was a bit of a surprise to me, but I knew it was His will. It would mean that the leadership of Project Hope would also cease to exist, and Vera and Sasha would no longer be responsible. They would still work at the orphanage, but could put in fewer hours. This would give them more time to spend with their parents and also give Vera more time to pursue holding seminars. It also meant that all of the staff of Project Hope would be put under the leadership of Children's Ark.

We met Vera and Sasha the next day and told them how we felt God was leading. They were both in agreement with the idea and wanted to pursue it. The following day we had a meeting with the president of the Children's Ark board of directors, Jack Kerbs. We told him about our desire to merge Project Hope fully into Children's Ark. We also told him that if we did do this, December 2009 would be the last month that the Kokomo Rescue Mission would receipt funds for Project Hope.

We would ask our supporters to send their support to the organization that receipts funds for Children's Ark starting on January 1, 2010. Project Hope's license with the Russian government needed to be renewed in July 2010, and we would not renew it. Project Hope would then officially cease to exist. Jack fully agreed with this plan to merge the two organizations together and for them to become one under the leadership of Children's Ark.

Under this merging, the ministry to the children would continue exactly as it was. The children would not even know anything had changed. We liked this very much. Vera and Sasha would have more time to spend with their parents and also in pursuing Vera's call to hold more seminars. Vera and Sasha's salaries would continue for six months, and after that they could continue to work at the orphanage or go full-time into having seminars. Children's Ark would have more funds to support their ministry because some or possibly most of Project Hope's supporters would support them. The staff of Project Hope would continue to work as they were, but under Children's Ark. We were confident this merging was of God, and as we saw it, everyone benefited from the move.

As I was thinking about the details of making this merging official, my mind wandered back to how God had blessed Project Hope for the past twelve years. God had greatly blessed us financially, but I can never say that it was because of my faith. As the ministry of Project Hope grew from the beginning, so did the need for funds to run it. By January of 1999, our expenses were five thousand dollars a month to run the center and several thousand dollars a year for the prison ministry. Our expenses included twenty-five hundred dollars-a-month rent for the building plus salaries for a staff of eight people, food for the children, medical cost to treat them, their educational cost, and cost for transportation, etc., on top of that. At times my heart would nearly sink as I thought about how much money had to come in to support the ministry.

I knew God owned the cattle on a thousand hills and that He could supply. I had seen Him do it many times, but each month I wondered if He would provide the money. Then He did it again, and the funds were there to pay our expenses. I would see it happen but then go back into my doubt, wondering if it would continue. In spite of my doubts, I saw God supply the funds we needed month after month. Then it became year after year. I started to be absolutely amazed by what I was seeing God do.

Where was all this money coming from? We never knew from one month to the next, but the funds were always there. Many times the funds came from people that we did not know. Here is an example. Many funds came from a man that lived in Texas. He and I talked on the phone many times, and neither one of us could remember how he got acquainted with Esther and I or our ministry. One husband and wife that are dear friends of ours gave thousands of dollars also. The church that helped us right from the beginning gave a thousand dollars a month for years. Many people gave to support the ministry.

The money just kept coming in month after month and then year after year. We were seeing not just thousands of dollars coming in, but rather tens of thousands and hundreds of thousands.

The longer this went on, the more amazed I became at God's ability to fund something He ordered. Our job was to just hear His still, small voice and then obey it, no matter what it meant to us personally. As I said earlier, Esther and I did not keep one penny of the funds for ourselves in any way. We used them for what they were given. I believe God honored this and trusted us to use His funds in a responsible way. We were seeing a miracle of God in the funding!

In addition to this, I started to see firsthand how much God cared for the children living in crisis in St. Petersburg, Russia. Otherwise He would not be doing the miracle of providing for their needs as He was. I think God looked down from heaven and saw children living in sewers. I believe this broke His heart, and He sent a little woman that grew up in the forests of western Canada and one that grew up in Finland to climb down into a sewer because they knew children were living down there. I believe God blessed their effort along with that of others, and a large ministry to these children was born out of it. Then God said, "I will provide for it," and He did.

As the years passed, I realized that there would come a time when Esther and I could not continue the ministry. I was nearly sixty-five years old when we went to live in Russia. When I turned seventy-five, I knew I was now considered an "old" man; however, I did not feel old. God had blessed me and I still could work hard all day without getting very tired. Even so, I thought of our age and many times wondered what would happen to Project Hope when Esther and I could no longer be the United States representatives of the ministry.

Our part of communicating with people and writing letters, etc., was very important. The fact that we were with the ministry from the beginning and had a heart for it was vital for what we were doing. If we spoke or wrote about what God was doing, we could do it firsthand because often we were there when it happened.

Each time I thought about what would happen to Project Hope in the future, God would speak to me in His still, small voice and give me a word of comfort, saying, "I will take care of it." This was always a comfort to me, but I could never figure out how He might do it. As time passed and I watched God supply the funds to run Project Hope, my faith grew to the place that I became like an excited child that knew his father was going to give him something very special.

God supported the ministry for 12 years, which is 144 months. As we look at the Word of God, we see that the numbers 12 and 144 are special numbers. The 12 years and 144 months were very special to Esther and me because we heard God direct us so many times by His still, small voice, giving us guidance on how to handle many events. We also had the joy of watching Him bring in hundreds of thousands of dollars to operate the ministry. The total amount that God brought in through the twelve years was about three-quarters of a million dollars.

In our wildest dreams, we could never have imagined that God would supply that much money after Esther went down into that dirty, smelly sewer to feed and minister to a few children. He did, however, and we look at it as a miracle of provision that God blessed us to see and experience.

Today is January 27, 2011. I am 77 years old. God has worked it out so that our responsibility to Project Hope is now transferred to people that are doing the same thing for Children's Ark. Esther and I will continue to be somewhat involved, but it will never again be the way it was for the twelve years after Esther went into the sewer.

Esther and I are still hearing and obeying the still, small voice of the Holy Spirit. We plan to do this for the remainder of the time the Lord has for us here on this earth. I know He has another work for us and we will continue to obey what He tells through His still, small voice.

Robert McCauley
January 27, 2011

Lightning Source UK Ltd.
Milton Keynes UK
UKOW05f1503110514

231478UK00011B/345/P